THE HOME ENERGY HANDBOOK

A GUIDE TO SAVING AND GENERATING ENERGY IN YOUR HOME AND COMMUNITY

Allan Shepherd, Peter Harper, Paul Allen
Nicky Ison and Jarra Hicks

The Home Energy Handbook:

A guide to saving and generating energy in your home and community

Allan Shepherd, Peter Harper, Paul Allen, Nicky Ison and Jarra Hicks

©Centre for Alternative Technology, 2012
Machynlleth, Powys
SY20 9AZ, UK
Tel. 01654 705980 • Fax. 01654 702782
pubs@cat.org.uk • www.cat.org.uk

ISBN 978-1-902175-71-3
1 2 3 4 5 6 7 8 9

Publisher and editor-in-chief: /
Editor: Hele Oakley
Typesetting, illustrations and c
Cover design: Annika Faircloth

Published by CAT Publications
Registered charity no. 265239.

Centre for Alternative Technology
Canolfan y Dechnoleg Amgen

Published with help from:

CarnegieUK
TRUST
CHANGING MINDS • CHANGING LIVES

Printed with the support of:

Good
Energy

FSC
www.fsc.org
MIX
Paper from
responsible sources
FSC® C005094

Printed in the UK by Cambrian Printers, Aberystwyth, 01970 627111.

Amadeus primo is made from 100% virgin fibre which is sourced from sustainable forestry guaranteed for peace of mind through an international chain of custody certification.

Foreword by Rob Hopkins, founder of the Transition movement

Stephen Prior

I spoke recently to someone who works for the government in the sphere of community resilience. When I asked about what thinking was going on around how communities might be supported in responding to peak oil, he said "we don't look at that. We put that in 'The Difficult Box'"

As a society, these vital issues of peak oil, climate change and the economic crisis, tend to be put in The Difficult Box. This book is about opening that box, and seeing the huge opportunities it contains, alongside the challenges.

For the past 6 years, I have been involved with the Transition movement. It is an experiment on a huge scale, one that asks "what would it look like if the best responses to peak oil and climate change came not from committees and Acts of Parliament, but from you and me and the people around us?" It is an invitation to be part of a collective figuring out of the best ways to build community resilience.

Energy is at the heart of what Transition initiatives do and *The Home Energy Handbook* describes many of the positive transition inspired projects that have emerged from the collective imagination of communities. These are ordinary people, doing extraordinary things, in extraordinary times.

At the heart of all these projects is the idea that communities should own and benefit as much as possible from the renewable energy generated around them. The exact models for how this happens will look different in each community, and the principle is also applied to a number of other areas of life such as food, building, economics and so on. It is important also to state that there are many other community-based organisations doing very similar work who aren't called Transition. Ultimately it doesn't matter what they're called, what matters is that their experience, their stories, are gathered and shared in as accessible and useful a way as possible.

What projects such as these do is to fill the void between what we can do as individuals, and what the government and big business can do. These are often presented as our only two viable routes to change. Yet as we are seeing up and down the country, when people come together with their neighbours and friends, and organise themselves around the purpose of building local resilience and localisation as economic development, they can do far more than they could do on their own, and they can show government what's possible. They can show how opening, addressing and creatively responding to the contents of our Difficult Box could actually be the key to the unleashing of entrepreneurship, community and resourcefulness that 'our time' needs in large amounts.

The Home Energy Handbook is a hugely valuable resource for individuals, households, communities and local and national decision makers. It is the first practical book to cover all the key subjects of home and community energy in one volume. It is a powerful tool in the hands of a community that wants to regain control of how it generates energy. It serves a vital role of allowing the experience of communities who have done this to be shared, and equipping them with the required technical information. There is a revolution afoot in terms of how we imagine energy generation. This is its manifesto.

Contents

Introduction

Allan Shepherd

Whilst working on this book I met an old man who had travelled from a tiny island in Scotland to give a presentation in South Wales. He had to be helped to the platform to speak. His name, rather improbably, was Willy McSporran. Addressing the 100 strong crowd (almost as big as the entire population of his island) he told the story of his people, how they had bought their island from the old laird under a community buy out scheme and were righting the wrongs of the past by creating community projects, renovating homes, re-organising farm land and starting new enterprises.

During what to me was one of the most impressive presentations I have seen: three phrases stuck out. The first was spoken by a member of the island community when the laird had gone: "who will look after us now?", to which his answer was "we will look after ourselves". The second concerned the economic success of the island. He said the island "had to wash its own face"; by which he meant there was to be no reliance on handouts and any projects had to pay for themselves. The third, the one he used at the end of his presentation: "better to try than to hope".

We will look after ourselves. The island must wash its own face. Better to try than to hope. These phrases struck a chord with me because all of the community projects I came across whilst writing this book shared three common characteristics: a sense of self-reliance and self-determination (but definitely not self-sufficiency), a sense of practical purpose (projects had an economic and social logic that created success) and finally a philosophy of positive kinetic energy (that although it might have taken a lot of work to get the project off the ground, once it was running it created so many positive benefits the hard work was soon forgotten).

Although this book is primarily about saving and generating electrical and heat energy it is also about creating energy for social change. As Rob Hopkins wrote in his foreword 'There is a revolution afoot in terms of how we imagine energy generation.' We can see it in the old way as being the preserve of big power companies, who take all the profit from the energy we use and lose, and hand it out to their share holders, or we can see it in a new way. That we each have an energy destiny, that we are better served by reducing the amount of money spent on energy, and keeping the profits from energy generation within our homes and communities. Energy = money = power to change things for the better.

Big companies will always produce more renewable energy than small communities (we definitely need them!) but they rarely seek to create community cohesion, resilience or friendship. This is not their job (although I for one wish it was!). But it is ours. And renewable energy generation provides us with a way in. A source of income we can use to good effect to create the kind of change we would like to see in our neighbourhoods. A new community garden, a play centre, loft insulation for people living in fuel poverty, better facilities in our village halls. But beyond the financial aspects, community energy projects bring people together. They can create a common bond which, once formed, sparks off all sorts of actions and activities, which may have previously been unimaginable.

Throughout this book I can point to places where the benefits of community energy projects have been felt by ordinary people in a tangible way. For example, in the village of Fintry, where a community shareholding in a wind farm helped the community to deliver numerous social programmes (page 98), in the Yard in Bristol , where a developer led housing estate was rejected in favour of community self-build (page 69), or in Vauban (page 110) in Germany, where a participatory approach to district scale planning delivered numerous benefits on a very large-scale.

In writing this book we wanted to say, this is what you can do to change your own home energy destiny but hey there's also these amazing community projects going on too. Could they inspire you? Because although sorting out your own home energy needs is a great thing to do it is not as rewarding or as useful as being part of a bigger community endeavor. As Willie Mc Sporran knows, individual action is not enough. We can't do what we need to do acting alone.

We also wanted to suggest when it might be more appropriate to take action on a national or global scale. Paul Allen's excellent introductory chapters (Our 21st century challenges and Rising to the challenge: where do we start?) give us the context we need. In them he takes us through a quick tour of our energy history, describing how we got to where we are, before going on to talk about the major challenges of the 21st Century and how we can face them at an individual, community, national and international level.

We also need to know whether our efforts are going to be worthwhile. We know we need to change but how do we make the right decisions? The answer to a large extent lies in how we calculate and cut our carbon emissions. Peter Harper takes us through this arena with his usual panache and humour in Chapter Three, tackling what could be a daunting subject with clarity and incision; harpooning *Guardian* reading greenies, himself included, for holding on to cherished and 'secret' non-negotiables that make true carbon reduction difficult, whilst introducing fresh new concepts to move the debate forward.

Part Two of the book was written by Nicky Ison, Jarra Hicks and I. We take you through the nitty gritty details of making it happen, both at home (me) and in your community (Nicky and Jarra). Dotted throughout this section are the case studies. Each one has been hand-picked to show off a different social or technological solution. There are rural and urban locations, big and small projects. Enough variety to give you a clear idea of what a community energy project could be. These have been an absolute pleasure to write!

You don't need to read them in a certain order but they are placed to match the chapters they sit near. The only exception to this rule is the first case study, an extended interview I carried out with Rob Hopkins, founder of the Transition movement, which I would recommend reading first. We think the Transition model needed and deserved to play a big part in this book because it delivers community engagement on a global scale. Reading it first gives good context for all that follows!

As with all books of this kind some time-specific information is bound to get a bit out of date. We've already had to change the information about one government scheme three times! Where information is obviously time specific double check using the various links or the Resources section at the back.

Thanks for reading and get in touch if you've got any suggestions about how we might improve things for the next edition!

Over to you!

Part One

The big challenges and what we can do about them

Chapter One
Our 21st century challenges

Paul Allen

How we got to where we are

In order to plot a course forwards, it is worth taking a little time to explore a brief history of our relationship with fossil fuels.

The story of fossil fuels began around 400 million years ago, when the earth's atmosphere was rich in carbon dioxide. The sun blazed down on this vast, fertile greenhouse. The abundant carbon dioxide and resultant high temperatures created an ideal hothouse.

At that time, the earth's landmasses were covered with a verdant mat of swamps filled with huge trees, ferns and other large leafy plants, and the seas and lakes were awash with algae and plankton. After these plant and animal remains decayed, they were heated and compressed under thick layers of rock.

This process went on for millions of years. The entire surface area of the earth acted as a solar collector, turning the sun's energy into plant and animal matter, then compressing and concentrating it into carbon rich black seams.

What is not immediately obvious in the story of fossil fuels is the sheer scale of the energy reserve that was stored away as the earth's surface area of 196,800,000 square miles lay basking in the sun for over 100 million years.

This massive 100 million year reserve of ancient sunlight lay slowly concentrating for further eons to make it, by far, the largest, most concentrated and most convenient energy store we have ever known or are ever likely to know.

Life before fossil fuels

It is not surprising we found this massive reserve of compressed ancient energy so useful. For the first few thousand years of human civilisation, before we began to tap into it, humanity's thirst for energy was largely restricted to an annual sunlight ration. We depended wholly and completely on the sun, the seasons, access to land and the strength of our horses, oxen and our own bodies. Both food and fuel were precious resources, and much blood was spilled in their pursuit. We lived at the mercy of the seasons, surviving by the axe and the plough, not only to grow our food but also to provide our energy – grazing for our horses, wood for our fires and so on.

Energy from the sun drove the earth's water cycle, which could be harnessed to power watermills. The uneven distribution of the sun's heat drove the winds and their energy was captured by windmills and sailing ships. Not forgetting also the direct heat of the sun, which made the summer time a much easier and less taxing time to live, especially in the colder parts of the world.

Any storing or concentration of sunlight could only be short term. Sunlight that fell on croplands provided food which could be preserved to feed families during the long, hard winters, or hay which could be stored over seasons to feed the horses and other beasts of burden. The sunlight that fell on woodlands could be manually harvested, dragged by horses to where it was needed, chopped and eventually burned as fuel wood.

'King Coal'

The coming of industrial coal was an energy revolution. Areas with the right mix of skills and resources, such as Wales and the north east of England, kicked off a global trend for drawing on our planet's massive deposits of ancient sunlight, captured and stored over millions of years. The ancient Chinese and the Romans certainly knew of it, but it was in Wales and the north of England that the coal revolution really began. There is evidence of

Björn Rantil

mine workings at Mostyn dating as far back as 1261, and of mining in the Blaenafon area going back to the 14th century.

Humanity had begun to make withdrawals from a massive and easily accessible 'energy bank account'. For the first time, the rate at which we were making withdrawals from our coal account far exceeded the rate of deposits. Coal quickly became the cheapest and most convenient 'miracle' energy resource ever discovered, driving change at an incredible rate.

It was during the 18th century that this new energy revolution really got going and the Welsh coal fields were well placed to drive it. Charcoal gave way to coal as the fuel of choice for smelting and, with new machinery becoming available, production could

continue to meet an ever rising demand.

From 1712 the rise of Newcomen's, then Watt's steam engines not only increased the demand for coal, they also made extraction easier, providing power for both pumping water and for raising the produce from mines. Major changes in agriculture, manufacturing, and transportation then swept across Britain, Europe, North America and eventually the world, triggering a process that marked a major turning point in human society; almost every aspect of daily life everywhere across the globe would be transformed.

The end of the 18th century saw the beginnings of a canal network across South Wales. This enabled the transport of coal to the coast or cities. Agricultural productivity rose ten- to twentyfold. Economic productivity rose a hundredfold. With the coming of coal powered steam ships, world trade really began to take off. Coal was so abundant that the supply could be stepped up to meet the rapidly rising demand. By 1840, 4.5 million tonnes of coal was produced, of which, 2.25 million went to the steel industry, one million to the domestic market and other industries and 750,000 tonnes for export.

Just 14 years later, coal production had risen to 8.8 million tonnes, with 2.6 million exported. By 1874, production had all but doubled to 16.5 million tonnes, with a quarter exported. The rise of the Welsh coal industry seemed unstoppable, with high quality coal available in massive quantities.

As the steam locomotive design was developed and the rise of the railways began, both demand and supply of coal were driven to new heights. Canals were at first supplemented, and then superseded, by the development of numerous competing railway branches which supplied the docks at Swansea, Cardiff, Newport, Llanelli and Barry, which all grew dramatically in importance as a result.

By 1913, Cardiff had become the largest coal exporting port in the world. The South Wales Coalfield, the Saudi Arabia of its day, provided one of the main sources of primary energy for industry and transportation. In all, some 232,000 men working in 620 mines produced 57 million tonnes of coal.

As Britain industrialised, her economy and the economies of her customers grew accustomed to dirt-cheap fossil fuel energy. Their captains of industry created a financial system built on the assumption that growth was the norm, and that growth would be both perpetual and unrestricted.

Oil – liquid ancient sunlight
The seeds of the next chapter in the story of our growing addiction to ancient sunlight reserves were sown in 1859 when the Pennsylvania Rock Oil Company of New York contracted 'Colonel' Edwin L Drake to drill for oil near a well known oil seep on Oil Creek in Titusville, Pennsylvania. On August 27, Drake struck oil at a depth of 70 feet. This was the first oil well in the United States, and the commercial era of petroleum extraction was born.

By 1877 the world's first oil tanker, the steam-powered Zoroaster, had been launched by the Nobel brothers to transport kerosene in the Caspian Sea, and by 1896 the first offshore oil well was drilled at the end of a 300 foot wharf in summerland, California.

A few years before that, in 1879, Karl Benz was granted a patent for the first internal combustion engine capable of powering a vehicle; the age of the motorcar began. This invention really tipped the balance and oil consumption escalated quickly, displacing coal as our most popular source of energy.

But energy is not the only use for oil. In 1935, Du Pont scientist Wallace Carothers invented Nylon, the first purely synthetic fibre to use petroleum-based hydrocarbons. Then in 1951, whilst working for Phillips Petroleum, research chemists Robert Banks and Paul Hogan discovered two new types of plastic – crystalline polypropylene and high-density polyethylene (HDPE).

These plastics, first marketed under the brand name Marlex, were responsible for many of the common plastic products we know today, such as milk jugs, carpeting and housewares. With this discovery, the role of oil extended from being just a source of energy to becoming the raw material for millions of products – from plastics, acrylics, cosmetics, paints and varnishes to asphalts, fertilizers, pesticides and medications. Modern life began to be designed around products and services underpinned by abundant cheap fossil fuels.

It's a short step from sufficiency to excess
The huge increase in productivity offered by fossil fuels led to people having access to more material goods than ever before. This opened up a huge potential for investment in further innovation, fuelling the rise of capitalism and the creation of 'consumer goods'. Great profits could be achieved in a growing number of industries creating the first 'mass culture of excess' amongst the expanding upper and middle classes. Humanity began the shift from sufficiency to excess. There were many reasons why this happened, but certainly the key driver was abundant access to

cheap fossil fuels.

Oil irrigates, fertilises, processes and delivers our food. It's the power behind our drinking water, home heating, manufacturing, communications and personal transport, and that's just the start! The western industrial world is now awash with abundant cheap fossil fuels – coal, oil and gas were both plentiful and profitable to produce – so all our living and working systems have been, quite literally, designed deliberately to use lots of the stuff.

Nowhere was this deliberately designed dependence on fossil fuels as marked as with the coming of the motorcar. The motorcar drove the post-war economy, so the development of the newly sprawling towns and suburbs were planned with the deliberate intent of maximizing the need for a car.

As the heavily subsidised road systems were laid out, the much more energy efficient rail systems were driven into decline. In Britain between 1963 and 1965 Lord Beeching's 'axe' saw the end of a large number of branch lines, closing much of the rural rail system. The aim was to make the rail system more profitable, whilst maximising car production, and so boosting the economy. The key problem with the plan was that the 'axed' branch lines acted as feeders to the main lines; that feeder traffic was lost when the branches closed. This in turn meant less rail traffic and less income for the increasingly vulnerable main lines. At its peak in 1950, Britain's Railway system had around 21,000 miles and 6,000 stations. By 1975, the system had shrunk to 12,000 miles of track and 2,000 stations, and has remained roughly this size ever since. With hindsight, many of the specific Beeching closures appear very short-sighted. Many of the 'axed' routes would now be heavily used, possibly even important trunk routes.

The globalised, highly material, modern lifestyle that we now take for granted is wholly dependent on access to abundant cheap fossil fuels. Without thinking twice, fossil fuels have pervaded almost every aspect of our lives.

As new uses for oil and other fossil fuels were found the amount used continued to grow. Beyond the basic level needed to provide food, clothes and shelter, use of extra energy does not necessarily make us any happier. Research by the new economics foundation has revealed that, since the 1970s, the UK's GDP has doubled but our perceived 'satisfaction with life' has hardly changed. Despite escalating energy use, not only has human happiness flatlined, our individual and national debt levels are going through the roof. In addition, we have become isolated from the systems that provide for us, creating a strange and brittle world.

Where we are now

Consider a typical modern day in a typical town. We wake up in a house heated by fuel brought to us in ways we are only dimly aware of, by an energy utility now owned in France. They have no fuel reserves beyond a couple of weeks. Our house is located in an area where we know few neighbours and is mostly owned by a German bank. We breakfast on food that was grown heaven knows where, by unknown hands, using methods we never see. Our lunch is bought from shops that would be empty in three days without fuel. We pay for it all through a Chinese bank over which we have little control.

We now depend for our continued existence on increasingly remote suppliers working through ever more distant systems that have no obligations to us, and indeed are not expected to have any. In Britain, just like everywhere else in the affluent West, the wellbeing of individuals and communities is now dependent on the continued reliable operation of a number of complex systems:

- Climate – our hospitable and stable climate.
- International relations – peaceful co-operation between nations.
- Energy – access to abundant, cheap fossil fuels.
- Economy – secure global and local economic systems.
- Ecology – stable biodiversity and ecosystem services.

All five are now stretched to breaking point and are approaching crisis. Left unchecked, their effects may compound each other.

In our report *Zero Carbon Britain 2030* (*ZCB2030*), in

order to estimate how far and how fast our transition away from fossil fuels needed to be, the Centre for Alternative Technology took a look at the science behind our most recent understanding of these key challenges. The full report is available free to download but here is a quick overview of what we found:

Climate

Even as far back as the end of the 19th century the forward thinking Swedish physicist Svante Arrhenius reasoned that adding to the greenhouse gas blanket by burning fossil fuels would cause the earth's temperature to rise. He suggested that this warming might be amplified, because, as the temperature increased, the air would hold more water vapour. In addition, the melting of ice would expose darker surfaces that would absorb more radiation. Arrhenius even produced quantitative estimates of the amount of warming that he thought might occur.

Since Arrhenius's time the earth has experienced a warming of 0.8°C in what is called 'average global temperature'. This may not sound a lot – the temperature in your garden at home varies by more than this every day – but when you consider the scale of the entire land surface and oceans of earth, you realise that to raise the global average surface temperature this much requires an immense amount of warming!

This warming not only manifests in the 'global thermometer reading' but in a multitude of changes to the natural world, including diminishing ice cover, altered plant and animal habitats and changing seasonal patterns. Data for the oceans, atmosphere, land and ice since 1950 has been analysed and it has been calculated that the entire earth system has been accumulating heat at a rate of about 6×10^{21} Joules per year – that's 6 x 10 with 21 zeros behind it!

Meanwhile, our scientific understanding of the problem has progressed immensely, and a large number of different lines of evidence has confirmed that the build up of greenhouse gases is the primary

One ought never to turn one's back on a threatened danger and try to run away from it. If you do that, you will double the danger. But if you meet it promptly and without flinching, you will reduce the danger by half.

Winston Churchill

cause of the warming, and that it has resulted from human activities. This has led to a strong scientific consensus – there is no longer any scientific body of genuine national or international standing that disagrees with this.

What exactly is it we need to do?
Since the industrial revolution, global atmospheric concentration of carbon dioxide has increased from 260ppm (parts per million) to around 380ppm. So far, by the greenhouse effect, humanity has raised the average global temperature by 0.8°C. But the earth does not behave quite like a greenhouse. In a greenhouse you reach a steady state by mid-morning. The earth is much more massive and takes much longer to warm up. Even if we were able to stick at 380ppm, we are locked into another 2 or 3 decades of warming which will take us up to around 1.5°C.

Below a critical threshold, we know the earth's natural 'carbon sinks' work to buffer us from the worst effects of our fossil fuel emissions, slowing climate change by helping reabsorb around half of the carbon dioxide we release back into the atmosphere.

Over recent years, clear and robust evidence has emerged that a global temperature rise above 2°C has a high likelihood of triggering an array of very

Key scientific evidence of climate change

- There is no other convincing explanation. Incoming solar radiation has been measured for decades and has not changed significantly, especially during the last 30 years. The trigger for the warming at the ends of previous ice ages is believed to have arisen due to changes in the earth's orbit that occur regularly about every 100,000 years, but the next such trigger is not due for another 30,000 years. Planetary movement alone would actually have produced a slight global cooling over the past 30 years.

- The lower atmosphere is warming, whilst the upper atmosphere is cooling. This effect cannot be explained without invoking the build up of a blanket of greenhouse gases.

- Unlike warming from other causes, an enhanced greenhouse effect should lead to greater warming at the poles – again, precisely what is seen to be occurring.

- Each of the greenhouse gases has a very particular 'signature' as they absorb particular wavelengths of light within the infrared spectrum. When satellite data was examined in 2000, it was found that the quantity of radiation leaving the earth in the wavelengths absorbed by CO_2 had fallen over several decades, as had those in the wavelengths absorbed by the other greenhouse gases.

- The sources of the additional atmospheric CO_2 have other types of fingerprint, since carbon exists in different forms (called 'isotopes'). By measuring the proportions of those different isotopes, the sources of that carbon can be identified. The isotopic fingerprint of atmospheric CO_2 shows an increasing proportion coming from fossil fuels, rather than from normal atmospheric sources.

much larger climate feedbacks, such as the release of methane from melting permafrost; these will trigger runaway climate change gas emissions which will be beyond our control, dwarf our human related emissions and unleash climate chaos.

Allowing this to happen on an earth supporting six to nine billion inhabitants would unleash widespread economic collapse, massive agricultural losses, international water shortages, dangerous rises in sea levels, food famines and widespread ecological degradation. It would also create tens of millions of environmental refugees and a global catastrophe that would make recent hurricanes or floods pale in comparison, and it would last for tens of thousands of years.

However, even a 2°C rise cannot be considered 'safe'. It would still mean we have made the earth warmer than it has been for millions of years. An alliance of the most vulnerable (Small Island States and Least Developed Countries) has called for the maximum negotiated permitted rise to be 1.5°C. So 2°C must be considered as the maximum absolute upper limit for an acceptable level of risk. It is imperative that this target at least is not exceeded.

In 2009, a group of scientists led by Malte Meinshausen at the Potsdam Institute for Climate Impact Research performed a comprehensive analysis to determine what must be done to limit warming to below 2°C. Because CO_2 has a long atmospheric lifetime, what matters for the climate is the total cumulative amount of CO_2 in the atmosphere, not the rate at which it is released.

However, based on the idea that emissions in 2050 are a good indicator of the likely total amount released in the intervening years, Meinshausen concludes that we will have about a 70% chance of staying under 2°C if total global greenhouse gas (GHG) emissions are cut by 50% from 1990 levels by 2050, and an 84% chance if we can achieve a global cut of 72%, as long as emissions continue to be cut after 2050 and approach zero before 2100.

Assuming the global population in 2050 to be about 9.2 billion, and dividing the total global emissions in 2050 equally among this population gives an annual personal allowance of about 1.96 tonnes of CO_2 equivalent per year for the 70% probability, or about 1.10 tonne per person for the 84% probability.

If all other things were equal, as UK emissions in 1990 were 797 million tonnes of CO_2 equivalent, we would have to achieve a per capita cut in the UK of about 92% or 85% from 1990 levels by 2050.

However, life isn't quite that simple. A small minority of the planet's population has caused the vast majority of the planet's problem. If we include a historical perspective, it is clearly insufficient to simply divide the 2050 global annual budget in this way.

Long industrialised countries such as the UK are responsible for the majority of the problem as we have been burning fossil fuels for over 150 years. During that time we have run vast empires, accumulated great wealth, and constructed the schools, railways, hospitals and other parts of the modern human infrastructure we enjoy today.

In light of the urgent need to reach a global agreement, the UK must aim for as close to a 100% cut as possible, as fast as possible. CAT's *ZCB2030* scenario was created to raise debate over how this could be achieved in just two decades.

International relations

We simply haven't been sharing out the energy, or anything else for that matter, very fairly. An average American consumes as much oil as 35 citizens of India. Here in the long industrialised West, we continue to use vastly more energy than is required to deliver our wellbeing, whilst the majority of the world strives to provide the basic schools, railways, hospitals and welfare systems which are not only a basic human right, but are a vital tool in stabilising global population. Despite record increases in global economic activity, the rich are still getting richer and the very poorest are being left behind.

This unfair distribution of resources has been going on for so long that the 'majority world' is now demanding the energy intensive consumer focused lifestyles the West has been flaunting for the past 50 years, and they are industrialising at a rapid rate to get it. Who are we to refuse them?

Competitive labour rates and eager fresh markets

have shifted global economic and political power. New gigantic markets such as those in India and China are opening up to modern consumerism and are driving global demand for oil through the roof. If China were to have three cars for every four people like the US does, it would use 99m barrels of oil a day. But the world only produces 84m barrels a day and current production is about as high as it is likely to get.

The long industrialised countries have the resources to invest in low carbon technologies for the future. The majority of countries do not and will therefore find it harder to adapt. While it is the majority world that will be hit the hardest by the consequences of climate change, historic responsibility rests overwhelmingly on the long industrialised world and so those who have already spent so much of the historic global carbon budget should set the pace in the transition to help foster a global agreement.

There is no time to delay. We urgently need an international agreement in order to move forward; the level of equity offered in the negotiations at Copenhagen and Cancun was not enough to broker agreement with the majority world. As the devastating effects of climate change destroy lives and livelihoods around the world we will face an increasing 'climate backlash', and which of us would not feel the same if we had lost our family or farms to the effects of overseas excess. Unless long industrialised countries begin to play their part in solving the problems they have created, the climate problem is unlikely to get the global agreement it so urgently requires.

Energy

Climate change is not the only reason we should embark on a transition away from fossil fuels. Our unstoppable oil economies are now being halted by the immovable facts of geology. For the first time in our history, just as demand is exploding across the globe, humanity will soon no longer be able to increase energy production year-on-year. Let's be clear from the start – no one is talking about oil 'running out', but rather the realisation that despite accelerating demand, global rates of production must inevitably plateau and go into decline, with

what remains being dirtier, harder to extract and considerably more expensive. This is not news; back in 1956 an oil geologist named M King Hubbert predicted that conventional production of US oil would peak around 1970. After decades of derision, Hubbert was proved right. US oil production did indeed peak in 1970, and it has declined steadily ever since. Even impressive discoveries such as Alaska's Prudhoe Bay, with 13 billion barrels in recoverable reserves, or the developments of new extraction technologies, haven't been able to reverse that trend – it is simply imposed by geology.

The peaking of conventional oil production is now a mainstream issue. In April 2010, even the US Military warned that 'By 2012, surplus oil production

The Swedish Government has set a new policy target: the creation of the conditions necessary to break Sweden's dependence on oil by 2020. And there is, indeed, an increased sense of urgency. If we prepare now, the transition to a sustainable energy system can be smooth and cost-efficient. If we wait until we are forced by circumstances, the transition may be costly and disruptive. No country can escape from this transition; to act sooner or act later are the only options.

Mona Sahlin, Swedish Minister for Sustainable Development, 9 May 2006

capacity could entirely disappear, and as early as 2015, the shortfall in output could reach nearly 10 million barrels per day' (this was outlined in a Joint Operating Environment report from the US Joint Forces Command, with a foreword by senior commander, General James N Mattis).

Peak oil shouldn't really come as a shock to the oil industry, which well understands the process of discovery, extraction and depletion. North Sea oil has peaked, as have the supplies of Mexico, Indonesia, China, Oman and Norway. The inevitable peak of world oil production is now imminent, and to compound the problem we are using oil quicker than ever before. There will be warning signs; set against escalating demand, prices will rise dramatically and become increasingly volatile. With little or no excess production capacity, any supply disruptions, such as hurricanes in the Gulf of Mexico, will drive world oil markets into a frenzy which governments and industry may chose not to cushion.

Despite continuous warnings from oil geologists and oil economists across the world, little action has been taken to deal with peak oil and its inevitable price shock. Why not? Because the prevailing belief is that the free market will take care of it. However, normal economics break down when it comes to oil.

In most cases, if the price of something goes up, more of it is produced. But the price of oil has no effect on how much oil there is out there to be found.

Of the 98 oil producing nations in the world, 64 are thought to have passed their geologically imposed production peak; of those, 60 are now in terminal production decline. Britain has now joined those in decline.

In 2005, after the 25 year economic and energy bonanza of North Sea oil and gas, the UK became a net energy importer again, as shown in figures 2 and 3. The principal reason for this is the decline in North Sea oil and gas production. Britain has been producing gas from the North Sea since 1967 and oil since 1975. The basin is now 'mature' (UK Oil & Gas 2009).

Our North Sea oil production reached its peak in 1999. It had suffered a previous peak and decline in the mid 1980s, linked to the Piper Alpha disaster and the subsequent remedial work that had to be

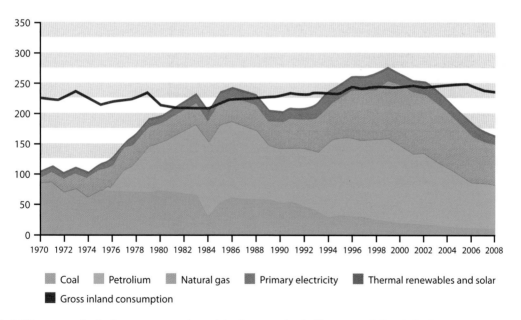

Fig. 1. UK energy production by energy type and gross inland consumption (million tonnes of oil equivalent), 1970-2008. "Primary electricity" includes nuclear and natural flow hydro-electricity but excludes output from pumped storage stations. From 1988, it also includes generation from wind farms. Production of "thermal renewables and solar" has only been recorded since 1988. It includes solar and geothermal heat, solid renewable sources (wood, waste, etc.), and gaseous renewable sources (landfill gas and sewage gas). Since 2004, the UK has returned to being a net importer of energy.
Source: Based on data from DECC (2009). Orignaily appeared in Zero Carbon Britain 2030.

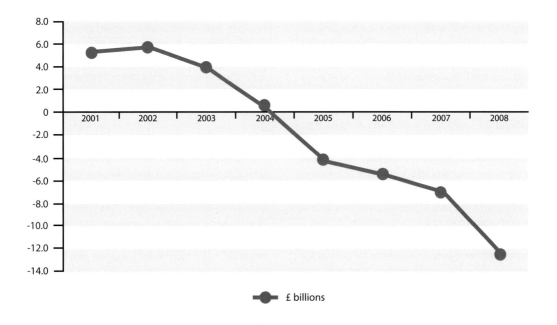

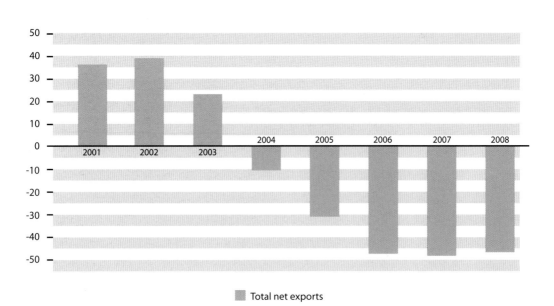

Fig. 2 (top), Fig. 3 (above). UK total net fuel exports, 2001–2008, based on (Fig. 2) balance of payments basis (£billions) and (Fig. 3) a quantity basis (million tonnes of oil equivalent). In 2004, the UK became a net-importer of fuel. Due to rates of currency exchange, the UK only became a net-importer of fuel on a balance of payments basis in 2005. However since then, the balance of payments for fuel has continued to decline.
Source: Based on data from DECC (2009). Originally appeared in Zero Carbon Britain 2030.

carried out. In contrast, the 1999 peak was caused by the declining size of newly discovered fields and the exhaustion of old ones. Oil production from the North Sea is now in terminal decline.

Our indigenous gas production is also now in decline. It is believed that UK gas production peaked in 2000 and is now declining at 2% per annum. If the UK continues to rely on gas, it will increasingly have to import it from Norway, the Netherlands, the former Soviet Union and Algeria. In addition, Britain now imports approximately 60% of its coal!

Ensuring our energy requirements can be met is not as simple as it first seems. Things take time and money to build, so strategic planning is vital in areas such as balance of trade, technology, policy and geology, if we are to ensure a reliable energy supply for the UK for the decades ahead. This means not only considering the balance between exports and imports, but also existing infrastructure, including plans for when it will be retired and replaced.

The UK is now at a critical crossroads in terms of its choice of future sources of energy. The relationship between investment in new generation capacity and the availability of supply is crucial to energy security. Any investment in new plant, whether fossil fuelled or renewable, must take account both of the security of its primary energy supply, and the potential price fluctuations expected over the duration of its design life.

If we can find, print or borrow the money, importing energy from overseas can, for now, substitute our failing domestic production. However, due to global geological constraints they cannot offer a reliable long term solution. There are other short term energy security options, such as a return to coal but this would of course accelerate climate change and is, therefore, not sustainable; it may also quickly become uneconomic if carbon pricing is deployed.

Once we take the long view, our well-being is clearly dependent on the development of indigenous sustainable sources, which can be powered up to meet the challenges of both climate change and reliable energy supply. It is sometimes suggested that the limits on fossil fuel availability may tackle

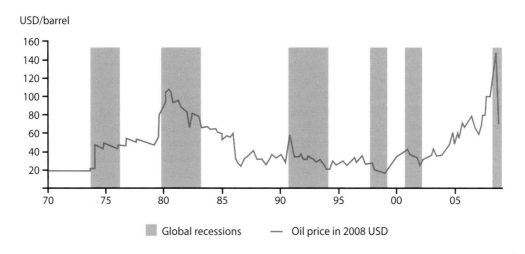

USD/barrel

Global recessions — Oil price in 2008 USD

Fig. 4. Recessions and oil prices since 1970.
Source: What's the Real Cause of the Global Recession? Jeff Rubin and Peter Buchanan, StrategEcon - October 31, 2008.

climate change without the need for any proactive intervention. However, according to current climate science, we will have to stop burning oil and gas long, long before the wells run dry!

Economy

The rules that determine the next two decades will be very different from those that have determined the last two. Communities across the world have been struggling to adjust to a new era of profound and abrupt change. Although not of their own making, these changes compel individuals and communities to reconsider how they move forward. For many, a reskilling in new attitudes and approaches to energy forms a fundamental part of that shift.

Since the late 1970s, North Sea oil and gas reserves have enabled the UK to be a net energy exporter. What's more, North Sea energy exports have made a significant contribution to the UK's balance of payments. Based on a rough estimate of 100 billion cubic metres of gas at 2p/kWh, 680 million barrels of oil at $78 per barrel and an exchange rate of $1.64 to the pound, replacing North Sea extraction with

The fiscal stimulus measures intended to pull the economy out of recession represent an invaluable opportunity decisively to transform the UK into a low carbon economy. A programme of investments in low carbon industries would help build a modern and sustainable economy, securing Britain's competitiveness and future prosperity in the new global economy that will emerge from this crisis.

Environmental Audit Committee, 2009

Our forecasts of the current balance from 2007-08 to 2011-12 are affected by one major change in the last year – the sharply lower levels of production and yet higher costs in the North Sea.

Gordon Brown responding on the decline in tax revenue from UK oil and gas production in his 2007 Chancellor of the Exchequer's Budget Statement.

imports would add £53 billion to the UK trade deficit. In addition, the Exchequer raised nearly £13 billion in tax from the offshore oil and gas industry in 2008. This would be gone too.

The long sleep of North Sea oil and gas has allowed us to fall into some very dozy practice. Before the North Sea bonanza, alerted by the 1973 oil crisis and the three day week, Britain deliberately focused on producing goods it could export in order to raise the foreign currency required to pay for the things we needed to import. Reading the headlines in the 1970s, the balance of trade deficit was never far from the top of the page. Today, as a net energy importer, we find that our so-called 'consumer retail economy' is virtually useless at raising the money we need to pay for the fuel we must import. In fact, rather than selling manufactured goods overseas, we are now a massive net importer of manufactured goods (especially from China). If you extrapolate the decline of our indigenous fossil fuel supplies – with 'business as usual' models – to 2030, it is easy to see that we will have a massive foreign debt problem, and by then energy will be in much shorter supply and more expensive.

Ever get the feeling we've seen all this before? An energy gap, rapid price rises at the pumps, then a recession, rising unemployment and the threat of savage cuts to public service spending? In fact, if you list all the energy price hikes and all the global recessions since 1970, it becomes clear that oil shocks are no stranger to recessions. Four of the last five global recessions were preceded by one.

But the current economic crisis is different. Previously, politically motivated supply blockages have been the problem. In 2005, world oil stopped being cheap and is very unlikely to ever be cheap again. In 2008, we learned by hard experience that $150 a barrel 'breaks the system'; it seems that the world economy can't function above that price.

This time there is an urgent need for solutions that deal proactively with the long term challenges of climate change and peak oil whilst also offering a practical route out of the current recession.

All these challenges, serious though they appear, are merely symptoms of a much wider and systemic problem with the current economic model. Instead of endless, stable growth and high and rising incomes, we have had inequity, volatility and crises. These are not anomalies, but a natural and increasingly severe expression of the 'normal' functioning of the system as it smashes into the 'limits of cheap oil' buffers.

But, astonishingly, this is precisely the paradigm that politicians were trying to return us to with their post-crash economic stimulus packages. Governments around the world have passed stimulus plans that total $3 trillion, but only a very small proportion of this has been used to bring us closer to the promised future low carbon economy. Instead, the recovery plans have been consumption-led – which rather than taking us away from a catastrophic climatic and ecological tipping point, will actually bring us closer to it. At the time of writing (spring 2012), Britain's economy was bumping along the bottom, having slumped back into recession (defined as two or more consecutive quarters of economic decline), making this recession the first double-dip downturn since the 1970s.

Brent crude oil was up in price yet again, averaging $118.60 a barrel during the first quarter, 12% higher than the same period in 2011. Also, despite the downturn in many western countries, global oil and gas production still increased 1.4 per cent to a massive 3.55 million barrels a day!

Any benefits of the consumer-focused economic stimulus have still yet to materialize, and we face a barrage of short-term cuts rather than a concerted focus on long-term investments capable of re-shaping the economy to rise to our 21st century challenges.

Never in our history has a closing window of opportunity been so vitally important to grasp. We have experienced market crashes, we have endured resource scarcities, fought wars and witnessed the collapse of empires. But never have the stakes been so high or the opportunities so vitally important.

The credit crunch has shown us the consequences of not reacting ahead of events. If we ignore the warnings and wait until the climate/energy crunch is really upon us before becoming serious about scaling-up the solutions, we might struggle to muster the resources required in the ensuing chaos and dislocation.

Now is the time for us all to mobilise our response.

Chapter Two

Rising to the challenge: where do we start?

Paul Allen

I f you've read the previous chapter you've already started to get to grips with the scale and seriousness of the challenges facing us. This is a key first step! Hard though it may be, recognition of the magnitude of our predicament forms the cornerstone of our response.

The urgent challenges of the 21st century cannot be solved with 20th century thinking; they require us to adopt a smart, conscious and integrated mindset. This means gathering the analytical tools we need to move forward to help us see through our long-held assumptions and misunderstandings.

As we set out to pioneer carbon descending lifestyles, we must learn how to 'do the numbers'; in other words, to take a baseline from which we can assess our performance and accurately count down our carbon. Peter Harper's chapter on carbon calculations will help you do this.

Hopefully, you are now champing at the bit to get started. In later chapters of the book we look at the detailed practicalities of implementing action on energy, but in this chapter we explore how changes at the local and community scale can synergise with actions at the national and international level, to accelerate nothing less than a new energy revolution.

Scanning the long horizon

At the turn of the new millennium, a group of us at the Centre for Alternative Technology (CAT) began a process of taking stock of the trajectory CAT had traversed over its first quarter century, and charting the likely path ahead. It had become increasingly clear that since the early 1970s we 'greens' had successfully identified a great many problems and a large number of solutions. So much so, that society faced a vast array of environmental challenges; recycling, acid rain, organic agriculture, volatile organic compounds in paints, disposable nappies and nuclear power to name but a few. It was clearly neither socially nor economically viable to expect all these challenges to be tackled at once.

The essence of success is to prioritise; gather from the thousands of environmental, social and economic challenges the really critical areas that are extremely urgent and devise ways to deal with these first. Peter Harper suggested that the criteria for such a prioritisation should be based around which challenges are irreversible, often because they feedback on themselves and runaway out of control. Getting to grips with our carbon emissions came top of the list!

Published in summer 2007, the first *Zero Carbon Britain* report was a first pass over a new and unfamiliar energy landscape. It offered a scenario that could be used as a yardstick to assess whether current progress was anywhere near on track in delivering the policy and technology transition required to meet the challenges we know lie ahead. This initial report was presented to all major British political parties in 2007 during the AGM of the All Party Parliamentary Climate Change Group. It was also presented in the Welsh Senedd, in Brussels, Washington, New York, and the UN COP 14 and COP 15 climate conferences in Poznan and Copenhagen. It helped to change how people were thinking about the future and inspired others to begin work on zero carbon scenarios for places as far apart as Ireland and Australia.

But soon after the launch of our first report, the credit crisis erupted. This radically changed people's outlook, not least due to the incredible energy price rises which preceded it. In response, CAT decided to embark on a new and much more detailed report – *Zero Carbon Britain 2030* (*ZCB2030*). This would update and add to our work, but also expand on the economic and employment analysis contained within the first report by synthesising cutting edge findings from leading researchers from a wide cross section of expert organisations.

Published in 2010, ZCB2030 presented a second and very much more detailed scenario. This demonstrated how we could integrate our detailed knowledge and experience from the built environment, transport, energy industry and agriculture sectors into a national framework, offering a common, coherent vision linking government, industry and citizens – endorsing, supporting and connecting actions across all sectors of society.

ZCB2030 generated an enormous amount of interest – with over 30,000 people downloading it or reading paper copies. It was featured prominently in national media and was adopted by the UK National Climate March.

At the time of writing (spring 2012), a welcome process of criticism, feedback and reflection, plus the emergence of new environmental technologies, has clarified what we need to do next. We are now excited about beginning a new period of research and investigation, being able to answer many of these detailed questions and build on the knowledge and networks acquired to date. Please visit www.cat.org.uk for the most up-to-date information.

Powering up and powering down

Decades of access to abundant, cheap fossil fuels have led us into some very wasteful practices. We know we are using a great deal more energy than we actually need to deliver our wellbeing, and burning that extra energy does not really make us any happier, healthier, richer or wiser. ZCB2030 demonstrates how – through taking an uncompromising new approach to energy use and by taking advantage of new technologies and efficient design – we can reduce energy demand by over 50% by 2030. We call this 'powering down'. By working together, we can pioneer new ways of living that are even richer, far more resilient and that use a lot less energy.

At the same time, through the widespread deployment of existing technologies, Britain can rethink its massive indigenous renewable energy assets to satisfy the remaining reduced energy demand. We call this 'powering up'. We are only now beginning to grasp the sheer scale of Britain's renewable energy assets. Where we are now is reminiscent of where we were in the 1960s when we first discovered our North Sea oil and gas fields. We know the energy is there, the technology to access it is developed and waiting, we just need to upskill and upscale the programmes to deliver it. Although the vast majority is national scale offshore wind, wave and tidal schemes, there is a vital role for community scale renewables.

The two simultaneous processes of powering down and powering up are core to the transition scenario. So rather than residing at the end of a peaking pipeline of polluting fossil fuel imports, a 'super energy lean' Britain can head its own indigenous renewable energy supply chain. Fields, forests, islands, rivers, coastlines, barns and buildings hold the potential to become power stations, with different technologies appropriate to every scale or region.

By their very nature these renewable reserves will not peak. In fact, as the technology matures and becomes economic in a wider range of applications, the available reserve actually increases whilst making the economy resilient to price hikes from overseas and preventing future financial turmoil as energy import costs spiral.

This energy transition is the cornerstone of a new economic approach that will move society on from doing the things that got us into so much trouble in the first place. By learning the hard economic lessons of the past few decades we can refocus the ingenuity of the finance sector on the actual challenges at hand.

Investment in such actions would not only create a vast carbon army of reskilled workers and inject money into the economy at ground level, it would also deliver very tangible returns to repay the investor – be they the taxpayer, an individual or a pension fund – from the price of the energy saved or generated. Additionally, such action would help to future-proof our economy against politically motivated energy blockades or price hikes and improve our balance of payments.

What lessons can communities learn from our vision of a Zero Carbon Britain?

Although there are no absolutes, it turns out that there is a tendency for powering down our energy intensity to be more accessible though a rethink of a lot of our individual lifestyle choices. On the other hand, a great deal of the powering up of renewable energy on the scale actually required means a wide deployment of regional, national or even international scale initiatives, such as offshore wind, wave and tidal schemes, or the EU supergrid.

Making your action plan

The next steps lie in clarifying your goals and mapping the road ahead, and deciding whom you would like to travel with. There are many different ways to move forward, in both powering down the amount of energy you use, and powering up your renewable sources. Here are four options to consider as you begin to draw up your plans.

1. **Being clear about who you are, where you are starting from and what else you want to achieve.** Your prime motive is clearly cutting your carbon dependence, but in deciding where to start you also need to look at where you are starting from and identify the additional benefits you want to maximise. For example, as well as cutting carbon are you also looking to save or invest money? Do you want to eat differently, get fitter, meet more people, declutter your life or just stay warmer in the winter? In fact, facing up to our oil addiction and decarbonising our diet, buildings, energy, water, work, clothing, heating, holidays and healthcare could actually increase our overall wellbeing.

2. **Looking for synergy in your solutions.** Once we join the dots and look for the bigger picture we find a great many solutions to one problem can also help to solve others. Just as the problems, if left unchecked, will compound and synergise, if we plan cleverly, the solutions we create can also synergise, but in a positive way to yield results greater than the sum of their parts. For example, saving energy in one place also saves money, which can then be reinvested to make other changes somewhere else.

3. **Working together.** There are already a great many people working together to mobilise solutions. We have learned from our history that communities often thrive in the face of pressures from the outside world, and do so by bringing together the graft and inventiveness of hard working local people. From establishing social enterprises to running a community housing initiative, from developing local food projects to inventing local money schemes, people are rolling up their sleeves and taking action to support the local economy, build social capital and take collective action to develop a wide range of community based assets. Working collectively helps you gain economies of scale and so reduce your costs. Larger community scale projects can also utilise technologies that don't really work that well at an individual or domestic scale. This book does not intend to duplicate the excellent group working advice provided by the Transition movement and other community networks; instead we will help groups redefine their attitudes and approaches to their energy choices.

4. **Fostering resilience.** As we plan changes in our homes, places of work and local communities, we can also build in the idea of deliberately redesigning things in such a way that makes them more robust and capable of standing up to the unexpected shocks and disruptions that lie ahead without simply falling to pieces. Fostering resilience is valuable at a personal, community and national level.

However, there is still a vital role for community scale renewable generation, particularly as it offers a double benefit; it not only reduces emissions but changes how we perceive and behave towards energy, changing our 'consumer attitudes'. The past decade has seen an unprecedented rise in the demand for local sustainably produced food, both for our personal and wider benefit. There is no reason why the coming years will not see growing demand for local sustainably produced energy.

Campaigning for change or being the change?

We can't wait for government, but can't ignore government either, nationally or internationally. Clearly there are many things that need to be done at national and international levels, and there are a wide range of campaigns and organisations we can join to make our voices heard. But there is also a wide range of actions we can take ourselves at domestic and community level. These are not opposing paths; in fact they are highly complementary. Pioneering projects demonstrate that we have both the will and the technology for change, which can of course influence policy. Better policies should make it easier to scale up the pioneering projects.

Although it will be locally rooted, a resilient future has aspects that require the creation of national and international plans. Everything cannot happen by happenstance, we still need to be working to a big picture, but this picture itself must be painted from the lessons learned by pioneering and integrating community scale projects. Through this two-way dialogue we create a platform for scaling up and accelerating the transition.

Mapping out your way forward

Exploring your way forward will depend on your individual location and circumstance, but there is a common approach:

- Get informed.
- Get a group.
- Get a plan.
- Get skilled.

- Get connected.
- Minimise demand.
- Rethink supply.
- Recycle the savings into your next action.
- Share your experiences honestly with others.

One of the best ways to begin mapping your route from fossil fuel dependence is to get to grips with the information that lies behind your energy use. Get your hands on your data; begin to understand the scale and speed at which the different types of energy flow into and out of your life.

This process can begin with a list of the types of energy you use in a typical week, month or year and what things you use it for. You can find out how much of each type you use and how much their costs have increased over recent years. You can do this as a group, family or on your own; the data is there in electricity and gas bills, petrol receipts and so on. Many of the new utility bills have your previous consumption printed on them in the form of a graph.

It is also worth doing a quick 'energy vulnerability' analysis for your current lifestyle. What would happen to your personal choices if any of the forms of energy you currently use became very much more expensive, or even intermittent? Assembling this picture is the first step to getting rid of that subconscious, outdated 1950s approach to energy, equipping you for the process of rationalising your energy demand and preparing you for price hikes, blackouts or any of the other assorted energy shocks which may lie ahead.

Please don't fool yourself – although they are important, your individual preparations are unlikely to be enough on their own. The only way ahead is to get through the energy challenge collectively, both nationally and internationally – but even being personally aware, and partially prepared, is a great deal better than being totally unaware and totally unprepared!

So how do we decide what to do first?

As a general rule, it is more effective to reduce the need for energy than to try and get it another way. We can switch energy suppliers, we can generate

What do we mean by fostering resilience?

In the act of globalising everything at the lowest cost option the profit driven free market economy has removed the diversity, variety and natural redundancy which underpin the 'bounce back' of local resilience. 21st century society must face the long emergency of breaching ecological limits whilst being stuck in a very 'brittle' society. 'Just in time delivery' becomes 'clean out of stock'; the 'least cost option' becomes the 'least available option', and as surely as one thing leads to another; failures quickly begin to synergise, carrying things far beyond any government or local authority's ability to cope, leaving us 'high and dry'.

Over recent years, communities across the Western world have struggled to adjust to a new era of profound and abrupt change. Although not of their own making, these changes compel communities to reconsider how they plan to move forwards into the 21st century.

Resilience is going to be an important factor in the transition. It can be defined in two ways – both of which highlight different properties.

The first is the speed and competence with which a household, town or ecosystem can recover from shocks or dislocation.

The second is a measure of how well a system can flip into a totally different but still workable living system should the original one become untenable. This could be driven by a change in the climate, or a radical shift in energy prices.

Both of these definitions are useful – but they both view resilience only as a means of dealing with negative impacts. I feel it is also useful for us to consider a third type of resilience: our ability to quickly adapt to, and embrace, good fortune.

As we begin to explore the new renewable energy assets we find on our doorstep, we need to be smart, flexible and adaptive, as we quickly harness this amazing and perpetual resource.

Resilience can become the new lens through which we filter our lifestyle choices. By working to develop our physical resilience we also build psychological resilience, both on a personal and community level. We are no longer in denial; we are actually working on the task at hand. Being on such a trajectory brings you into relations with others and so builds pathways into a new community. This alone can do wonders to improve our quality of life, as many of the Transition Towns demonstrate so well.

Building real resilience is of course rooted in interpersonal networks and linking into your wider community is clearly going to be important, but developing a closer affinity group is also invaluable. These people will form the group you build deeper trust with; they will be your first port of call in times of difficulty; they will be the group who share your investments in energy efficiency or renewable generation systems.

Resilience can create a powerful new driver for engaging more deeply with our friends and neighbours. Of course, a group of resilient individuals does not necessarily make a resilient community. But once they come together in common purpose they become a powerful force for change.

Of course, shifting our attitudes to energy is not the only action needed to increase our resilience, it also embraces a wide range of areas including health, skills, confidence, equity and community cohesion. Another very tangible way of increasing your personal and community resilience is to work together to reduce your debt. The short term economic thinking of the 1990s meant that living with increasing levels of debt became the norm. The economic reality of recent years has left many of us with levels of personal secured and unsecured debt far above what is good for us. Many of the paths for carbon descent, energy descent and debt descent run a very similar course. Using less energy and buying fewer things requires less money, releasing more funds to repay debt as quickly as possible.

Resilience is going to play an increasing role as we reshape our lives in the coming years. Creating resilience in the communities that surround us cannot only help deliver tangible benefits, it can be a creative and empowering process.

energy ourselves, but far and away the most powerful tool for cutting carbon and increasing our resilience is to reduce our energy excesses. The powering down section of this book takes us through this in great detail via insulation, smart appliances and so on. Suffice to say, even more than putting panels on our roofs, cutting our energy demand is a powerful first step for increasing our personal and community resilience in the face of an increasingly turbulent world.

For example, the winter of 2010-11 was a wake up call for the UK. We had weeks of -15°C for the first time in a number of years. Because our homes and offices are poorly insulated, UK gas consumption rose to an all time high, with many newspapers warning of only a few days' reserves in the network.

In 2020 or 2030 a period at -15°C could be a lot more challenging. Currently we still get a lot of the energy we need from our own North Sea oil and gas reserves, but these have now peaked and their output is declining annually. By 2030 these reserves will be just a small percentage of the current production capacity and our supplies will be coming from much further afield. We would be foolish not to take action now, particularly if the same actions actually save us money too! We are clearly more resilient when we have a super insulated home and a heating system incorporating the option of a backup fuel for at least one room should all else fail.

Although there are some good quick wins to starting off by powering down, no one is suggesting you have to take it to its limit before beginning to power up: the two processes must run together. Particularly at the moment, the Feed-in Tariff and Renewable Heat Incentives offer powerful drivers to becoming an energy generator. We hope this book helps ensure the choices you make are well informed.

Looking forwards

As we make our own changes, and explore the changes others have made, we are beginning to glimpse a sustainable future, dappled in the present. Replicable beacons of good resilient practice are beginning to multiply, harnessing economies of scale and multiplying it by community ingenuity

and courage. This in turn begins to change our wider culture.

Reality TV is actually a long way from reality. The messages of impending 21st century challenges and the solutions they demand have so far been largely restricted to scientific papers and independent media. They are absent from mainstream television culture, in the films or on the radio, although you might just catch a mention on the Archers. We are constantly bombarded with an unbroken torrent of 'infotainment' utterly divorced from our physical reality.

I have yet to see a significant work of popular art that captures the modern aspirations of our transition and more importantly of a post-transition society. No novel, song, painting, docu-drama, soap or movie has come close to portraying what living in a Zero Carbon Britain might look or feel like. But together, we can pioneer it. We can see it if we squint. We can see dappled rays of the future here and there, which will, over time, become commonplace.

Make no mistake, the transition from fossil fuels will mark a turning point in our history every bit as remarkable as the Agricultural Revolution or the Industrial Revolution. We need to harness the same grit, determination, and ingenuity of those pioneering times, to build a new energy revolution capable of yet again creating a new world, as yet unimagined.

In pioneering real physical changes in our own living systems, whilst also projecting our collective achievements, we also play a special part in breaking the dangerous deadlock of politics as usual and generating a new solutions driven mass movement which can help lever vital international agreement by demonstrating we have both the technologies and the will for change.

Chapter Three

Calculating personal carbon: are you responsible for your own emissions?

Peter Harper

Counting and cutting carbon – finding a game plan that works

In the previous chapter we started to think about 'doing the numbers'; about setting out a baseline from which we could measure our carbon descent and then measuring that descent as we make it – rather like counting the number of steps down a long flight of stairs.

Of course, unlike a real staircase where people generally start at the top and make their way down to the bottom, most people are starting at, and travelling to, different places on the staircase. Some can only easily make it part of the way down, whilst others need to go further than the bottom.

Measuring where all these people – six to nine billion of us – are on the staircase and where we all need to get to is not going to be easy, so we need some common agreement from the start. In this chapter I look at some of the tools that exist for calculating carbon and talk about which ones work best, before going on to look at the areas where we need to and can make the most important changes.

This chapter is designed to make you think more deeply about carbon calculation; to help you prioritise your own actions so that you know that what you are doing is effective and essential.

Vanquishing the vague

Most prescriptions for personal energy descent, or 'how to be greener', are contained in unranked and unquantified lists of 'Good Things To Do', often hundreds of items long. It's hard to do even a fraction of them. Often enough, would-be-green households, businesses or government departments simply pick a few easy items and consider their responsibilities discharged.

'Environmental calculators' challenge this hit-and-miss approach. They bring some crucial numbers to the table and help you make appropriate choices; where the 'jugulars' are and which things are not really worth bothering with. For example, they might show you that flying is more important than recycling, so it would make sense to spend more effort on the one than on the other. Over time a calculator can also be used to monitor and record any changes, so you know whether your efforts are succeeding, and how quickly.

Ecological footprinting and carbon accounting

Out of dozens of potential environmental indicator systems – in other words, analysis techniques that show us the impact we are having on our environment – each with its own strengths and weaknesses, two have emerged as being particularly helpful for personal calculators: Ecological Footprinting (EF) and Carbon Accounting (CA). Their key quality is that they reduce everything to robust *quantities* that can be compared with some measurable limit and thus give you a clear indication of your overall sustainability. In the case of EF this standard is the so-called 'bioproductive capacity' of the earth itself.

An EF score is a measure of land *area* (hence 'footprint') and can be given a sharp meaning in terms of the 'number of earths' needed to support it if everybody behaved in the same way. This gives us the unforgettable target of 'One Planet Living'.

A 'footprint' is a dramatic metaphor evoking several images, for example, of a human squashing something, perhaps inadvertently; and at the same time the idea of definite limits, connecting with those striking images of the earth from space. That there is 'only one earth' is so fundamental a piece of knowledge, if the EF shows that 'you' are in some sense using up more than one Earth, you know you've got to shape up.

On the downside there are one or two methodological difficulties with EF that make it a bit fuzzy, and since climate change has emerged as a kind of grand 'proxy' for all other environmental problems, there has been a tendency to use the easier-to-measure greenhouse gas (GHG) emissions (we often say 'carbon emissions' as a rough shorthand) for the main parameter, with various IPCC targets or emission standards setting the limits rather than the size of a country or of the earth (IPCC being the authoritative Intergovernmental Panel on Climate Change).

In fact the GHG component is almost invariably the largest element in an EF score anyway, and the two match each other very well in most areas. As a result, carbon accounting is very often used as an easier and equally meaningful substitute for EF, and (somewhat to the annoyance of the EF community) the 'footprint' metaphor has been stolen as well, so now pretty well everybody speaks of 'carbon footprints'.

For these reasons, we'll concentrate on the carbon measure rather than the EF measure. No disrespect to EF! We'll also be concentrating on UK rather than global emissions, which are regrettably beyond the scope of this book.

What is the carbon problem?

First, we have to step back and look at the wider picture. What is the 'carbon problem' and how do actual people fit into it? It's all rather new to the scientific and policymaking communities, so there is no one single obvious way to look at it or measure it. But to get involved you have to take a view, to take certain opinions on trust, and perhaps ignore others. Not easy, and there is more 'philosophy' than most people are comfortable with. But we try to do the best we can.

The first thing to appreciate is that it's an *all-the-world* problem and that little Britain, and even more so, little you, cannot solve it all on your own. We can 'do our bit', but what *is* our bit? The commonest idea is that we should try to work out what level of GHG emissions the earth can stand on a permanent basis, call that a limit, and then divvy up the total so everyone on earth gets the same allowance.

This seems very reasonable, but you can imagine how difficult it is to decide *what* a reasonable limit is. In fact, some climate scientists argue we have already gone past a reasonable limit. There is also a question of whether 'equal fair shares now' is actually fair, because the people in the rich countries have essentially caused the problem through the emissions they generated during their modernisation process. Don't the developing countries deserve the same whack of low-cost energy to get them out of poverty and into the modern world?

We can go on debating these questions, but for the purposes of this discussion we need to make some assumptions, bearing in mind that they are no more than that. Let's assume a 'moving to fair shares as soon as possible' principle, of which the most well known expression is 'Contraction and Convergence' (discussion of which is beyond the bounds of this book but can be found in great quantity on the internet and in Aubrey Meyer's writings on the subject).

Limitations of EF and CA

Perhaps we should note in passing that neither EF or CA embrace all possible environmental impacts. They do not cover quality of life or visual impacts or 'pollution' in the classical sense (smogs, chemical spillages, air quality and so on). Significantly, in both systems nuclear power comes up smelling of roses (as it were). This means that if you don't like nuclear power you have to invoke criteria other than area or GHG emissions. Having said this, GHG emissions do correlate remarkably well with most other classes of environmental impact. See figure 1.

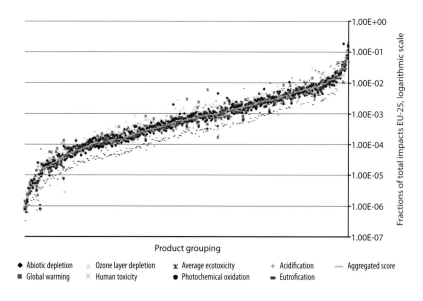

Fig. 1. *The different environmental impacts related to the final consumption of products (full set) and aggregated scores, product groupings ordered as to increasing aggregate score.*

The graph above shows a large range of products ranked according to a range of environmental impacts. The first thing to note is the very high correlation between the different kinds of impacts. The second thing is that there are very few 'purple squares' (global warming scores) that are 'outliers': they cluster near the centre of the distribution. The conclusion is that to a very good approximation, global warming can be used as a proxy for that vast basket of troubles airily referred to as 'environmental impact'.

Indirect and direct carbon emissions

Basic carbon calculators for individual householders are quite easy to create, and there are lots of them. The easiest items to measure are 'direct emissions' covering travel and energy use in the home. By 'direct' we mean that the CO_2 is emitted right there and then, from (for example) the gas stove or the exhaust pipe of the car, or through air travel. Electricity is also considered 'direct' since although the CO_2 is not actually emitted at the point of use, we know fairly precisely how much was emitted at the power station just a few moments before.

Because these emissions are so easy to measure with a good degree of accuracy, many calculators stick with them, and give you the results as 'your carbon emissions' or 'your carbon footprint'. This is rather misleading, because these direct emissions actually account for *less than 40%* of the national total.

We're already into some philosophy here, because you could say, 'alright, I accept that this 40% is our bit, householders and consumers: but the other 60% surely belongs elsewhere'. But where is 'elsewhere'? What is the difference between consuming petrol or gas and consuming food or clothes or hospital services?

More sophisticated and 'realistic' calculators accept that there isn't really a difference. They show all the emissions, including the *indirect* emissions due to purchases of food, goods and services, plus a household's or individual's share in the background investment and physical infrastructure over which an individual has little direct control.

Very broadly speaking, we can divide emissions into three huge classes:

The 'basket' of greenhouse gases

A proper comprehensive calculator includes *all* GHG gases, not just CO_2. This is important because a significant fraction of the warming effect – perhaps as much as 25% – is unconnected with CO_2. It is important in this context to note the terms that are used in various places. In some, the reference is entirely to CO_2 emissions, and confusingly this is sometimes given not as CO_2 but as carbon alone. Since carbon makes up 37% of the weight of the CO_2 molecule, the two measures can be converted by multiplying or dividing by 3.7 accordingly.

The simple carbon measure, however, does not take account of the fact that some carbon containing molecules have much higher (or lower) warming effects than CO_2 itself. The only reasonable measure is the 'CO_2equivalent' or 'CO_2e' for short, that measures the warming (or 'forcing') effect of each GHG relative to CO_2. Each greenhouse gas is given a Global Warming Potential (GWP) score relative to the CO_2 value of 1, which is multiplied by the amount emitted to give the overall effect.

For example, Nitrous oxide (N_2O) has a GWP of about 300, so a mixture of 20 tonnes CO_2 and 1 tonne of N_2O would have a GWP of $20 + 300 = 320$ tonnes CO_2e. Thankfully, N_2O is not emitted in anything like the quantity CO_2 is; however, that which is emitted is 300 times more dangerous than the equivalent amount of CO_2. Note that not all GHGs contain carbon, even though colloquially we speak of 'carbon emissions'.

There is one final complication in relating the GHGs to CO_2. The effect of each gas's GWP is different over different periods of time, so strictly speaking the time should be specified.

Over 100 years, methane has a GWP of 25, but over 20 years the value is 72. For the present discussion we can leave this debate on one side, but be warned that as opinions and policies crystallise on a target date such as 2030 or 2050, the agreed GWPs are likely to be adjusted and might well change the ranking of which measures to prioritise. That's why I said earlier, 'a significant fraction of the warming effect – perhaps as much as 25% – is unconnected with CO_2': on current accepted conventions adopted for the purposes of the Kyoto Protocol, it's given as about 15%, but this is essentially a legal convention.

You often see the bald statement that 'methane is 25 times more powerful than CO_2'. This is only true by convention, and for the purposes of mitigating climate change before 2050, the effective value should be considerably more than 25.

1. Direct emissions from the fuels and other energy you consume in the home – about 21%.
2. Direct emissions from fuels used to move you about – roughly 10%.
3. Everything else – the indirect emissions – about 69%.

The emissions in this last class are usually referred to as *embodied* emissions, because although the actual GHGs were released at some other time and place, they are considered to be 'embodied' in the goods and services that engendered them. They remain embodied, a bit like a genie in a lamp, until they reach their final consumer, when – metaphorically speaking – they emerge and are deemed to be the responsibility of that consumer. This question of 'responsibility' is discussed in the box on page 26.

The estimated range for the UK's annual consumption related emissions is as wide as 720 million tonnes (Mt) to 934Mt. To cut elaborate discussion short, we will adopt a figure of 862Mt, giving a per capita footprint of nearly $15tCO_2e$ per person per year, or 33 tonnes per year for the 'average household' of 2.3 people.

Who is responsible: the emitter or the consumer?

The UK government collects statistics on the emissions that arise in their own territory, as do most other governments. These are taken very seriously and reported under the terms of the Kyoto Protocol. The total is often called the 'territorial emissions' and makes up the headline figure regularly announced by the UK government – usually falling, and accompanied by self-congratulatory fanfares.

Because the territorial emissions are carefully measured, analysts like to use them. But they are in some fundamental sense rather misleading because almost anybody would agree that 'responsibility' for emissions should belong, not to the *producers* of emissions, but to the *consumers* – those who ultimately benefit from the emissions.

On this 'consumption basis', the emissions for which the UK (and its citizens) can be considered responsible, are much higher. They include, for example, the UK's share of emissions from international shipping and aviation, and the emissions required to produce the goods imported into the UK.

There are, therefore, two ways of assessing national carbon accounts, a 'production perspective' and a 'consumption perspective'. From the point of view of constructing a personal or household emissions calculator it is definitely the consumption perspective that we want.

Unfortunately, it is much harder to measure the consumption accounts, and any measurement requires a fair amount of fudging and 'informed guesswork' that is sensitive to a broad field of assumptions that many analysts don't even know they're making. The result is that there is quite a wide range of estimates for the UK's total consumption emissions, and anybody who is trying to construct a domestic carbon calculator has to 'take a view' on which estimate to use.

Carbon calculators – footprints and fingerprints

In spite of these conceptual difficulties it is usually possible to create a calculator that will reflect the basic carbon realities of modern life and tell you very useful things. CAT's approach is simply to divide the total national consumption emissions – the national carbon footprint – by the whole population. That gives us the average emissions per head, or the 'carbon footprint' of the average person. This is a very important statistic. We can go further. Because national emissions statistics are collected on a very wide range of categories, it is possible to break the basic footprint into a series of useful categories to give what we might call the 'fingerprint': the allocation of emissions to particular 'sectors' of the economy. This is usually done by means of 'Input-Output' (I-O) tables produced by the Office of National Statistics (ONS).

Unfortunately, the ONS tables, like so many official statistics, prefer to use data that can be verified and replicated, rather than less clear data that are closer to the underlying reality. So constructors of calculators that strive for 'reality' are forced to 'interpret' or 'second guess' many of the official figures.

Just to clarify our terminology here, we use 'footprint' to mean the whole of a person's, (or household's, or nation's) emissions. 'Fingerprint' is a more qualitative measure, used in analogy with forensic fingerprinting, referring to the proportions of different subcategories, different for each case. Two households might both have a carbon footprint of (say) 15 tonnes, but have completely different carbon fingerprints, just as two people might have the same size of finger but completely different fingerprint patterns.

An interesting feature of the 'national fingerprint' (using consumption-based accounts) is that by definition it must precisely map onto the 'personal fingerprint' of the average citizen. This means that the sum total of each component of the personal fingerprints adds up exactly to the corresponding national footprint. We could refer to the nation's footprint as the 'macro-footprint' and the average citizen's as the 'micro-footprint'.

The effect of this mathematical mapping assumption is to relate an individual's score to the national total and to national targets. This has significant educational and political value by indicating who it is that is responsible and what kind of action should be taken, and by whom.

In particular, it clarifies the see-saw relationship between sustainable consumption and sustainable production, and plugs into fundamental environmental debates on affluence and economic growth.

Some numbers: figure 2 shows the UK's consumption based emissions 'fingerprint', or in other words, how the 'footprint' breaks down into components. This is therefore – by definition – also the fingerprint of the 'average citizen' and the 'average household'. These 'averages' don't refer to any household in particular, but the statistical average generated by the simple arithmetic.

Principal categories of carbon emissions

We noted before that the average footprint could be anywhere between 12tCO2e and 16tCO2e, depending on assumptions and how you do the sums. The 'fingerprint' – the way a household's footprint is made up – is possibly a more helpful tool. But even this is a little bit elastic. You will find in different calculators considerable differences in the fingerprint, even though the size of the whole footprint is the same. This is because statistics are collected in all sorts of different ways, without necessarily having carbon emissions in mind, and carbon assessors have to make decisions about which categories to put them in.

Let's take some examples. Does 'transport' include the emissions in making the vehicles or aeroplanes? Or in servicing them? Or the journeys to work of the bus drivers and car assembly workers? Does 'food' include journeys to buy the stuff? Or the emissions from retail shops? Or the energy for cooking and refrigeration? Or the disposal of wasted food? Does 'clothing' include shopping trips? Or washing and ironing?

You can choose to have a narrow interpretation or a wide interpretation of each category but, of course, all that is happening is that the boundaries are shifting: you are moving emissions from one category to another. Washing and ironing can be under 'clothing' or 'electricity'. Food shopping can be under 'food' or 'transport'. The total footprint is the same, but the allocations are different. This can be a real head-scratcher from the point of view of trying to create a helpful personal calculator, and personal prejudices can easily affect the result. 'Food' for example can range from about 12% of a footprint to twice as much, depending on what you decide to include.

The carbon cost of the public sector

There's another decision to be made as well: what about the bit relating to the government? Some calculators put it in, others leave it out. This is very confusing. The reason for leaving it out is that it is not under the direct control of householders or consumers, so why bother showing it in the calculator? The reason for showing it would be that you would then get (ah!) the whole picture: your own country's emissions, and by extension your own 'default' emissions in one exact 1/62,000,000 scale, including your share of responsibility for the emissions of your country's government.

House energy 21%

Transport 25%

Food 18%

Goods and services 21%

Infrastructure 15%

Fig. 2. A consumption-based CO₂e 'fingerprint' of the UK. It applies to the average household and the average citizen. These are the big categories that we shall use in the rest of the discussion. 'Infrastructure' refers to all the services provided by government, and public investment.

Figure 2 shows a basic split into five principal categories: house energy, transport, food, goods and services, and infrastructure.

To aid the discussion we have colour-coded the main categories. Red and yellow, are the direct emission categories, house energy (HE) and transport. Green and light blue are the indirect emissions categories, food (green) and goods and services ('G&S', light blue). In black are the emissions generated by the government on your behalf in providing schools, roads, hospitals, pensions and so on. As a consumer you pay for the coloured bits in cash, while the black bit is paid for through taxes.

We like this difference between consumers and government because it reminds us of our 'civic obligations' and that sustainability is mainly a collective matter that cannot be achieved entirely by heroic personal efforts. It also introduces another useful distinction. We could say that as citizens we are all *ultimately* responsible for the UK's emissions. If not us, who? But we are not *effectively* responsible for the government bit. The only way we can influence that is through political activity and, of course, we should engage as vigorously as possible in that. But in the short run we have virtually no power to change the government's share.

Carbon emissions and business

At this point, someone is going to ask; hang on, what about industry – the business sector? Don't they have

some responsibility too? This is another tricky matter. If you are trying to construct a consumption rather than a production account, you are not asking 'who emits?' but 'who benefits?' In a modern democracy the entire economy is run for the benefit of its citizen consumers. That is why the entire 'micro-footprint' is allocated to consumers. The business sector does not 'benefit' so, in principle, it has no footprint at all!

OK, in some ways this is obviously a daft thing to say, because businesses certainly do have a certain amount of discretion in how they operate, and what processes they choose to provide their products. So, similar to the government sector, we could say that businesses have some *effective* responsibility even though they have no *ultimate* responsibility.

The problem is how to fit this into the calculator, because the emissions categories are all accounted for. We can't add anything, we can only subdivide existing categories. But how do we do this? How *much* effective responsibility should be awarded to businesses in each subsector? It might well be possible but would take an enormous amount of research and thousands of heroic assumptions. And it would be highly political.

The right-wing view would be that the consumer is sovereign, and businesses only supply what is demanded. If a product has high emissions, consumers should consume less of it or buy something else. Therefore business has negligible responsibility.

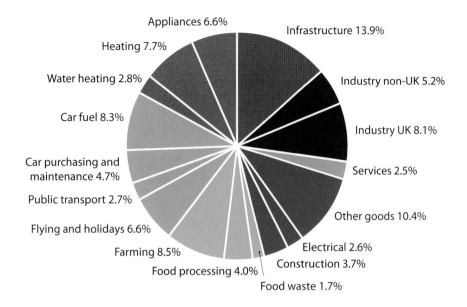

Fig. 3. Another way of representing the averaged 'fingerprint' with the main categories of figure 2 subdivided. It also includes an allocation for 'industry' both in the UK and overseas (grey).

In complete contrast, the left-wing view would be that consumers are helpless playthings of ruthless capitalists who have mastered the dark arts of generating demand for things that are not actually needed. Therefore they, not the consumers, should take most responsibility for the emissions.

How do we decide which view is more appropriate? Let's side-step this question and ask for each category of consumption: what are the highest and lowest emissions generated to produce a given unit? The difference between the highest and lowest could be used as a measure of the 'discretion' available to manufacturers and providers, and hence a measure of their effective responsibility for emissions. An example of the results is shown in figure 3. But for reasons of presentational clarity, we'll abandon this way of cutting the cake for the rest of the chapter.

Figures 2 and 3 apply to the statistical average. Any real person is going to differ both in their micro-footprint and in their fingerprint – the way their footprint is made up. There are lots of influences on both measures, including the composition of the household, age, family customs, type of work and so on. And, of course, there are deliberate carbon

reduction measures that we'll discuss later. But by far the largest influence on a household's emissions is *expenditure*, and in turn that is very closely related to income. Richer households emit more, and the relationship is remarkably close, as you can see from figure 4.

Other things being equal, a household with a disposable income of £900 a week would have about twice the emissions of one at £300 a week. This reminds us that spending money into the UK economy generates GHG emissions in one way or another – mostly embodied – and it is much harder for the wealthy to decarbonise than for those who are less well off.

How does spending relate to the emissions categories?

Figure 5 shows the standard categories of emissions compared with the amount spent on the same categories by the average household. The comparison is striking, because it shows we tend to spend relatively little on some of the bigger emitting categories. We pay a lot for our public services and for commercial goods and services, and relatively little

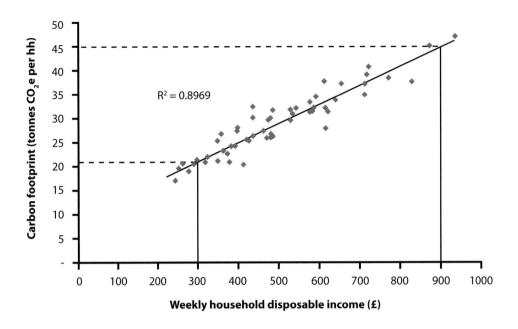

Fig. 4. *Correlation between household disposable income and overall carbon footprint. From Minx et al. (2010). The blue dots are the data-points collected by the researchers. R^2 is a measure of the correlation between the two variables. The highest possible score is 1, so this score of 0.8969 shows a remarkably strong correlation.*

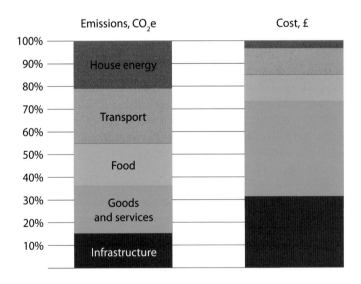

Fig. 5. *Yet another way of representing the basic fingerprint, comparing the categories by emissions and by expenditure, which is very different.*

for the real basics, HE, transport and food. It is quite surprising to hear that expenditure on household energy is less than 4% of the average household's budget, but we have got so used to cheap energy that 'fuel poverty' is defined as having to spend more than 10% of a household budget on HE. It is consumer goods, and above all *services* that cost a lot.

Economic carbon intensity

The relationship between emissions and expenditure is the basis for a very important measure in carbon accounting, the *economic carbon intensity,* usually measured in kilograms of CO_2e per pound sterling or kgCO_2e/£. We'll be calling it just 'intensity' and leave the 'carbon' understood. The intensity of a product or service can vary a lot. This means that in carbon terms, a pound spent on one item might entail very different emissions from a pound spent on a different item. This is shown in figure 6 for the average household.

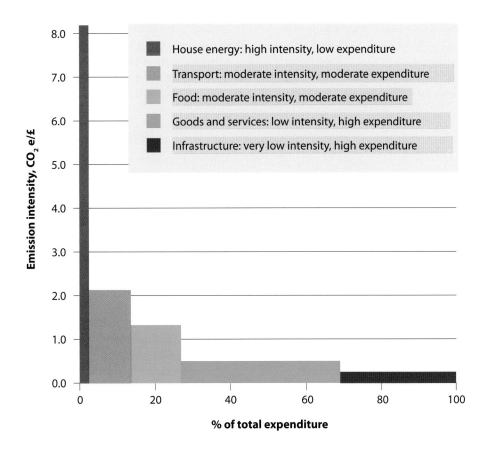

Fig. 6. Emissions intensity plotted against expenditure in each principal category for the average household. The areas of the blocks are proportional to the total emissions of that category.

Why carbon intensity is important

Figure 6 shows several things. The main categories are ranked in intensity pecking order from left to right. The most intense is HE at 8.3, followed by transport at 2.2, food at 1.3, G&S at 0.5 and government services at 0.2. The expenditures for each are shown along the horizontal axis. Plotting intensity against expenditure in this way reveals the total emissions from each category through the *area* of each rectangle. This is the micro-footprint and fingerprint at a glance, with much more useful information. It shows that high total emissions can arise from high *intensity* (like HE) or from high *expenditure* (like G&S) or a bit of both (like transport or food).

This is important for transitional households to get a grip on: you won't save a lot of money by saving energy, because you don't spend much on it anyway. But on the other hand each small reduction in energy spending (along the bottom axis) has a really big effect on your emissions. The opposite is true for the G&S section: reducing spending by the same amount won't make much difference. Here you should pay attention to the intensity of what you buy (the vertical axis).

Switching to lower intensity spending

These principles are expanded in figures 7a and 7b, using transport as an example. 7a shows that the averaged intensities of figure 6 actually consist of a mixture of subcategories, often with starkly divergent intensities. This is important from a carbon reduction perspective, since you can't usually swap one of the major categories for another, but you can choose lower intensity ways of providing the same, or at least similar, services. It is often possible to choose different subcategories to lower overall emissions. This is not particularly surprising. In transport, most money is spent on private vehicles with a high intensity component (fuels) and a lower intensity component (buying and maintaining the vehicles). Private

---

The carbon intensity of flying

Flying is an unusual activity in that, while it emits GHGs directly and measurably (you just weigh the fuel) the emissions have some odd effects when emitted in the upper atmosphere. They might accentuate global warming by various cloud forming and other effects, or they might help to mitigate it. Experts argue furiously, but there is no universally agreed conclusion. This is very tough for calculator makers because once again they have to 'take a view' in calculating an effect to match a particular clutch of air miles.

Ten years ago it was widely thought that the effects of aviation were so bad that the raw GHG effects should be multiplied by 3, or even more. This meant that, for example, a trip to Australia could well outstrip all your other emissions for the whole year. Subsequently the IPCC has reduced this 'uplift factor', and in the latest *Assessment Report* it is effectively abolished altogether, not because we know the answer but because we don't: the data do not point to any definite conclusion one way or the other.

For this reason the examples given here do not contain any uplift factor, but current UK government practice is to apply a multiplier of 1.9. Many calculators do this, and it means that aviation will figure nearly twice as much and will actually increase the footprint a bit (because the 'uplift' does not represent extra GHGs). Older calculators might well still have an uplift of 3 or even 4, and in these cases a few trips can dominate the whole fingerprint.

There are other non-GHG effects as well: for example, soot depositions from inefficient combustion processes might well make a big difference overall. The theorists are working on how to assess and mitigate such effects but we ignore them here.

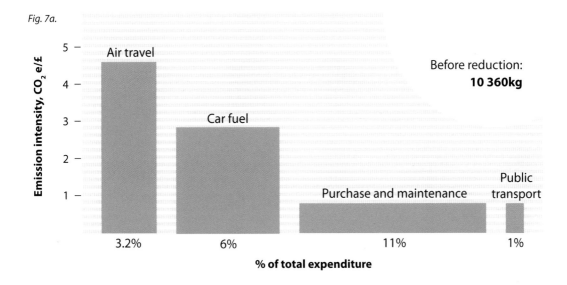

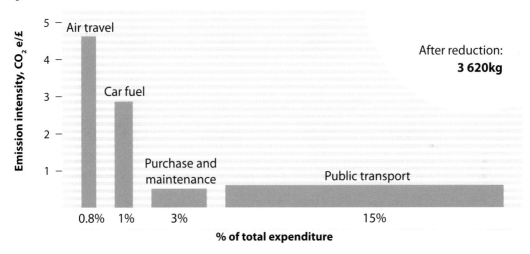

Fig. 7a & 7b. Example of how emissions might be reduced in the transport category, by switching spending to lower-intensity modes. The total miles travelled are virtually the same. Costs are lower, but of course it is important the money saved is not spent on higher-intensity categories.

transport costs you hard both in carbon and cash. Public transport has an intermediate intensity, so switching is likely to save both emissions *and money*.

But note that this doesn't work very well if you have a car and don't use it: a really big lump of carbon – and cash – is embodied in the car itself and the services needed to maintain it. It is important however to spend this saved money on items lower down the intensity hierarchy, not higher up – like flying or heating a less efficient house.

Food is slightly different from the other categories in being less 'elastic'. To a reasonable approximation

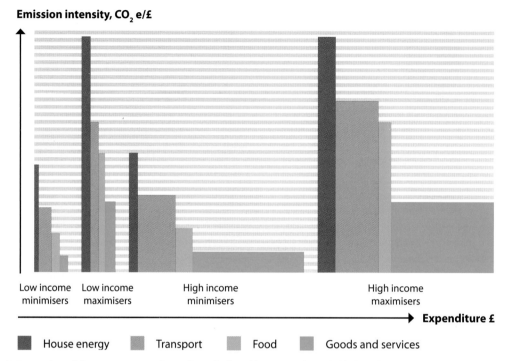

Emission intensity, CO$_2$ e/£

Low income
minimisers

Low income
maximisers

High income
minimisers

High income
maximisers

Expenditure £

■ House energy   ■ Transport   ■ Food   ■ Goods and services

Fig. 8. Comparison of divergent patterns of spending in high and low income households, based on observed cases. Expenditure/ emission categories run from right to left, HE, travel, food, G&S. Government and infrastructural spending is deemed to be equal for all households so is omitted. The areas of the categories are proportional to emissions and show potentially large differences within any given income class. They also show the large differences in emissions attributable to expenditure, which is, of course, greatly correlated with income.

we all need, and consume, similar quantities of food, so 'consuming less' is not such a viable strategy as it is in the other categories. Instead you have to concentrate on intensities in a different sense: the *material intensity* or CO$_2$e/kg of product.

For example, livestock products usually have higher material intensities than crop products, so switching even partially from one to the other (while maintaining the same nutritional value) can lower intensity and therefore overall emissions. The contrast in economic intensity is not usually so great, so dietary changes don't always save you money.

Rule of thumb: if your aim is to reduce emissions, shift expenditure from high intensity to low intensity goods and, if possible, into the lowest intensity services category.

How income relates to fingerprint

Households with different levels of income tend to spend slightly differently, and might have different strategies for reducing their emissions. Poorer households have little choice but to spend a large proportion on energy, food and essential transport, and after the rent or mortgage is paid have little left over.

Well off households spend proportionately less on the 'essentials' and have a large fraction of discretionary income. Some of this goes on better quality food, heating larger houses, and fashionable gadgets, but there is a particularly strong tendency to travel more by car and air, and these are high intensity activities.

On the other hand, shrewd well off households can choose to invest in low carbon technologies such as solar heating, heat pumps, electric vehicles. Very often these do *not* save money, but this simply means there is less money to spend on potentially intense goods so, paradoxically perhaps, it helps to reduce the overall intensity of the household.

Although income is a good predictor of household carbon emissions on average, there can be a wide range of emissions for households having the same size and income. This is demonstrated in figure 8, which shows two pairs of (hypothetical but credible) households at two different income levels, each with different habits and spending patterns and, therefore, widely divergent emissions.

As figure 4 (on page 30) shows, for any given level of income, there are households above the line and some below it. We know from other surveys that there can be as much as fivefold differences between households of the same size and income. Figure 8 shows this range is represented at each of the two income levels by exceptionally high emitters ('maximisers') and exceptionally low emitters ('minimisers').

This suggests that householders have considerable power to reduce their emissions, especially if they start above average, and there are plenty of anecdotal accounts that support this idea.

Can householders make a difference?

Is there any documented evidence to support the idea that householder action can make a big difference to their household footprint? Angela Druckman and Tim Jackson at the University of Surrey devised a 'reduced consumption scenario' based on typical 2004 emission data.

They drew up a list of plausible and 'sensible' measures open to most householders and found a hypothetical reduction of 37% in the footprint. Their proposals are summarised in figure 9. It is important to note that this reduction is achieved without a great deal of cultural effort or what might be called 'lifestyle change'. Food, for example, is not considered a changeable element.

Prashant Vaze, a former civil servant, in his excellent

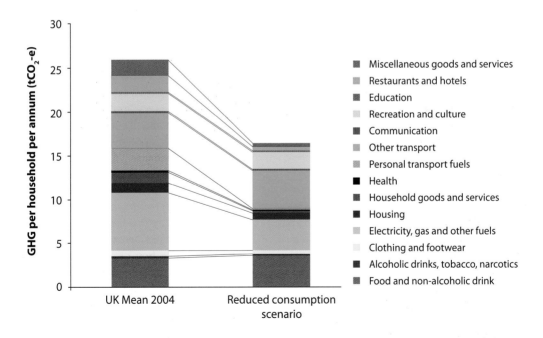

Fig. 9. Comparison of 2004 emissions fingerprint with proposed 'reduced emissions scenario', from Druckman and Jackson (2009).

The Economical Environmentalist, logged a 34% reduction in a single year, using rational measures marred only by an unavoidable long haul plane trip. Had he not taken this trip, the reduction would have been over 50%. He claimed it did not damage his quality of life, although there was a certain amount of resistance from the rest of the household!

I have myself carried out similar exercises, both on paper (Harper 2008) and in reality (Harper 2002), with results that suggest even greater reductions are feasible while maintaining what we might describe as 'modest modern standards of living'. The results are extremely sensitive to household income: I was poor and. in an odd way. that made it easier. It's much harder if you are wealthy. Rich people simply have too much money and, try as they will, they cannot find any way to spend it without generating emissions somewhere. What are they to do?

The wealthy environmentalist

One possibility is that wealthy people could shift responsibility onto the government. If only the government would act decisively to decarbonise the energy supply, then a large part of the emissions would be painlessly removed! Is this really the case? *Zero Carbon Britain 2030* (*ZCB2030*) succeeds in reducing UK emissions down to 10% across the whole economy (and the rest by sequestration processes).

The right hand stack in 10a applies most of the decarbonisation measures envisaged (in other words the Power Up and Power Down approach described in Paul's earlier chapter) to a hypothetical 'high income maximiser' household of 2030.

There are too many unknowns at this stage to be able to apply credible numbers, but figure 10a suggests some possible patterns. Note that these high income maximisers have enough money to pay the expected very high carbon taxes in any category, rendering the goods essentially inelastic.

Wealthy homeowners would probably achieve near-zero home energy emissions in *ZCB2030*. The other categories however are more problematic. Most surface travel would be fully decarbonised, but flying depends on biomass-derived aviation fuel that would have small but unavoidable positive emissions.

The food system cannot be fully decarbonised, and if the maximisers maintain a standard diet they will inevitably score high in this category. As far as goods are concerned, we are unsure what the major source of goods and services will be in *ZCB2030*, but probably it would not be fully decarbonised, so indiscriminate expenditure will result in higher emissions.

Figure 10b by contrast shows high income minimisers, that is, carbon-conscious households deliberately targeting their expenditure and also embracing certain lifestyle changes in categories that cannot be fully decarbonised. The likelihood is that in spite of their higher spending, such households would be able to achieve a micro-footprint below the 10% delivered by public policy in *ZCB2030*.

One might ask, this is all very well, but what can wealthy households do *now*? Let's rule out one thing: that they could simply give their money away to very low intensity 'good causes', thereby becoming low income minimisers instead of high income minimisers. They could, but few are likely to do this!

There is something the better off can do though that is far more effective than simply giving money away, and that is to invest it deliberately in carbon reducing or even carbon negative activities.

Just as people can spend their money 'badly' on high intensity goods, or 'well' on low intensity goods, they can do even better by spending on goods, services or activities that actively reduce emissions elsewhere (like renewable energy) or, even better, that actively withdraw CO_2 from the atmosphere. In terms of adding up our carbon emissions, these can be regarded as 'negative emissions' that are deducted from, rather than added to, the totals. Their intensity values would be expressed as negative kilograms of CO_2 per £ spent, for example, -5kg/£.

We can categorise these activities in two classes that I shall call 'onsets' and 'offsets'. An onset (derived, slightly facetiously, from offset but also mimicking 'on-site') is an investment in a household's on-site fabric or activities that reduces emissions. Many of these are extremely cost-effective and are open to most householders. Many, however, are expensive and unlikely to 'pay back' in cash terms.

Never mind, these investments reduce your

Fig. 10a. *Fig. 10b.* *Possible effects of top-down decarbonisation measures such as those envisaged in Zero Carbon Britain 2030, for high income 'maximisers' and 'minimisers'.*

emissions in the longer term and mop up cash that would be likely to cause higher emissions if available to spend in the UK economy – or worse, in some other economy with a higher overall intensity than that of the UK. Further, these investments help build markets and contribute to the 'learning curve' that improves products and brings down prices. Remember when compact fluorescent lamps cost £9 each? Now they give them away.

So much for onsets. *Offsets* are investments in low, zero or negative carbon processes somewhere else (or 'off-site'). You don't do it yourself, you pay someone else to do it. Now let us acknowledge that a certain kind of dubious offsetting activity has given the idea a bad reputation: sending a fiver to an organisation who promise to plant a tree to cancel out your trip to the Seychelles. I am not talking about this. I am talking about taking part in the grand background decarbonisation of the British economy. This is for those who cannot wait for the government to get round to doing it, and to put taxes up to pay for it – even though, of course, to meet its own targets it should. The process has to be catalysed, and this is a

vital role for the eco-wealthy.

The effects of both onsets and offsets are illustrated in figure 11b (page 39). The figure shows a fictitious household with an expenditure of £1,200 a week and a micro-footprint of around 60t a year. The household can halve this micro-footprint by cost-effective carbon reduction measures and investment in onsets, the most obvious being on-site renewable energy generation with net export to the national grid (in other words, producing more electricity than the household needs), and low-emission vehicles. It can also earn a 'credit' against the rest by investing as little as £100 a week in off-site renewable energy. This is a possible general model for how would-be-green, wealthy households 'should' behave in the transition period.

What if you are not wealthy? Investment in the new low carbon economy is open to 'average' households too. For example, a few years ago I bought a £500 stake in a local community wind power project, which amounted to about 3% of my extremely modest disposable income (about half the UK average).

At an intensity of -8kg/£, probably more in many

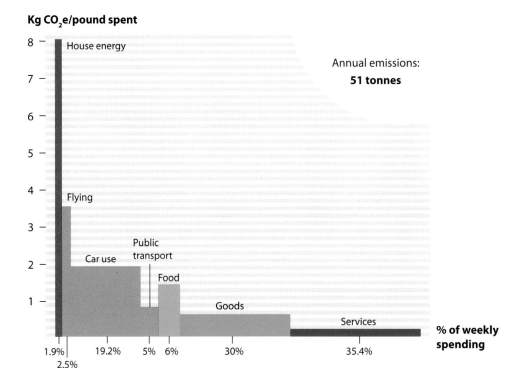

Kg CO$_2$e/pound spent

House energy

Annual emissions:
51 tonnes

Flying

Public
transport

Car use

Food

Goods

Services

**% of weekly
spending**

1.9%   19.2%   5%   6%   30%   35.4%

2.5%

Fig. 11a. *Wealthy families carbon emissions before comprehensive carbon reduction strategy introduced.*

cases, this sort of investment is something of a bargain for would-be decarbonisers. £120 buys you a 'negatonne' and makes a much larger impact than most other things you can do. But, of course, it would be idiotic to spend your £120 and undo its benefits by heedless high carbon spending.

Habits, customs and commitments

Have our experiences with the CAT calculators taught us anything about the most cost-effective measures to reduce our carbon footprint? A great deal of emissions arise from habit, custom and what we might call *commitments*. Commitments are what we feel obliged to do, like visiting relatives, providing our kids with the best schooling, giving Christmas presents that match the customs of our family, however carbon hungry. If you can alter

your commitments, you can start tackling the 'five pillars of modern life' that account for most of your carbon emissions. They are kept up by customs and commitments, and for most households are *non-negotiable*. If you can get these sorted out you can potentially relax and enjoy the rest of life. The pillars? They are:

- A warm cosy house – heated to shirt-sleeve temperatures throughout, most of the time, and no limits to electricity use.
- A family car (or three!).
- Meat and dairy products with virtually every meal.
- At least one annual holiday abroad.
- A constant flow of nice new stuff.

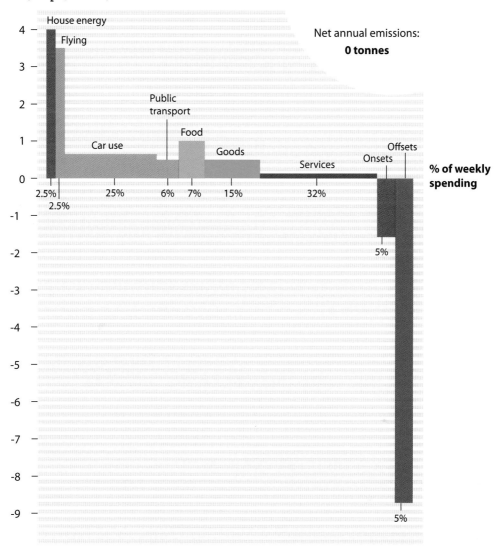

Kg CO₂e/pound spent

Net annual emissions:

0 tonnes

House energy

Flying

Public transport

Food

Car use

Goods

Services

Onsets

Offsets

% of weekly spending

2.5% 25% 6% 7% 15% 32% 5%

2.5%

5%

Fig. 11b. Wealthy families carbon emissions, after comprehensive carbon reduction strategy completed, including 'onsets' and 'offsets.'

I found personally that once I had worked out how to demolish these pillars not only was my carbon footprint cut by about 60%, but my quality of life actually improved. Sounds easy? No: I would suggest two important caveats. The first is that there is nearly always fierce resistance from other members of the household with their own preferences and commitments.

The second is even more significant. Anybody who manages to demolish the classic non-negotiables almost invariably has another set of hidden non-negotiables arising from habits and commitments characteristic of what we might call 'middle class *Guardian* reading greenies' These themselves might be high intensity or scarce-resource goods that put your carbon footprint right back where it started. Some of these non-negotiables are listed in the box. Do you recognise yourself?

Even if you don't, you almost certainly have different non-negotiables you'd find near impossible to demolish because they represent something integral to yourself. Either something to do with the vision you have of yourself or about status and social signalling. I planned a 15-year transition from previous commitments to a new low carbon set but still fell foul of nearly all *the Guardian* non-negotiables.

This is why *ZCB2030* is so interesting: it does nearly all the work from the top down and doesn't mess with a person's sense of identity or their social signalling systems. All we ask of the rich is that they don't obstruct legislation, don't be NIMBYs, pay up for the new infrastructure (buy bonds if they like) and pay their carbon taxes without grumbling.

Prioritising personal and community emissions reduction: doing things that really work!

Most of what we have learned is not very new: it's in most of the books on the subject, and sometimes quantified, but let's just go through a few hot tips in the main categories.

Remember that if you succeed in reducing one area drastically, the proportions of the other areas will increase, changing your perspective on what's the best thing to go for next.

Travel

No flying, or at least keep it to an absolute minimum. This will make a really big dent in your potential emissions, since flying is so cheap it's almost irresistible.

On personal vehicles, although it's good to have a clever efficient one and to reduce mileage wherever possible, you still have to pay the high fixed costs of purchase and maintenance, and experience shows

The secret non-negotiables of *Guardian* reading greenies

- Generously-sized house, probably bigger than you really need:
    - with character,
    - with garden,
    - in a pleasant location,
    - in a suitable neighbourhood.
- Compliance with family obligations:
    - including visits to relatives,
    - 'love miles' include friends and paramours,
    - advantageous choices for children.
- Having children is OK, as many as you like:
    - but not lodgers, too disruptive of family life,
    - although pets are OK, even quite big ones.

- Having a rewarding job, even if it's a long way away, entailing big commutes.
- Work doesn't count for carbon emissions.
- The right to split up and start a further household.
- Maintaining a civilised discourse:
    - no unseemly or illiberal proposals.
- Quasi-recreational travelling:
    - to South America, or maybe Far East, from time to time….ecotourism!

that if you have a car you'll use it – for pretty well everything. It's hard not to. So the biggest single step is to be a car-free household, and recycle the enormous savings into lower-intensity forms of transport. Here are a few ideas of how you can manage without a car. Most car-free households adopt a combination of these measures to allow them to carry on with convenience:

- Join a car-share club.
- Rather than owning a car, hire vehicles, or use occasional taxis where necessary.
- Get superb bicycles, and use them for routine short journeys, perhaps commutes. Spending extra money on bikes is worth it if you can afford it. Don't struggle with an old crock that is cheap but makes life hard!
- Find out about new electric-assist bikes. They extend practical commute lengths.
- Learn your way around the cheap deal systems on the rail network.
- Try to synchronise work/education and dwelling to minimise commutes for all members of the household. Live in a place where public travel links are good.

Food

Given that most people buy nearly all their food, the key choices are in terms of diet and what you buy. It obviously doesn't make sense to eat more than you need, and certainly not to *buy* more than you need and throw it away. Eating smaller amounts is good and healthy, and developing a culinary culture of using up leftovers extends your range. Most households waste 20% more food than they need to, the worst up to 50%.

So this is a big one. Any unavoidable waste can be fed to low carbon pets or composted using rat-proof bins, tumblers, digesters or wormeries. Don't forget to compost your cardboard too.

The largest emissions factor in the standard diet is associated with livestock products – in this order: beef>lamb>cheese>pork>poultry>eggs>fish>milk.

Reducing as much as you can, working from the front of the list, can have a big impact. No need to be vegetarian as such; a diet with small or occasional amounts of meat has lower emissions than a non-meat one with large quantities of dairy produce. Having said this, nobody beats the strict vegans.

Note that carnivorous pets, especially large dogs, can have a similar impact to an extra person. From a carbon perspective, best to stick to guinea pigs or gerbils.

The next ranking food emissions factor is in the post-farm-gate phase (in other words processing/preserving/transporting/distributing/cooking). It points to a shift away from highly processed foods and towards simpler raw or dried ingredients. Keep freezing to a minimum. Things eaten raw obviously need no cooking energy, but for cooking you should opt for pressure cookers, slow cookers and microwave ovens where possible.

Does growing your own (GYO) make a big difference to your food emissions? In direct terms, usually not. What!? How can this be? The reason is that GYO provides only fresh fruit and vegetables, not carbohydrates, proteins, oils/fats or exotic foods, and fruit and vegetables have such low carbon emissions anyway that there's not much to displace.

If you want GYO to make a bigger difference, you will have to shift your diet so that a much higher proportion comes from vegetables and fruit, say 50%, and this really does displace other categories to some degree. I have recorded meeting 25% of my food expenditure from an allotment-sized plot, assuming organic prices, and I try to build meals round seasonal vegetables, with the higher carbon foods added for variety, flavour and general oomph.

There is probably a fivefold difference in emissions between the lowest and highest types of nutritionally adequate diet. Usually the low-emission diets are healthier too.

Remember that for the average household home energy is only about 21% of your footprint and 4% of your expenditure. It is important but needs to be seen in context. The cornerstone is to have the smallest house you can and share it with as many people as possible (see previous box).

Obviously, if you have the chance to build a new home you can get heating pretty close to zero and reduce electricity to a very low level. That's beyond the scope of this chapter. The following suggestions assume you live in an existing non-eco dwelling:

- Keep room temperatures as low as you can feel comfortable with after a week.
- Back this up with high quality thermal underwear and chunky sweaters and fleeces.
- Draughtproof, insulate and double-glaze when and where you can.
- Get a new boiler if yours is old, and invest in the most up-to-date control systems. These will allow you to run the house elegantly without heating any spaces unnecessarily.
- Try to get some kind of monitor system on display in the kitchen – at best a full smart meter doing both gas and electricity, for example, AlertMe, but at least a real time read-out for your electricity. The feedback helps you understand what's going on and nearly always allows you to reduce unnecessary consumption.
- If you're having a major plumbing upgrade, you might as well do solar water heating if your roof is suitable.
- 'Technically, installing a pellet stove to run your central heating makes you carbon neutral for heating, and for a minority this is probably almost true. But we couldn't all do it, and in the long run it might be better to use plants for sequestration (giving negative intensity) rather than to create energy (at best, zero intensity).

- Heat pumps – in the right conditions, installed and operated with care and intelligence – are a better bet in the long run if you have the right site and have already carried out substantial insulation improvements. Heat pumps align you with the predicted low carbon electric future outlined in *ZCB2030* and other reports.
- Green tariff electricity? Yes, always do it, but don't regard it as a magic wand to dissolve your footprint.
- Micro-wind turbines? No (except for very remote sites where there is no electricity): use the money to invest in large-scale installations.
- Photovoltaics? At the moment solar PV is a very poor use of your money in terms of £ spent per $kgCO_2e$ saved, but since electricity is one of the most intensive items in your fingerprint, and there are official subsidies, it is worth looking into. In practice, PV owners also tend to get much more tuned in to their energy usage and end up with a much reduced consumption. The existence of the Feed-in Tariff system means that there will be an income stream, and all you have to do is not spend it on high emissions things, like air flights.
- Community energy is currently a rare option for most householders but, as the case studies in this book show, it is definitely possible and potentially rewarding in terms of social cohesion and building quality of life at a community level. Most interesting possibilities include community owned wind turbines, district heating system using biomass, or mixed technology approaches to housing developments incorporating energy saving and production. There are some exciting exemplar schemes that have the potential to be rolled out across other communities. A good moto is: *remote investment is easy and fun.*

Goods and services

This is the catch-all category that accounts for 20-25% of emissions and 40-45% of expenditure. It is a complete ragbag consisting partly of material goods, generally high intensity, and services with a low intensity. Mathematically, it is better to shift spending from the other three categories into this one, and within this one, from goods to services.

Notice it's no good saying 'buy less', because we all spend what we have. If you don't spend it on consumer goods the chances are you might find you have enough for that weekend break in Malaga, a snip package at £250. Even if we save, the money still goes into the UK economy: pension funds, supermarkets, investment in tar sands. That is, unless you invest in ethical banks and building societies such as the Coop, Ecology or Triodos.

The key is probably to reduce intensity by raising the cost or, in other words, investing in the very best quality of things that will last a long time. This particularly applies to household refurbishment and maintenance. Invest in low energy on-site features. And, of course, keep repairing things. Buying second-hand is good but, since it saves you money, you have to be careful what you do with the saving.

Starting with home energy

Figure 6 on page 31 showed the carbon intensity of the four main areas of personal emissions you could readily do something about. The graph is useful because at a glance it shows us that home energy has four times the carbon intensity of its closest rival – if you spend one pound on home energy, that pound will create four times more emissions than if you had spent it on transport.

Reducing the intensity of home energy expenditure is a priority for anyone serious about controlling their carbon emissions, not to save money but to save energy! This is why we have spent so much time explaining how home energy relates to the other four sectors and why we've chosen it as the focus of this book.

Reducing the *intensity* is also actually fairly easy and within the grasp of most people, given that they have access to some upfront funds and also to the levers of change – in other words, if they own their own property or can influence their housing association, council or local community.

All the technologies involved are tried and tested and readily available. Some need technical support from specialised installers or designers but many can be done DIY or by general builders, electricians, plumbers or energy engineers.

Following the principles outlined in this chapter, spending your money on these technologies will:

- Reduce the economic intensity of your energy use.
- Deliver substantial quality of life improvements (either within your home, community, or both).
- Create energy resilience by curbing reliance on imported fossil fuels.
- Substantially reduce your annual carbon emissions (thus helping you to avoid carbon taxation, or preparing you for any possible future carbon rationing scheme).
- Allow you to turn expenditure away from fuel and put it into the fabric of your home and community (instead of spending on something you don't like, you're investing in property, social networks and people that you do like).
- Encourage investment in technological innovation to make the technologies affordable to more people, accelerating the rate of change.

Bear these principles in mind when reading through the rest of the book. They will help you refine your decisions about which technologies to choose and which personal and community energy projects to venture forth with. Good luck. Plenty to be getting on with!

Part Two

A practical guide to home and community energy

Allan Shepherd

Chapter One

Power down and power up – working out energy priorities

Early on in the book we introduced two key phrases: 'power down' and 'power up'. We could have used words such as energy saving and renewable energy production, but power down and power up are phrases that contain dramatic momentum, like you really mean it. Which I hope you do!

This part of the book shows you how to put power down and power up into practice. It's divided into nine chapters: one chapter to describe the power down home, another for the power up home, and seven chapters tackling the nitty gritty of 'doing it!'.

Each of these seven chapters expands on one of seven key questions:

- Have I draughtproofed and ventilated correctly?
- Have I insulated?
- Am I making the most of passive solar gain?
- Do I have an energy efficient heating system and energy efficient electrical appliances?
- Should I switch to a renewable heat source?
- Can I generate my own renewable electricity?
- Could I scale up to community level energy generation?

Remember this phrase too:
insulate, triple-A, generate
(the triple-A refers to energy efficiency labeling); it quite clearly sets out the priorities in the right order.

Here are the same questions written as direct actions:

✓ Control air flows: use ventilation not infiltration.

✓ Slow down the rate of heat loss using insulation and improved glazing.

✓ Retain as much heat from the sun as possible using passive solar techniques.

✓ Become energy efficient with modern heating systems and electrical appliances.

✓ Switch to renewable heat (where possible!).

✓ Become a renewable electricity generator.

✓ Scale up to community level energy generation.

This is a simple home energy checklist to carry with you through the rest of the book.

Have I draughtproofed and ventilated correctly?

The controlled release of fresh air into a building is essential for health and wellbeing but uncontrolled draughts waste energy and are bad for you. The technical term for draughts is infiltration, a word I like because it gives a visual picture of air getting in where it's not wanted. Air flow should be controlled through ventilation, not allowed to happen by chance through infiltration. Eliminate infiltration by draughtproofing and use good ventilation techniques instead.

Have I insulated?

Insulation slows down the speed at which heat is lost through the fabric of a building; the materials that make up the external walls, floors, windows and roof. Heat will always be lost through these materials, but slowing down the rate of heat loss cuts fuel consumption. Draughtproofing also prevents heat loss so it makes sense to do this when (or before) you insulate. There is no point insulating well but not draughtproofing. Double and triple glazing is another form of insulation; the air gaps between the layers of glazing slow down heat loss.

Am I making the most of passive solar gain?

Passive solar gain delivers a cut in fuel consumption by trapping and storing heat from the sun. Rooms are warmed using energy from the sun rather than heat from a heating system. Passive solar gain exists to some degree in most houses (unless you live in a cave!) but can be improved using techniques described more fully in chapter five.

The three essential ingredients are:

- Large double or triple glazed windows facing somewhere between east and west, but preferably south (windows that face north should be smaller in size to minimise heat loss).
- Walls and floors with a high thermal mass – in other words, a capacity to absorb and store excess heat when it is sunny and release it back in to the room when it is not.
- A fast reaction heating system, to respond quickly to changes in the weather.

It is possible to overheat a house using passive solar heating techniques, so ventilation, heat storage control and shading are all important aspects of any passive solar design process.

Do I have an energy efficient heating system and energy efficient electrical appliances?

Energy efficiency is different to energy conservation. Energy conservation is about keeping heat in using insulation and draughtproofing techniques. Energy efficiency is about using less energy to do the same amount of work. We can increase energy efficiency by changing habits, switching appliances and establishing better control systems. Improvements in the energy efficiency of some products mean they now represent some of the easiest and, often, most cost- and environmentally effective changes you can make in a home.

⏻ Should I switch to a renewable heat source?

The three primary renewable heat choices – solar thermal, heat pump and biomass – are all site specific, meaning that not all households will be able to install them. In CAT's *Zero Carbon Britain 2030* (*ZCB2030*) report, renewable heat was identified as a key way for households to reduce their household carbon emissions, but those already connected to mains gas may be advised that installing a more efficient gas boiler (perhaps along with solar thermal panels where appropriate) is a better bet than switching over to a biomass boiler or ground source heat pump.

⏻ Can I generate my own renewable electricity?

The three main renewable electricity generation technologies – solar PV, wind and micro-hydro power – all work on a household and community level. However, most people opt for solar PV, as it is the least 'picky' of the three technolgies when it comes to location. Wind and hydro power require very specific conditions which are typically only available in rural areas. Solar PV only requires an unshaded position (usually but not always a roof) that faces somewhere between east and west, preferably between south east and south west. This makes it the option of choice for urban areas.

⏻ Could I scale up to community level energy generation?

Fixing your own home is great but you can achieve more with a community project. Working with others allows you to combine resources to save and generate energy on a much bigger scale, earn money for your community, strengthen bonds between neighbours, create local jobs and keep money spent on energy in the local area. It also allows you to take on or be part of projects that you could never possibly be involved with as an individual. Read the special case study sections peppered throughout the book, the chapter on community renewables written by Jarra Hicks and Nicky Ison and the resources section at the back.

Financial support

Although there have been plenty of commercial, local and national government grants, plus incentives and schemes for energy over the last decade or so, there has never been one comprehensive plan which could deliver the kind of carbon savings everybody wants. Industry and environmental lobbyists have been pretty much united in demanding a centrally organised programme that would deliver stability, direction and enough worthwhile incentive to allow consumers to play their part.

We now have three (not entirely comprehensive) national programmes delivering financial incentives through targeted, accredited technologies. Each of the schemes has its critics, and there are certainly many people who will find themselves excluded (perhaps because they don't have the right site for a particular technology, or they can not yet find the upfront investment needed) but the schemes do and will deliver substantial carbon gains.

Here's a quick list of some of the key organisations and institutions that can provide the support you need. There are many more in the resources section on page 213:

Centre for Alternative Technology (CAT). CAT provides information, publications, consultancy and a wide range of professional, academic and leisure courses on all subjects covered in this book. As an independent charity working in the sector for nearly 40 years CAT has an established earth-friendly ethos combined with excellent training facilities.

Energy Saving Trust. The Energy Saving Trust provides a formidable range of practical action guides plus online tools for assessing the appropriateness and value of different power up and power down technologies. It provides financial and planning guidance and will keep you up to date with all the latest developments.

Plan Local (also Local United and Community Energy Scotland). All three organisations provide valuable support for community energy initiatives, including online resources, advice packs, case studies, videos, training and direct one-to-one support. Plan Local is part of the Centre for Sustainable Energy.

Department of Energy and Climate Change (DECC). DECC is responsible for energy policy in Britain and as such provides all the detailed information you need about energy legislation, including the three key financial incentives – Green Deal, Feed-in Tariffs and the Renewable Heat Incentive.

English Heritage. English Heritage looks after a wide range of historical properties and has experience of tackling many of the problems commonly associated with retro-fitting old homes. Thankfully for us, English Heritage have published much of what they have learnt in free downloads on their website, including advice on using traditional materials.

The Feed-in Tariff incentive scheme for renewable electricity

The Feed-in Tariff (FIT) was the first of these schemes to be introduced: by the Labour government in 2010. Popular in several European countries, the scheme pays renewable energy generators a fixed fee for every unit of electricity they produce and a further payment for every unit exported to the national grid. This guarantees a market for both the electricity produced and the products and services that support its generation. In this way, both the consumer and industry benefits.

Over the lifetime of the programme the cost of renewable installation will fall and the subsidy will be reduced, the idea being that it will eventually be cost competitive to install renewable technology without subsidy. To be eligible for Feed-in Tariff payments systems under 50kW must be installed by an accredited installer using accredited technologies under the Microgeneration Certification Scheme

FITs is a green energy 'cashback' scheme. Rather than getting a grant upfront you pay for the installation yourself and receive payments over time. The payments are inflation linked (from a level set at the time of installation), last for twenty or twenty-five years depending on the technology and are paid for every unit of electricity produced, plus every unit fed into the national grid (if grid-connected). Houses must have an Energy Performance Certificate (EPC) Level 4 to qualify. Visit the DECC website for up-to-date details.

Whenever production exceeds consumption the excess electricity generated is exported to the grid; whenever you need more than you produce, you buy electricity from the grid. A meter is fitted with every system, measuring the electricity generated and the amount bought. The amount sold is rarely metered; instead it is 'deemed'. Payments for the energy you generate are made via your FIT provider.

Over time (exactly how much time will depend on your system) your initial investment will be paid off and you will start earning money from the FIT payments, as well as continuing to benefit from a reduction in imported electricity. The technologies eligible to receive FITs are solar PV, wind and hydro power, with solar PV being the most likely choice for most households. The rate of payment varies between the technologies and the size of return will vary depending on the size and effectiveness of the system (in other words, how well it is working). Visit http://info.cat.org.uk/fits, www.decc.gov.uk or www.fitariffs.co.uk for more info.

(MCS). This guarantees standards but also makes DIY installations (which do not qualify) financially unattractive.

The scheme is paid for by a levy on existing electricity bills so there has been some criticism that it is a tax on the many for the benefit of the few, or even on the poor for the rich; as most household renewable energy schemes cost upwards of £6,000 the biggest problem for most households is access to capital.

Some PV companies have developed roof rental schemes, whereby the installer pays for the installation and maintenance of a PV system in return for receiving the Feed-in Tariff payments: the benefit for the consumer being reduced electricity bills. The Energy Saving Trust believes these schemes provide far greater financial benefit for the installer than the consumer, part of the problem being that the consumer only gets the benefit of free electricity during daylight hours when the PV modules are generating but when most people are not at home to make use of it. As such, perhaps as much as 75% of electricity produced by the modules will be exported to the grid. Also, some people have reported finding it difficult to re-mortgage their home once a rent-a-roof scheme has been set up, so please check with your mortgage advisor, bank or the Energy Saving Trust before going ahead.

Communities have also started to benefit from the tariff by installing generation capacity in the grounds of community properties, the money for the installation sometimes being raised from a community share issue (of which more on pages 202-204).

The Renewable Heat Incentive

The Renewable Heat Incentive (RHI) was introduced by the coalition government. It was launched in the autumn of 2011, but only for the commercial sector. An interim grant scheme called the Renewable Heat Premium Payment was launched for householders at the same time (apply via www.energysavingtrust.org.uk).

Details about the domestic RHI, including the launch date, are still unknown, but it is likely that it will follow some of the same principles as the non-domestic RHI and the FITs:

Only schemes, installers and equipment accredited by the MCS will be eligible.

How the Renewable Heat Incentive works

The RHI is available for five different types of renewable heating system: solar thermal (water heating), heat pumps (but not air-source) and biomass (but not wood stoves), biomass combined heat and power and anaerobic digestion (both of which can produce heat and electricity, are eligible for the RHI and FITs and are only ever likely to be used on a community or commercial scale). Most householders are likely to find solar thermal the most appropriate technology. As many heating systems combine different types of renewable heat and conventional heat in a number of different combinations it will be possible to boost your renewable heat output and RHI payments by using more than one technology. Visit http://info.cat.org.uk/rhi

Payments will be made through a tariff for energy generated over many years so the cost of any initial investment will have to be met by the consumer.

Tariffs will be differentiated by technology and size of the installation, with the idea that all technologies and sizes should be equally financially viable.

The Green Deal

The government claims that the Green Deal (see next page for more information) will revolutionise the way we think and make decisions about energy by making money available through low interest loans that are paid back via energy bills. So long as the measures are approved and installed by an accredited advisor and demonstrably make financial savings equal to or greater than the loan repayment, consumers can make their houses energy efficient without having to put their own money in.

The government admits that there are cases where energy efficiency measures will not pay for themselves, either because the measures are too expensive (for example in the case of solid wall insulation) or because the household is in fuel poverty, and increased energy efficiency would deliver a higher quality of living (warmer, healthier homes) rather than lower bills. For these cases, large energy companies will be required to offer financial support under the Energy Company Obligation (ECO).

Will everyone be able to take advantage of these schemes?

There are many people who will not be able to take advantage of these schemes. Those who don't own their own house; can't persuade their landlord to do the right thing; live in an area with very little community cohesion; don't have access to an appropriate renewable energy site; do not meet the financial criteria for Green Deal: they will be left out.

Nevertheless, FITs, the RHI and the Green Deal are and/or will allow hundreds of thousands of households and community groups to easily and cheaply save and generate energy. It will also establish a dynamic, competitive home power sector, which will bring down prices and make energy saving and generation more affordable for others.

Those who find it difficult or impossible to access money made available through these schemes should check with the Energy Saving Trust to see what other financial support mechanisms are available, in particular in relation to the Green Deal, details of which, at the time of going to press, were still being formulated. The Energy Company Obligation (ECO) should provide measures to help the most vulnerable low income households and will offer support to those with expensive to treat properties.

Eligibility, affordability and installers

All applications for these schemes must be confirmed by an accredited installer. For FITs and the RHI the accreditation is run by the MCS; the Green Deal has its own accreditation. At the time of writing there were approximately 3,000 companies offering MCS accredited services, so shop around and find one you feel comfortable with. The MCS website – www.microgenerationcertification.org – has an installer search facility allowing you to find the one

Apart from the householder, a Green Deal installation will typically involve three parties:

- An assessor – to carry out an independent property assessment and then recommend the most appropriate measures.
- A green deal provider – to propose the financial details (including repayment rates), pay an accredited installer to actually carry out the work, and then receive repayments through the electricity bills.
- An installer – to do the work!

The three roles – assessor, provider and installer – could be carried out by the same company, or three different companies. In any case, to protect the consumer from "cowboys", each of these roles will be carried out by an accredited professional.

Those of us who like DIY will be disappointed by this because some energy saving measures can be done more cheaply DIY-style – draughtproofing and loft insulation, for example.

Once the work is complete the loan repayments are attached to the household electricity bill. The "Golden Rule" of the Green Deal is that repayments should not be higher than the savings the customer can expect to see. In other words, even with the repayment added, energy bills should not be higher than they would have been without. In theory,

this should not only make the Deal attractive for consumers but also give security to providers: if a household can pay their energy deals today then it will also be able to afford the repayment of the loan. Another interesting aspect is that repayments are made by the energy bill payer, who is not necessarily the owner of the property.

Thus, landlords can install energy saving measures and attach the costs to the bill payer (though only with their express permission). Landlords can be notoriously reluctant to make improvements of this kind because they never get a return; with Green Deal they will be able to pass the bill on to the tenant, the hope being that the tenant saves money on fuel bills and enjoys an increased level of comfort.

The government is also proposing powers to bring properties up to a defined threshold before being rented out again, subject to there being no upfront financial costs to the landlord (using Green Deal or equivalent). It is also worth noting that there is also a tax allowance for private landlords, allowing them to claim the costs for a range of insulation measures against tax (www.hmrc.gov.uk/pbr2006/pbrn12.htm).

When a property is sold the debt is sold on, so the new owners must be made aware of the commitment they will take on, the theory being that the savings in energy bills will more than pay for the debt repayments. Check with your mortgage advisor before going ahead!.

nearest to you. As a minimum, get three quotes and ask to see a portfolio of existing work from each.

You should always insist that installers actually visit your site and take a good look at everything before they give you a quote or tell you how much energy you can produce. It may sometimes be advisable to pay an independent consultant for an impartial opinion on the technical and financial feasibility of a scheme, especially in the case of larger and more expensive projects.

Site surveys for solar PV, solar water heating, passive solar gain, biomass, heat pumps and most energy saving measures are relatively straightforward and typically only require a single site visit. This is not true for wind and hydro projects, which require long periods of onsite wind speed and water flow monitoring.

It is possible (and also useful and lots of fun) to make your own energy assessments, but you will not be able to use these DIY assessments to apply

for funds. This is because the calculations you make are unlikely to be as precise as those made by the installer. This is particularly so in the case of renewable energy generation, whose success is dependent on numerous variables (about which there will be more detail later).

However, it is useful to be able to rule technologies in or out for yourself without going to an installer, and for this reason I have provided some very simple assessment tools with some pointers to more in-depth explanations for those who prefer a deeper understanding (see following chapters).

As far as possible I have also tried to give sample costings for most of the possible projects you could carry out, plus some idea of possible paybacks. This may also allow you to rule out some options before contacting an installer, although please be aware that these samples should be treated as ballpark figures.

When the installer has completed the site survey they will give you a quote for installation as well as a rundown of what the proposed changes will mean for you; in other words, how much energy you will save or generate, how much money you can expert to earn from generation tariffs, how long it will take to pay off the initial investment, how much CO_2 you will save and how much maintenance will need to be carried out.

They should also tell you what legal requirements you will have to fulfill, for example, whether or not additional planning consent or Building Regulations approval is required. They will take you through the various payment plans on offer and help you fill in all the paperwork. For generation projects they will need to give you annual and lifetime generation targets. These are important indicators for the financial and technical viability of any installation. If for any reason your system doesn't meet its targets you should be able to go back to the installer and ask them why.

When an installer gives you a quote they should also be able to supply you with a schedule of works and a completion day should you decide to go ahead. At this point you would be wise to see if there are any savings to be made by carrying out additional or complementary works on your property at the same time. For example, if you have to replace your roof

anyway, it will be cheaper to fit PV or solar thermal when the scaffolding for the roof renovation is already in place and, in the case of PV, possibly to fit roof integrated modules (see chapter nine). Likewise, if you are planning a major renovation of an existing plumbing system, it would be advisable to fit your solar thermal system at the same time.

In fact, there is a useful rule of thumb here, a final note before moving on to the next chapters; energy saving and generating projects are always cheaper if the work is carried out:

- When a building is being constructed.
- When a building is being renovated.
- When essential work on part of a building needs to be carried out anyway.

New build or retro-fit?

There are 24 million homes in Britain and nine out of ten of them will still be in use in 2030. Most of these do not meet current building standards, let alone come close to the performance of advanced eco-house designs such as 'Passivhaus'. So, although new build eco-houses are impressive in their technical specification, it is more important to create a national renovation programme to make good the housing stock that already exists. Let us be clear, knocking all the old houses down and starting again is not an option!

Wall insulation in the UK						
Construction	1970	1980	1990	1996–2002	2003–2006	From 2007
Solid wall (SW) U-value	1.7	1	0.6	0.45	0.35	0.3
SW thickness	240	250	270	300	300	300
Cavity wall (CW) U-value	1.6	1	0.6	0.45	0.35	0.3
CW thickness	250	260	270	270	300	300
Timber frame (TF) U-value	0.8	0.45	0.4	0.4	0.35	0.3
TF thickness	270	270	270	300	300	300

Changes in required U-values (W/m²K) and thickness (mm) of different wall constructions since 1970 for new build properties. Source: various Building Regulations and construction guidelines. Originially appeared in Zero Carbon Britain 2030.

The insulation level of the building envelope has gradually improved over time. The table above shows changes in U-values since 1970 (the higher the U-value (see page 66 for detailed explanation) the lower the insulating quality of the material). It illustrates the need to upgrade the existing building stock to meet current standards.

If you are planning a new build construction there are several existing statutory and voluntary codes for new build housing, including Building Regulations Part L, Code for Sustainable Homes (CSH), the Standard Assessment Procedure (SAP) and Energy Performance Certificates (EPCs). It is also worth noting that by 2016 the government will demand that all new buildings be zero carbon (although the exact definition of zero carbon as laid down by the government still remains undecided at the time of going to press).

Case study

The Transition movement: global network of local groups sharing ideas and energy

Most of the case studies in this book are relatively simple community projects with a single aim, an easily defined organisational structure and clear local ambitions. This one is different. The Transition movement is a cultural phenomenon. It has spread across the globe, spawned a whole wave of individual community projects in its wake, revitalised the way we view the future and, for many people, changed the way we engage with one another.

It is positive, forward thinking, ambitious but also pragmatic and flexible. Perhaps the most important thing about the Transition movement is that it allows its participants a framework to draw together disparate social and environmental activity under one banner with one direction – all those engaged heading towards a localised, post-growth, post-peak oil and, most importantly, resilient local economy.

To get a sense of why Transition has become so popular, I visited Transition founder Rob Hopkins in his suburban Devon home for two hours of in-depth conversation. By coincidence, I happen to visit the day he launches his new book *The Transition Companion*, the follow up to his hugely successful *The Transition Handbook*. This gives me a chance not only to talk to him about how the Transition movement has evolved over the last five years, but also to participate first hand in a Transition event; albeit, I suspect, an atypical one.

Although Rob would be the first to say that the Transition movement is the product of all of the people participating in it, to the point where his new book was subject to an open collaborative review process involving many hundreds of people, there's no doubt that Rob's affable, engaging personality is embedded throughout the processes and structures he, along with a key group of supporters, have developed.

I find this out first hand during our two hour conversation, sitting by his kitchen table crunching apples and drinking tea. Rob is welcoming, open and honest, but also driven, determined and focused. He believes he has come up with a

Transition initiatives in London, as of June 2011.

formula for community engagement and social change that deserves to be tested on a global scale, whilst admitting that he doesn't know whether it will really work.

In fact the new book starts with 'A Cheerful Disclaimer': 'Transition is not a known quantity. We truly don't know if Transition will work. It is a social experiment on a massive scale. What we are convinced of is this:

- If we wait for governments, it'll be too little, too late.
- If we act as individuals, it'll be too little.
- But if we act as communities, it might just be enough, just in time.'

Some critics believe that Transition definitely won't work. In fact, you can find several online critiques of the Transition movement suggesting that popular protest and campaigning are more effective tools for social change, pointing to movements throughout history that have forced the pace of change by acting as a thorn in the side of the establishment rather than a feather floating alongside it; the suffragettes, Gandhi's campaign of non-violent direct action, the Arab Spring – these are three examples that come to mind.

It's an interesting debate to have because, collectively, we only have a limited number of years left to make the changes we need to make and we each have to decide how best to spend our time. We want to be effective and we don't want (and actually cannot afford) to waste time. Rob believes that our existing political and economic system is so near to collapse that we are much better off spending our 'now' time building the alternative (becoming ready for the collapse) rather than fighting against something that is already on its way out. Others believe 'the system' will not collapse without a great big shove from 'we the people'. Some think that system collapse is the worst thing that could happen and that what we really need is controlled change based on national and international action plans (*ZCB2030* and others).

The reality is that we will need responses based on each of these beliefs to develop and run alongside each other at the same time. No one is sure that their plan will work and the best outcome for everyone is a plurality of tried and tested ideas that harness, from a wide range of places, an enormous amount of energy from many, many people. Only then might we find something that knits together to give us a reasonable stab at getting through this period of immense change.

Personally, I like the Transition movement because it provides a popular alternative to the warrior model of social change; which, for whatever reason, many people are unable or unlikely to be a part of. It is non-threatening, allows voices to be heard equally and finds common ground between people of very different backgrounds. Moreover, people like Transition. They have fun. They learn new skills, develop their thinking, make new friendships.

At a time when (according to Ofgem) half our waking hours are spent watching TV, using our mobile phones or sitting in front of a computer, Transition gets whole swathes of people off their sofas doing something different: planting a tree, making a community garden, starting up a renewable energy company, creating their own currency…the list goes on. I'm sure as a kid Rob must have watched *Why don't you just switch off your television set and go and do something less boring instead'*?

It's important to say at this point that although Rob provides a central vision for the Transition movement, it's up to the Transition initiatives themselves to deliver their own individual plans of how the vision will work in practice. They set their own agendas, work towards change at their own pace and decide what's best for their community. To help them do this there is support from the Transition Network (primarily a web based resource offering connections between groups – www.transitionnetwork.org) and Transition Training (which offers courses for Transition group members – www.transitionnetwork.org/training). There are also regional and national conferences and now eight books, of which *The Transition Companion* is the latest addition.

The Transition Companion shows how much the movement has moved on in the last few years, but also how much it is capable of adapting itself as information about how groups work comes from all around the globe. The first book, *The Transition Handbook*, set out a very clear twelve step programme for groups to follow, culminating in the development of an Energy Descent Action Plan (EDAP), a detailed piece of work setting out the way a community would decarbonise and re-localise.

Unfortunately, many found the twelve step approach too restricting and unrealistic, whilst EDAPs have proven to be beyond the grasp of almost all groups; Transition Town Totnes has one, but it was only possible with substantial funding and a full-time member of staff.

The Transition Companion has liberated groups from the twelve step programme and instead given them a larder of ingredients to pick up and combine in a way that works best for them. This allows groups to develop in their own way without having to think about creating an Energy Descent Action Plan, although this option is still there for groups if that's the way they want to go. This is a pragmatic acknowledgement that this part of the early Transition vision has failed to take hold; the failure in this area has led Rob to reassess the purpose of Transition:

'When we started doing Transition I thought it was an environmental process, but five years on, looking back, I've realised it's a cultural process. The question is: how do you shift a culture to be more prepared for times of uncertainty and rapid change? And can you, through all kinds of ways, through obvious and really subtle ways, in ways perhaps that you don't even notice, start to change the story a place tells about itself? So that when you come into a situation where everything is changing very rapidly and everything is very fluid and uncertain, Transition is in the blood stream; in the DNA.'

As we talk about this subject during our interview, Rob rather unexpectedly uses a quote by right wing neo-liberal economist Milton Friedman to illustrate his point:

'Only a crisis, actual or perceived, produces real change. When that crisis occurs the action taken depends on the ideas that are lying around; that I believe is our basic function, to develop alternatives to existing policies, to keep them alive and available until the politically impossible becomes the politically inevitable.'

I think I prefer that quote in Rob's hands rather than Milton Friedman's, but the point is well made.

'Is the mission – when you look at resilience and the idea of being ready for shocks – to embed the story of Transition sufficiently in the local culture that it creates a very different kind of thinking about what we need to do?'

In this organisational model Transition groups are freed from the responsibility of coming up with all the answers and allowed to concentrate on the job of changing what they can, in the knowledge that these changes will strengthen communities in preparation for a time when those communities will need to draw upon that strength.

Rob has already seen this happening in several disaster areas where the existence of Transition groups made a return to post disaster normality easier: in New Zealand after the earthquakes, in Brazil following mudslides and in Japan after the tsunami and nuclear disaster. In these places, existing Transition networks were able to step in to support the rebuild process, bringing new thinking and creating stories of resilience and hope.

The power of story is now central to Rob's understanding of how Transition works. In Rob's version of the Milton Friedman worldview, people are allowed to develop and embed stories without being constrained by dogmatic goals; they don't have to ask permission to create or follow rules, they have the freedom to develop projects that work for them. Moreover, each project carries with it an enormously powerful story that encourages more experimentation and creativity.

Transition Heathrow hosting the Sipson Golden Conker Championship, October 2010.

One of Rob's favourite Transition energy stories is the tale of the Gasketeers of Malvern Hills, which features a world famous author, some beloved listed gas lamps and a small group of energy 'nerds' working within Transition Malvern Hills. Anyone who has read C.S. Lewis' 'The Lion, the Witch and the Wardrobe' will be familiar with the gaslight that greets the children as they enter Narnia. This gaslight is actually based on real gaslights that still exist in Malvern. Unfortunately, the 104 gaslights were poorly maintained, produced very little light and each one every year cost the council £580 in gas and maintenance.

Enter stage left – almost certainly via the wardrobe – the Gasketeers! Using local and international expertise they developed ways to refurbish the lamps, improving their light output and reducing gas consumption by 84%. The new low maintenance lamps now require just one visit a year, the work carried out by Lynn Jones, who cycles round with a fold up ladder on a specially built trailer. Each lamp now only costs £70 for gas and maintenance per year. The council is very happy, especially as the work transforming the lamps was carried out for free and would have cost an estimated £20,000 if carried out by a professional company. For their next project, the Gasketeers are seeing if they can set up their own biogas plant to provide the gas for the lamps!

Most of the energy projects that have emerged as part of the Transition process come during what Rob calls the 'building' stage of Transition groups. This is the fourth of five stages that seem common to most groups – the others being 'starting out', 'deepening', 'connecting' and lastly 'daring to dream'. Some groups never make it to the building stage, perhaps because they don't have the skills to overcome conflict, or

they lack clarity and direction, or organisation. Some groups start with small numbers and can't seem to gain traction with other people, sometimes one driven person gets things moving but has to move away. At other times the group simply runs out of steam.

One problem common to most groups is momentum. Groups usually start with a feeling of overwhelming excitement, but this is usually followed by a plateau where nothing much appears to be happening. It's important to remember that plateaus, setbacks and disappointments are inevitable, and to be successful community groups, have to play the long game. As Rob points out, 'If we were wildly dizzy and giddy all the time it would be exhausting. It would be like being Kylie Minogue, all the time.'

Because each Transition group is made up of several subgroups, each exploring its own area of interest, it's also possible that some things emerge from the Transition process stronger than others, 'In Totnes at any one time, half of the groups are flying and half are moribund. After the initial rush stage people tend to think it will happen like magic, but then maturity sets in, when people with experience of making things happen get involved.'

One of the most useful things to take away from the Transition process is the toolkit that has emerged for motivating and moving groups forward. The five stages described above are similar to the old adage for group dynamics: form, storm, norm, perform. Groups need to recognise these stages and find navigation channels through them. *The Transition Companion* is full of good advice on how to do this, even down to providing tips on how to be a good listener, an incredibly underrated skill.

Transition Network also provides Transition Training workshops to further develop these skills, but not specific

The power's in **your** hands

468 households have joined the neighbourhood programme
141 solar pv installations
45% of those on low-income household roofs
Saving energy - cutting costs
www.transitionstreets.org.uk

energy related training courses. I asked Rob about this and he suggested that it wasn't necessary for Transition to offer this sort of training because it exists elsewhere and the skills often emerge from within the group, or can be brought to the group from outside. It's more important for the Transition groups to create the right space to enable people to do what they want to do. You can see from the case studies below that this is an approach that seems to be working.

Transition Streets

Transition Streets emerged from Transition Town Totnes as a way of enabling Transition at a street-by-street level through informal social get-togethers. The project was funded by the Department of Energy and Climate Change to the tune of £625,000; it has to be said, this level of funding for a Transition project is very unusual (even more so now). It was part of DECC's 'Low Carbon Communities Challenge', the point of the challenge being to test various delivery methods for changing energy use at the community level. With this remit in mind, Transition Streets was carefully audited and shown to have made total carbon savings of 576 tonnes (an average of 1.2 tonnes per household), with total financial savings of £273,000. An estimated 35% of the Transition

Streets participants were low income households, which made them eligible for a £3,500 grant and low interest loan package for the installation of PV panels. One of the most important benefits to participants turned out not to be the energy saving and generation but the feeling of getting to know their neighbours.

Transition Linlithgows's solar bulk buying scheme

Joining together solar thermal heating systems on a community scale is very unusual and difficult to achieve, but the bulk buying of materials for numerous separate installations is a very good way of saving money and increasing community participation. Transition Linlithgow began a bulk buying programme in 2010 which has now developed into a social enterprise, giving part of its revenue back to the community. The project involved selecting a manufacturer (based on all aspects of manufacturing and the environment as well as performance and ethical business approach) and negotiating a discount to encourage participation. The project was linked to home energy audits so that whenever someone was interested in renewable technology the group carried out an in-depth audit. As the project has grown there has been a lot of interest from neighbouring community initiatives, some asking for training in how to arrange their own bulk buying schemes. Now the group also bulk buys PV panels and ground source heat pumps.

Bath and West Community Energy

Bath and West Community Energy (BWCE) came out of a meeting of the Transition Bath energy group when people in the meeting looked at one other and said, 'we could actually do something about this'. Rather than looking for grants, the group decided from the outset that it wanted to function as a social enterprise and deliver renewable energy generation on a large scale. It has been set up as an Industrial and Provident Society. Profits will be returned to the community and the society will be locally owned, locally controlled, will generate local income and provide local jobs. BWCE formed a partnership with the local council and Scottish and Southern Energy to install PV arrays. This will give the group a solid foundation for creating a £500,000 community share issue. In the long term the group hopes to generate £500,000 for the community by developing an £11 million wind and hydro project. Impressive stuff.

Chapter Two

The power down home

Fig. 2.1. The power down home

Four steps for cutting home energy use

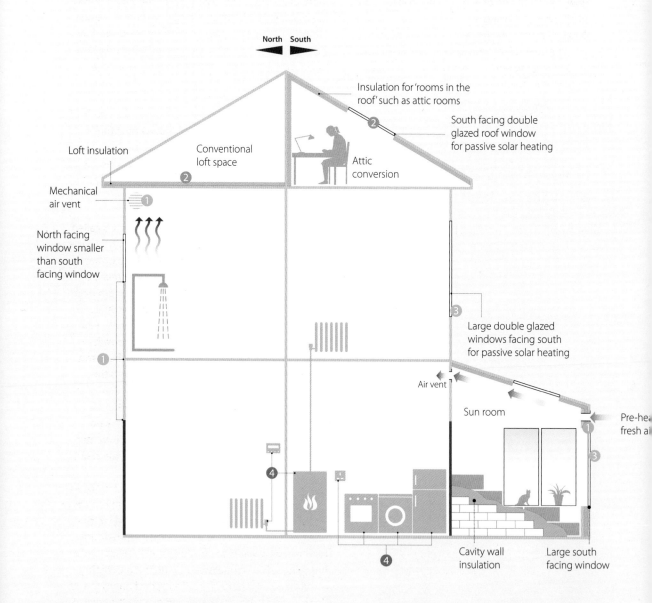

North   South

Insulation for 'rooms in the roof' such as attic rooms

South facing double glazed roof window for passive solar heating

Loft insulation

Conventional loft space

Attic conversion

Mechanical air vent

North facing window smaller than south facing window

Large double glazed windows facing south for passive solar heating

Air vent

Sun room

Pre-he[...] fresh a[...]

Cavity wall insulation

Large south facing window

① Draughtproof your home and use effective ventilation techniques.

② Slow down the rate of heat loss using insulation and double glazing.

③ Retain as much heat from the sun as possible using passive solar techniques.

④ Become energy efficient with modern heating systems and electrical appliances.

The illustration opposite shows four steps to power down your home:

- Control air flows: draughtproof your home and use effective ventilation techniques.
- Slow down the rate of heat loss using insulation and improved glazing.
- Retain as much heat from the sun as possible using passive solar techniques.
- Become energy efficient with modern heating systems and electrical appliances.

Thermal comfort is more important than heat

Some people make the mistake of equating thermal comfort with heat, but raising levels of thermal comfort is not the same as turning the thermostat up. An overheated house with poor ventilation can give you as little thermal comfort as a draughty house with numerous cold spots.

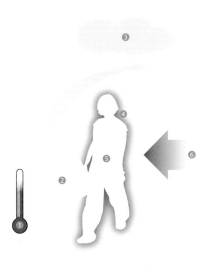

1. Air temperature
2. Air movement
3. Humidity
4. Heat from activity
5. Insulation from clothing
6. Mean radiant temperature

Fig. 2.2. The six variables affecting thermal comfort.
Source: The Whole House Book, Harris and Borer.

Thermal comfort is little understood by most people but it can be easily defined as the physical sensation of wellbeing that is felt in well designed and appropriately heated buildings. Those who enjoy thermal comfort are healthier, happier and more productive. Those who live in conditions where thermal comfort is difficult to achieve find life harder. Although the environmental purpose of power down is to reduce energy consumption and CO_2 emissions the human purpose is to raise levels of wellbeing.

Creating thermal comfort – six variables that affect thermal comfort

Figure 2.2 shows the six variables that affect thermal comfort. Two of these are individual or local (activity and clothing), the other four are environmental (air temperature, mean radiant temperature, air velocity and humidity).

Activity

We all produce heat. The metabolic rate, as it is called, is measured in watts per square metre (W/m^2) of body area or in 'mets', one met being the metabolic rate of a seated person ($58W/m^2$). Buildings can relate to the heat produced by movement using modern heat control sensors linked to central heating systems. A dance class in a community hall, for example, will produce a considerable amount of extra warmth for a small period; it makes sense to have a heat and ventilation control system that can cope with this.

Clothing

Clothing is our own personal insulation and is measured in 'clo'. When we are naked we are a no clo area. Shorts and T-shirts are about 0.3 clo, winter clothing 2.2 clo. Wrapping up warm really does help!

Air Temperature

Air temperature is linked to heat loss (see page 66), as the thermal comfort you experience in your home or building will depend on the difference between the internal temperature and the external temperature. Heat naturally wants to evenly distribute it's self, so a hot thing wants to migrate to a cold thing until they are at an equal temperature. If a room changes from a hot to a cold state repeatedly and quickly the level of discomfort will be high.

Activity	Metabolic rate in 'met'	Clothing in 'clo'	Comfort temperature in °C
Sleeping	0.8	2.2	18+/-3
Bathing	1.4	0.0	27+/-1
Sitting	1.0	1.5	20+/-2.5
Light work	2.0	1.0	16+/-3
Heavy work	3.0	1.0	10+/-4
Walking	1.2	2.2	14+/-4

Fig. 2.3. Table showing the sort of temperatures that 90% of the population will find comfortable. Source: The Whole House Book, Harris and Borer.

Mean radiant temperature

The mean radiant temperature is the mean of the temperatures of surrounding surfaces weighted by area, ability to emit heat and proximity. This relates to experiences such as feeling uncomfortably cool when sitting next to a large single glazed window though the air temperature is perfectly adequate elsewhere in the room. In practice, a well insulated house can be kept at a much lower air temperature than a poorly insulated one because all the surfaces inside are warmer and kept at a more constant temperature.

Air movement

An increase in air speed will increase cooling of the body by convection and evaporation. Ideally, air movement should be between 0.1 and 0.25 metres/second – below this air becomes stagnant; above this and air is experienced as draughts. Draughtproofing and controllable ventilation help to regulate the movement of air.

Humidity

Humidity should be kept below 65% to prevent mould and above 40% to prevent the membranes in the eyes, nose and throat becoming too dry. There are several ways of modifying relative humidity:

- Using ventilation techniques.
- Constructing with materials (known as hygroscopic) that can absorb liquid in periods of high humidity and release it when humidity is low. These include porous earth materials, such as clay and plaster, and organic materials, such as timber.
- Using vapour permeable constructions which allow moisture to wick away from the inside and pass through to the outside of a building.
- Using electrically powered humidifiers and dehumidifiers.

Thermal comfort tolerance

Figure 2.3 shows the range of typical activities that might take place in a house and the comfort temperatures (acceptable for 90% of the population) for each activity in °C based on the metabolic rate in 'met' and clothing in 'clo'. These figures are for a house that is well insulated, with no draughts, low air velocity from any fans and no large cold surfaces (with temperature differences of not more than 10°C). You'll see that even a small range of activities requires a wide heat range – from 10°C up to 27°C.

Interestingly, thermal comfort is also linked to the level of control (or even perceived control) people feel they have over the heating, cooling and ventilation of 'their space', plus the level of connection occupants have between the indoor space and the outside world. For example, our comfort tolerance is greater in unheated spaces, such as conservatories – the proximity to the outdoors seems to reduce our intolerance to discomfort.

Heat: losses, gains and loads

Figure 2.4a shows that heat is not a static entity but in fact constantly changing. The temperature of a room can change rapidly and dramatically just because the activity within it changes. Controllable heating and ventilation systems that can respond quickly to these changes deliver greater levels of thermal comfort, preventing overheating as much as under heating. The following sections help explain a little more how heat losses and gains can determine the required heat load of a building. We go on to talk about heating and heat loads more fully in chapter six, but it helps to understand these processes now.

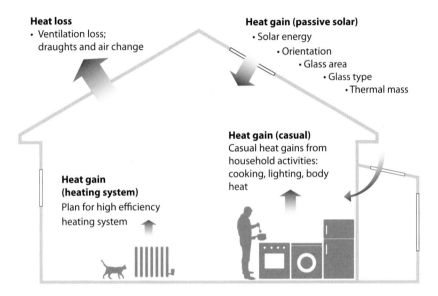

Heat loss
- Ventilation loss; draughts and air change

Heat gain (passive solar)
- Solar energy
- Orientation
- Glass area
- Glass type
- Thermal mass

Heat gain (casual)
Casual heat gains from household activities: cooking, lighting, body heat

Heat gain (heating system)
Plan for high efficiency heating system

Fig. 2.4a. Planned and casual heat gains and losses for an average house. Source: The Whole House Book, Harris and Borer.

Fig. 2.4b. Where a home loses heat. Percentages will vary depending on the house.

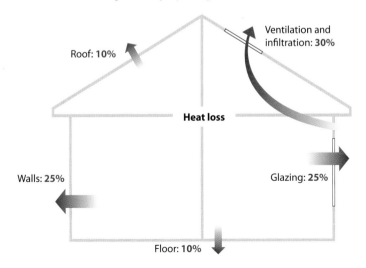

Roof: **10%**

Ventilation and infiltration: **30%**

Heat loss

Walls: **25%**

Glazing: **25%**

Floor: **10%**

- 11 C
- 8 C
- 4 C
- 1 C

Fig. 2.5. Thermographic image showing heat loss from typical houses. Source: Insulation for Sustainability, 2002.

What is heat loss?

Heat loss is the rate at which heat escapes from the inside to the outside of a building (expressed as watts per metre squared (W/m^2)). Heat is lost in three different ways, through:

- The fabric of the house – in other words the walls, roof, floor, windows and doors.
- Ventilation – controlled movement of air. We have to breathe!
- Infiltration – unwanted movement of air through cracks and inefficient detailing in the construction.

It's quite easy to see these losses with an infrared thermal imaging camera. The camera measures long wave infrared radiation (heat) and displays it as a visible picture, making it easy to detect defects in insulation, air leakage, cold bridging (see page 93), dampness, hidden objects (such as flues and air ducts) and blocked heating distribution pipes. Figure 2.5 shows houses in the same street with very different problems. The houses on the right have cavity wall insulation but single glazing. I'll let you guess what's going on with the neighbours.

The rate of heat loss is determined by three factors:

- Outside and radiant air temperature.
- Inside air temperature.
- The heat transmission value of construction materials – known as the U-value (expressed in W/m^2K).

The heat transmission value is a measure of the rate at which energy passes through an area of material when there is a 1°C difference in temperature between inside and outside. For example, the U-value of a single glazed window – $4.80W/m^2K$ – means that 4.8 watts is escaping through each square metre of glass when the temperature outside is 1°C lower than that inside.

Obviously, in winter the speed at which heat leaves the building is vastly accelerated, as is the demand for fuel. Materials with lower U-values are better at preventing heat loss (see figure 2.6) so a double glazed low E window (of which more later) has a

Location	Construction	U-value (W/m²K)
Roof	Uninsulated loft	2.00
	With 100m insulation	0.30
	Room in the roof 200mm (2002 UK)	0.20
	Loft with 250mm insulation (2002 UK)	0.16
	Superinsulated 300mm insulation	0.12
Wall	Solid brick 225mm	2.20
	Uninsulated cavity brick	1.30
	Uninsulated cavity lightweight block	0.96
	Cavity of timber frame wall with 50mm insulation	0.45
	With 100mm insulation (2002 UK)	0.35
	Superinsulated 250mm insulation	0.14
Floor	Timber floor uninsulated	0.83
	With 150mm insulation (2002 UK)	0.25
	Superinsulated 250mm insulation	0.14
	Solid floor uninsulated (average house)	0.70
	With 100mm insulation (2002 UK)	0.25
	Superinsulated 200mm insulation	0.15
Timber window	Single-glazed	4.80
	Double low-E 12mm airspace (2002 UK)	2.00
	Double low-E Argon fill 16mm airspace	1.70
	Triple low-E Argon fill or double super low-E	1.30

Terms used for U-value

W Watts, the rate of energy loss

m² Square metres

K Temperature in kelvin, each interval being the same as a degree Celsius or centigrade.

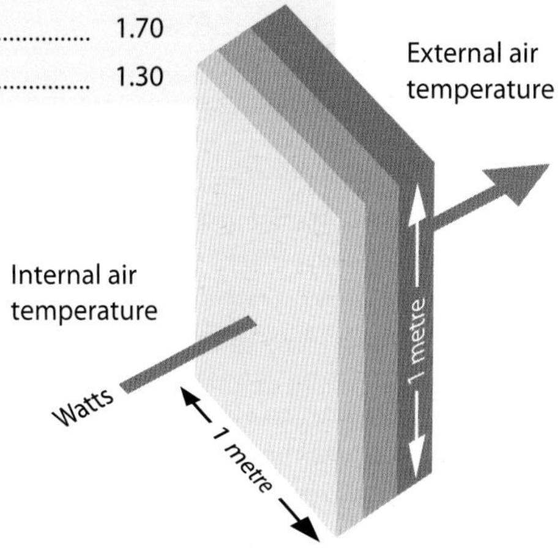

External air temperature

Internal air temperature

Watts

1 metre

1 metre

Fig. 2.6. U-value Is the rate of heat loss in watts per square metre of construction multiplied by the temperature difference.
Source: The Whole House Book, Harris and Borer.

U-value of 2.00. Interestingly, drawing a thick curtain makes a huge difference – the combined U-value of both curtain and single-glazed windows being 3.60.

What is heat gain?

Houses are also capable of generating heat – of creating a heat gain.

The three potential heat gains in any house are from:

- Solar energy (passive and active solar heating).
- Casual heat gains as a result of activity within the house (from people, lights, cooking and so on).
- The heating system.

Thus, it makes sense to:

- Conserve first – in other words, improve the fabric of the building; insulate, draughtproof, double glaze and control ventilation.
- Capture heat from the sun and keep it in the building.
- Use fossil fuels as efficiently as possible by using the most efficient heating technology available; where possible use a non fossil fuel heating system such as a wood stove, biomass burner or heat pump.

Reducing national heat demand

In Sustainable Energy Without the Hot Air, David Mackay estimated that heat demand could be reduced by 40% just by only heating spaces as they are used rather than keeping heat on all the time. Another idea might be to encourage the construction of tiny houses. The idea of the tiny house has emerged from a movement in the US as a reaction to a massive growth in average house sizes over the last 30 years. People who can, commit to living in smaller (mostly self-build) spaces that are cheaper, easier to manage, require less heating and are very cute. Check out www.tumbleweedhouses.com

- Decrease the thermostat/air temperature and the area requiring heat (that is, only heat rooms when they are used). You can also use modern programmers to 'zone' different areas with a heating demand appropriate to their use.

What is the heat load?

The heat load of a building is the amount of energy required to raise and maintain the temperature of the structure to the desired level – usually expressed in kilowatts (kW), one kilowatt being a thousand watts. It is determined by a number of factors, including number and size of rooms, type of material used in construction, infiltration and ventilation and external and internal design temperatures, which is defined by the location and use of the building – the external design temperature of a building in Inverness will be lower than the external design temperature of a building in Bristol.

Getting the heat load figure right is important because it determines the size and type of heating 'plant' needed – plant means the whole heating system, which could include a boiler, a wood stove, solar water heating panels and so on. Energy conservation and efficiency measures help to reduce the heat load, and so will save you money on both the initial purchase of plant as well as on continual fuel costs (for example, wood, or electricity in the case of heat pumps).

There are many computer programmes available for energy assessment (and many professionals proficient at operating them), but you can do a basic calculation using the table on page 118. Also recommended is the government's Standard Assessment Procedure for Energy Ratings of Dwellings 2009 (SAP) which can be downloaded free of charge from www.bre.co.uk/sap2009

These contain professional level (sometimes quite technical) guidance for energy conservation measures, as well as sample worksheets. Set up your own spreadsheet to make the calculations – you can instantly see the results when you 'fit' double glazing or 'add' an extra layer of insulation. Life suddenly seems a lot warmer!

Case study

The Yard, Bristol: community housing scheme combining power down and power up features

Ecologically speaking, Bristol must be one of the most creative cities in Britain. Home to numerous groundbreaking schemes, organisations and initiatives it has a strong network of community risk takers, by which I mean people who are prepared to go out of their way to create projects that benefit the community.

One such group of people came together to create a community self-build project in St Werbughs, known already for its city farm and extremely popular allotment site. I met up with Jackson, one of the directors of the Ashley Vale Action Group (the community company set up to facilitate construction), to dicsuss the project's past, present and future.

The story of the Yard begins in the year 2000 when a site occupied by a local scaffold company came up for redevelopment. Concerned that the site would become yet another bland corporate-owned housing estate, a group of local people got together to create an alternative vision for the site based on community participation and sustainable development. The idea of a large self-build scheme came up, which evolved into a design, a logistical plan and an awareness raising campaign.

At the same time a developer put in a bid but needed to obtain planning permission prior to buying the site. This gave the group time to mount a campaign to stop the rival development, establish a legal entity with which the existing landowner could negotiate (AVAG, a not-for-profit company limited by guarantee), and begin to raise interest in potential self-builders who could stump up the cash to buy the site.

After a successful community campaign the rival application was rejected by planning and AVAG employed a lawyer to negotiate a deal with the landowner, also successful. The group then set about finalising a masterplan for the site, to aquire planning permission themselves, and to allow self-builders to take control of their plots as quickly as possible.

Self-build house at the Yard, part of phase one of the project.

Interestingly, most of the people involved in the campaign and AVAG were not looking to self-build themselves, they just wanted the site to be used in a community orientated way. The self-builders had to be recruited from outside the core group.

The group made sure that the project had a strong environmental ethos by using as many existing resources as

possible (including a large concrete slab on which the houses could be built, without the need for additional foundations); and by creating eco-construction criteria for each self-builder. The overall idea being to reduce the amount of energy used during the construction phase, as well as through the life of the building.

The criteria stipulated that all materials had to be category A, as specified by BREEAM (Building Research Establishment Environmental Assessment Method). If other materials were to be used the self-builders had to get permission from AVAG. The planning application also stipulated that designs had to

be made in accordance to consideration of the other houses around them and be less than ten metres high, a specified height which later proved to be a point of contention for the householders who lived opposite, many believing it to be too tall.

'In hindsight it would have been better if some of the houses opposite the existing terrace could have been lower. Because the limit was ten metres, people built to ten metres, rather than thinking about what was the most appropriate size.'

The project plan was divided into three phases, the last phase only being completed in 2010. The first phase was a ring of large self-build houses around a central green space, the second phase a collection of smaller self-finish houses (where the external shell of a building is built by a contractor but the internal walls, decoration and fittings are supplied by the owners), and the third phase, the transformation of a disused office block into refurbished self-finish flats.

During the first phase each self-builder was sold a private plot. Unlike some other self-build schemes there was no formal agreement for builders to help one another, but informally they did, sourcing and ordering materials together, sharing labour and so on. Because each plot was a private scheme it did allow people to work within their own time capacity and budget. 'Some people finished very quickly and employed contractors, some people did it all themselves, some people are still building now.'

The height issue was not the only point of conflict to arise during the project. Some of the original directors, each of whom had put in a huge amount of voluntary work to make the project happen, pulled out following disagreements about what the project should be. Jackson likens this to parent-sibling antagonism through the teenage years, 'Part of that was to do with self-builders being given a kind of authority in their own right, being a force in their own right, and having their own desires over and beyond what some of the directors originally set out to see.' There were also considerable delays in elements of the whole project caused by partners dropping out at critical moments (specifically, a housing association), the banking crisis (which left some buyers without access to mortgages), and at times funding gaps.

Environmentally, the third phase of the project – the office block conversion – is the most advanced. Although the self-build projects have a high environmental standard – all but two have timber frames and many have features such as PV and solar thermal, warmcell insulation, lime render,

cedar cladding and Heracliff board – the environmental criteria has improved over the years, incorporating improved technologies as they've come along.

The office block conversion represents a masterclass in eco-retrofit. So much so that in 2009 it won the REGEN South West Renewable Energy Award for Best Housing Scheme. All the original single glazed windows were replaced with low-E double glazing (it would have been triple glazed but for a supply problem). On the north side the overall window size was reduced and some of the previous window spaces filled in to reduce heat loss. 120mm of external wall insulation was put in place, along with cavity wall insulation. In addition, two large wood pellet boilers and $27m^2$ of solar thermal panels were installed to provide the whole building with domestic hot water and heating (with six flats, a community centre and several office spaces sharing the hot water). A 2.5kW solar PV array provides electricity for the community centre.

This final phase of the project also tested a new type of collective structure – a so-called commonhold arrangement. Under commonhold, all occupants of the building share ownership with the community group. The community group sold the apartments to the occupants but the common hold collectively had responsibility for the delivery and design of the building, as well as choices regarding how the project should be renovated.

The Yard is interesting as a project because it has managed to overcome numerous financial, logistical and social hurdles to fulfill its vision. It's taken ten years and lots of dedication and free labour on the part of unpaid directors and volunteers, as well as self-builders and self-finishers. But what it has achieved is a unique and beautiful housing project in the middle of an urban area, delivering what Jackson believes to be a very strong social network and high quality of life.

'Most people know each other very well. This doesn't

Self-finish houses (with turf roofs) in foreground. Part of phase two. Larger self-build houses behind, part of phase one.

Jackson also believes the quality of the build is better than in many developments; the emphasis on long term well-being over short term profits has created better choices for residents whilst still delivering cheaper houses. A very different ideology has resulted in a different type of home.

Before and after: run down office block becomes state-of-the-art eco dwellings in phase three of the project.

mean we all get on very well but I think this is part of having a very strong community. Everyone has their own connections within the site so there's a very strong network. There's a common sense of sharing the space. We're undergoing a quality of life assessment at the moment. It's already showing that the sense of wellbeing on the site is much higher than the average for the local area and the whole of Bristol. People [living in the Yard] feel ownership of where they are. Having the chance to create their own space makes people feel very proud.'

What next for the Yard?

Although the Yard has now been completed AVAG wants to create a legacy of self-build activity that goes beyond the site. Two new companies – Ecomotive and Bright Green Futures – have been created to support other self-build schemes, and some people from Ecomotive have helped to create the National Self-Build Association, which has already begun to shape policy through the government's new Self-Build working group. There is also a community build social website to help people get in touch with one another: www.communitybuild.org.uk

Chapter Three

Draughtproofing and ventilation

Fig. 3.1. Draughtproofing

Thirteen places where draughts get in

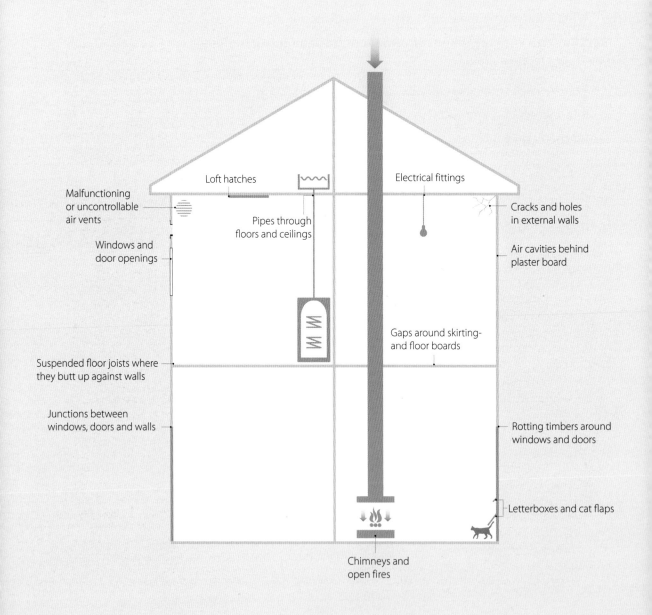

Loft hatches

Electrical fittings

Malfunctioning or uncontrollable air vents

Cracks and holes in external walls

Pipes through floors and ceilings

Windows and door openings

Air cavities behind plaster board

Gaps around skirting- and floor boards

Suspended floor joists where they butt up against walls

Junctions between windows, doors and walls

Rotting timbers around windows and doors

Letterboxes and cat flaps

Chimneys and open fires

Ventilation – the controlled movement of fresh air into a building

Ventilation is required to remove stale air and humidity and to bring fresh oxygen into a house – both for the inhabitants and also for any heating system that requires oxygen, such as wood stoves. Of course, ventilation brings cold air into the building and any ventilation technique must be controlled so as not to unnecessarily increase the heat load (the amount of heat required).

SAP worksheets allow you to calculate the optimum amount of ventilation for your building, giving a different weighting for each method of ventilation. Alternatively, an accredited advisor will do these calculations for you. As a rule of thumb, a conventional modern building needs to be ventilated at a rate of 0.8 to 1.0 air changes per hour – almost twice that for a super insulated building. Since infiltration rates in many traditional buildings have as many as 4 air changes per hour, draughtproofing is very beneficial.

Trickle ventilation
Trickle vents are usually found in modern window casements. They are small draught-free openings that can be open and closed according to need.

Passive stack ventilation
You'll see the word 'passive' used a lot in this book and it generally refers to a lack of movement or mechanical and electrical parts. For example, passive solar heating differentiates itself from 'active' solar water heating or electricity generating PV systems. A passive stack ventilation system does its job without requiring any fans; they are mostly used to remove stale or humid air from 'wet' areas, such as kitchens or bathrooms. Pipes running from the ceilings of these rooms to a roof opening draw the air out.

Because the stale air needs to be replaced by fresh air, the SAP recommends that passive stack ventilation be used in conjunction with trickle vents. Ideally these trickle vents will bring air into a 'buffer zone' such as a conservatory or draught lobby (see box on page

80) before it passes into the main part of the house. This allows the air to be pre-heated using passive solar techniques. To prevent ventilation when it is not required, stacks should be fitted with humidity controlled valves so that ventilation will only occur when there is a potential problem with damp.

Intermittent-running extractor fans
These are designed to do the same job as a passive stack system and are generally used when passive ventilation is either not possible or inadequate. They are switched on and off when needed – automatically by a humidity sensitive switch, manually by the user, or in conjunction with some other function, for example, when the light switch is turned on.

Mechanical ventilation
Mechanical ventilation systems use fans that run continuously. They bring fresh air into the house (input only), take stale air out (extract) or do both (balanced).

The ventilation air change rate

The ventilation air change rate is the rate at which outside air enters/leaves a building. This table shows standard rates of air inflow for different ventilation techniques. These are used to assess total heat load in a building.

Item	Ventilation rate m³/hour
Chimney	40
Open flue	20
Fan	10
Passive vent	10
Flueless gas fire	40

Source: SAP, 2005 edition, revision 3.

Draught lobby and porches

An unheated porch (with an internal and an external door) provides a buffer zone between the inside and the outside of a building – absorbing cold air before it can enter any heated room. The inside door of a porch will need to be as well draughtproofed as the outside door. Ventilation air can be drawn from a porch – even though porches are unheated, porch air is always warmer than the air outside, especially if glazing is used to maximise passive solar gain. Under SAP the term 'draught lobby' has a particular meaning: it describes an enclosed space leading into a cloakroom with a floor space at least 2m² where the door arrangement is such that a person with a pushchair (or similar) is able to close the outer door before opening the inner door.

Positive input ventilation (PIV) – bringing air into the house

Positive input ventilation is a fan driven ventilation system that will often use a loft space as a pre-heat area before allowing air to enter the main part of a building – the air drawn in from the loft is slightly warmer than the cold air coming direct from outside (if the insulation is good there shouldn't be much heat at all in the loft). Fans that run continuously obviously use a lot more electricity and so the SAP expectation is that the pre-heat saves more energy than the fan uses. The SAP calculation for systems that use a loft to pre-heat ventilation air is the same as for natural ventilation, including a 20m³/h ventilation rate equivalent to two extractor fans or passive vents.

Mechanical extract ventilation (MEV) – taking air out of the house

MEV systems remove air from a building – either centrally using a network of ducts and one central fan, or from each wet room (kitchens and bathrooms) using individual fans.

Whole house mechanical ventilation with heat recovery (MVHR)

An MVHR system provides balanced ventilation. They take the warm, humid air extracted from wet rooms and pass it through a heat exchanger which draws fresh air from the outside. The heat exchanger manages to pick up around 85% of the heat that would have been lost to the outside. The warmed fresh air is then introduced into the living rooms and bedrooms. An MVHR will provide a high standard of draught-free comfort but it should be fitted carefully so that the energy used to power it is not greater than the heat saving. Unnecessary energy use can be reduced by installing humidity sensitive extraction grilles and by taking fresh air from a loft, sun room, draught lobby or conservatory. An alternative to the whole house system is to have humidity-controlled heat exchange fans in the kitchen and bathroom.

How to air a room in winter

If you don't have good ventilation in a room, turning the heating off and opening a window for a five minute burst of fresh air can help. This is much better than leaving the heating on and the window half open for a long time.

Case study

Most of the case studies in this book are big projects, but if you want to get started with something small yet incredibly effective, read the case studies below. All are in inner city areas but the ideas can be applied anywhere.

Bristol Green Doors

Bristol Green Doors was set up in 2010 to give householders the chance to open up their energy efficient homes to members of the public and to share their retrofitting experiences, both of saving and generating energy. Over one weekend thousands of visits were made to over 50 homes, with an average of 50 visits per home. Visits were pre-registered via the website to avoid overcrowding and to protect households. Case studies of many of the homes were then made available on the Bristol Green Doors website (www.bristolgreendoors.org). The weekend was followed by a two month programme of courses, talks and workshops, and

Home owners show visitors what life is like living with renewables.

two more technology focused events; Insulation Celebration and Solar Saturday. If you haven't got the resources to put this kind of event on yourself it could be possible to link up with existing providers instead. If you don't want to organise an event yourself but would either like to open your doors to others or visit an open doors house, visit www.superhomes.org.uk. Superhomes are older homes that have been refurbished to the highest standards of energy efficiency, leading to at least a 60% reduction in carbon emissions.

Draughtbusters

'If you've got fresh air, leaking into your house, who you gonna call? Draughtbusters.' Watch the youtube videos made by the Hyde Farm Climate Action Network (Hyde Farm CAN) and you'll get a good idea of what Draughtbusters is all about. But here's a quick summary; Draughtbusting is a way to get together with your friends and neighbours to work one house at a time on fixing draughts. You'll need someone who knows what they're doing to start things off, but once you've fixed one house together the knowledge should spread easily between people. Hyde Farm CAN (www.hydefarm.org. uk) offer a local draughbusting service to identify low-cost measures and work with you to install these measures. The only thing they ask is that the householder pays for the materials and invites some of their friends and neighbours to join in. This way the skills are passed quickly between households. There are local Draughtbuster initiatives all over the country. Look for one near you.

Energy monitoring hire

Energy monitoring equipment can be expensive to buy so why not share the cost with your neighbourhood? Transition Town Brixton applied for a grant to buy 10 Efergy Electricity Monitors to lend to the community. To borrow one, local residents have to sign up via www.transitiontownbrixton.org.

Chapter Four

Insulation and improved glazing

Fig. 4.1. Insulation

Four places to insulate: floors, roofs, walls and windows

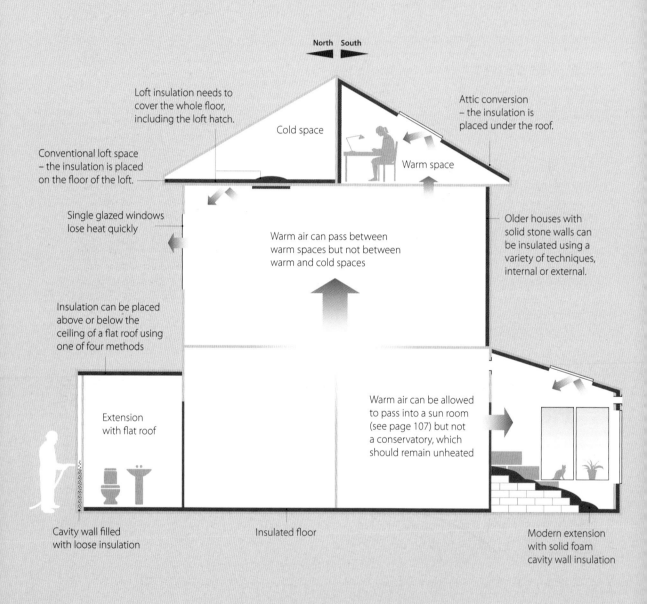

North South

Loft insulation needs to cover the whole floor, including the loft hatch.

Cold space

Attic conversion – the insulation is placed under the roof.

Conventional loft space – the insulation is placed on the floor of the loft.

Warm space

Single glazed windows lose heat quickly

Warm air can pass between warm spaces but not between warm and cold spaces

Older houses with solid stone walls can be insulated using a variety of techniques, internal or external.

Insulation can be placed above or below the ceiling of a flat roof using one of four methods

Extension with flat roof

Warm air can be allowed to pass into a sun room (see page 107) but not a conservatory, which should remain unheated

Cavity wall filled with loose insulation

Insulated floor

Modern extension with solid foam cavity wall insulation

What is insulation?

Insulation relates to the fabric of a building, or the building 'envelope' as it is also known. It prevents heat loss by slowing down the transmission of heat from the inside of the building to the outside. In other words, it lowers the U-value of a construction (see page 66 for explanation of U-value). For example, 100mm of roof insulation well laid across every part of a loft floor can lower the U-value of a roof from 2.00 to 0.30W/m²K (though this is dependent on the type of insulation). Ideally, every house should be super insulated, a term used to describe levels of insulation thought to be the optimum for a cold climate (see figure 4.2). However, current Building Regulations instead specify a 'worst acceptable standard', although they do point out that 'the achievement of the TER (Target CO₂ Emissions Rate – also part of Building Regulations) is likely to require significantly better fabric performance'.

To give you an example of how the difference plays out, a super insulated loft (with 300-450mm of loft insulation) has a U-value of 0.12 but the worst acceptable standard (only 200mm of loft insulation) has a U-value of 0.20. Likewise, the best window you can get is a Passivhaus standard window (with a U-value of 0.8-0.6) whereas the 'worst acceptable' window is a double low E 12mm airspace with a U-value of 2.00. This is still considerably better than a single glazed window – which has a U-value of 4.80.

Thickness of insulation and financial payback

Financial payback depends on use of building, type and cost of fuel used, how quickly the cost of that fuel is rising, where the insulation is being put, whether you are retro-fitting an existing building or building from scratch, and whether you are doing the job yourself or paying a contractor. The cost of a contractor is relatively high compared to the cost of the materials themselves so if you already have a contractor in to do the work you might as well ask them to quote for super insulation at the same time.

Having said this, the benefits of insulation reduce as the insulation gets thicker – the first inch is very beneficial, the next slightly less so – until there comes a point where adding extra insulation is pointless. For example, the optimum thickness for loft insulation is around 600mm but the benefits of insulation flatten off at around the 350mm mark. This is why super insulation is regarded as being about 300-400mm and no more. Financial payback becomes more significant when fuel prices rise and when the heat load (demand) of a building increases. It is worth considering how the use of a building may evolve over time when making these decisions.

	Worst acceptable	Super insulated
Roof	0.20W/m²K	0.12W/m²K
Wall	0.30W/m²K	0.14W/m²K
Floor	0.25W/m²K	0.15W/m²K
Party wall	0.20W/m²K	0.14W/m²K
Windows, roof windows, glazed rooflights, curtain walling and pedestrian doors	2.00W/m²K	1.3W/m²K

Fig. 4.2. Worst acceptable standards compared to super insulated for fabric parameters. Source: Building Regulations Part L1A (2010).

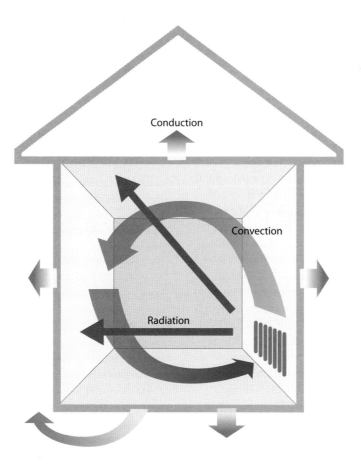

Fig. 4.3. Heat movement by conduction, convection and radiation. Source: The Whole House Book, Harris and Borer.

To insulate or super insulate? The answer will mostly come down to cash and environmental consciousness. Sometimes it will be physically impossible to insulate a building to the max (perhaps because doing so would uncomfortably shrink the size of rooms, for example), or sometimes regulations (such as those specifying National Park or listed building renovations) will prevent it. But when it is technically and legally possible to super insulate a house you might find yourself making a cost analysis based on how much additional energy you will save.

How does insulation work?

No matter what you do to stop it, heat will leave a building. This is because it is naturally drawn towards the cold air outside. It has four clever ways of getting through the materials that are supposed to keep it inside:

- Conduction.
- Convection.
- Radiation.
- Evaporation.

To understand how these four differ from one another light a candle and place your hand above it (at a sensible height - no burnt palms please!). The heat you feel on the palm of your hand reaches you by convection. This is because hot air expands and rises, pushing the cold air out of the way – allowing it to get to your hand.

Now place your hand to the left of the flame. You still feel the heat but this time the heat is reaching you by radiation – the heat is carried to your hand by electromagnetic waves created by energetic electrons in the wax in the wick of the candle. Now pick up a teaspoon and hold it above the flame. It won't take long for the iron particles in the spoon to transfer the heat along, right to your fingertips (ouch!), at which point you will instinctively know to drop the spoon or move it away from the flame. This process is called conduction.

Finally, once the spoon has cooled down, fill it with water and place it above the candle. The heat goes into the water first rather than along the spoon. The water turns into steam and rises into the air. This is evaporation. Eventually, when all the water has evaporated the heat will then transfer along the spoon via conduction.

All materials relate to these processes in different ways. Why do we have wooden handles on metal pans? They conduct heat poorly. If we used wood for the pan itself it would burn rather than transfer the heat through to its contents. Metal pans on the other hand love to let the heat through them. Air conducts heat poorly and thus makes a good insulating material between two panes of glass. However, it will pass heat on through convection, so airspaces used in insulation must always be small enough to suppress convection currents.

Shiny materials are good at dealing with radiation as they reflect radiant heat. This is why foil is placed behind wall radiators, to reflect heat back into a room. Evaporated vapour will evenly disperse in the air in the room. Therefore it will come into contact with the cold walls (assuming poor insulation).

The materials in a building need to be able to absorb moisture and allow it to make its way to the outside – which is what it wants to do. This process is known as hygroscopic regulation and some materials are better hygroscopic regulators than others. They are said to be breathable. Many modern insulating materials based on hydrocarbons (such as polystyrenes and polyurethane) are impermeable to water vapour. Other materials (such as aerated bricks or hempcrete) are good hygroscopic regulators. As are breathable paints and lime wash (used in both the interior and exterior finishes in order to avoid creating a watertight barrier). A natural lime plaster coating will let through 300 grams of water vapour per m^2 per day ($300g/m^2/day$). A cement based plaster only allows 45 to 50 grams through.

Insulation, condensation and breathable constructions

If a room is well insulated there will be no surface condensation as the surfaces will all be near room temperature. Instead, any water vapour will make its way through the construction until it reaches a cold layer near the outside of the insulation where it will condense (this is known as the dew point). This process is called interstitial condensation. In masonry constructions, where fungal growth is not supported, no damage is done. This is not true of timber frame constructions where great care must be taken to prevent interstitial condensation. There isn't space to go into detail here but remedies for this problem are covered in great detail in CAT's *The Whole House Book* (Harris and Borer).

Insulating roofs

Insulating lofts

Loft insulation is easy to install and the payback time is quick. Over its lifetime it also saves a significant amount of CO_2, depending on the size of house and type of fuel used. In all cases it improves thermal comfort and decreases draughts. When buying insulation look out for the Energy Saving Trust logo, which selects products according to set criteria. A full list is available from http://www.energysavingtrust.org.uk/In-your-home/Energy-Saving-Trust-Recommended-products

Loft insulation can be blown-in by a professional installation company, or rolled or laid as boards either DIY or professionally. Contact the Energy Saving Trust or the National Insulation Association (www.nationalinsulationassociation.org.uk).

Blown insulation

Blown-in insulation includes Warmcell, a product made out of recycled paper. Required depths are sectioned off with timbers and the insulation blown-in using machines. If the loft space is needed for storage, boards are placed on top of the sections. All blown-in insulation must be handled by trained contractors, although loose fill available in bags for small spaces can be self installed. Contact the Energy Saving Trust for details.

Rolled insulation

Rolled insulation is generally referred to as quilts or batts. These are sold in tightly wrapped rolls and are

How much CO_2 could loft insulation save?

Installing 270mm of insulation in a loft which previously had no insulation will save around 730kg of CO_2 per year. If there was already 50mm of insulation and you topped this up to 270mm, the extra saving would be around 210kg of CO_2 per year (figures from the Energy Saving Trust based on a three bedroom semi-detached house).

Loft insulation

If everyone in the UK installed 270mm of loft insulation, we could save around £520 million and nearly three million tonnes of CO_2 every year.

sized according to depth and square metre coverage. They are made from a wide range of materials, the most natural being sheep's wool, the most common being mineral wool (sometimes made from recycled glass bottles). Sheep's wool feels more comforting when you lay it but the recycled glass insulation is almost as pleasant and definitely not as sharp as it sounds! In any case, it is advised to cover your skin and to wear a face mask and goggles when laying insulation – particles of any insulation can be abrasive, inside or outside of the body.

Insulating attic conversions, flat roofs and other unusual roof spaces

The phrase 'rooms in the roof' describes a situation where the warm part of a building connects directly to the roof without any cold loft space in between. This could refer to loft conversions, but it would also include community halls, old schools, barns and chapels, disused workshops or factory spaces, attic flats and so on. Retro-fitting these spaces with insulation is more complicated.

There are two ways of doing it:

- Build the insulation into the roof structure as close to the roof tiles as possible. (Increase the depth of the insulation by hanging ceiling joists off the rafters.)
- Create a loft space using a suspended floor.

A description of the second option is beyond the scope of this book as the detailing of major construction work is necessary, but it is possible to fit insulated suspended timber floor systems or to buy ceiling insulation pads that rest on top of light weight suspended floors. Examples can be seen at

Insulating flat roofs

Because there are a wide range of different types of flat roofs and insulation solutions for them, it is impossible to give anything other than a brief overview here. In most cases it will be necessary to call in a flat roof specialist. Quite often flat roofs are built on top of modern constructions which have little in common with the older building they find themselves attached too. It is important to insulate flat roofs well – even in a small area like a porch – because these attachments can quite often form a cold bridge to the main building.

The area where the two buildings connect should be well insulated but also kept moisture free. It's easy for water to seep into flat roofs if the connection is not good and any dampness in insulation will destroy its effectiveness. Flat roofs typically have a simple structure, with the waterproof covering laid over timber decking on timber joists. There are four main types of flat roof insulation:

- Cold deck – where the insulation is below the decking and above the ceiling.
- Warm deck – where the insulation is above the decking and below the waterproof layer.
- Inverted flat roof – where the waterproof layer is placed above the insulation (also water resistant, for example, cork), which is kept in place by slabs, pebbles or turf.
- Internal – where insulation-backed plasterboard is fixed internally in a similar way to internal wall insulation.

For more information try *Insulating Flat Roofs*, a free download from the English Heritage site www.climatechangeandyourhome.org.uk and *The Whole House Book* which contains a selection of different approaches to flat roof construction.

www.greenplanetinsulation.co.uk/prodtype. asp and http://www.celotex.co.uk/Applications/ Floor-Insulation (though this does not constitute a recommendation). English Heritage produces a very good downloadable guide, *Insulation of suspended timber roofs,* available for free from www. climatechangeandyourhome.org.uk/live/content_ pdfs/783.pdf

The first option is the only practical option for small spaces and existing loft areas. It is also an attractive option when converting old buildings when you want to maintain a large open plan living space. High levels of roof insulation can be difficult to achieve though.

Remembering that you're working upwards (against gravity) and not downwards, all the insulation you fit has to be contained by some sort of timber and board structure that can bear the weight of the insulation – conventional trussed rafters are just built for the job of holding light weight tiles above them in place. They are not deep enough to contain 270mm of loft insulation, plus the required amount of free air space that must be kept around the insulation (50mm above the 'between-rafter' insulation, 25mm where the

insulation butts up against the eaves and a continuous 5mm gap where it butts up against the ridge).

Thus it is often necessary to have two layers of timber: the first to support the roof finish (in other words, the tiling felt and the tiles) and the second to support the insulation and ceiling finish (for example, plasterboard). These two sets of timber are separated to prevent a cold bridge to the outside. In new constructions, timber I-beams can be used. In an existing traditional roof, with rafters supported on roof beams, the second layer of timbers (ceiling joists) can be hung off the rafters using hardboard, ply or timber hangers.

It is possible to use thinner rigid insulation boards in place of a thick layer of insulation. These can generally be fitted into existing rafter spaces and provide a substantial energy saving (if not quite as good). Boards must be very carefully cut so that they fit snugly between the rafters. You can then add extra insulation by using insulated plasterboard. These are attached to the ceiling joists so take up a little more of the room space (see *The Whole House Book* for more information).

Examine your loft

Can you see the joists – horizontal beams that make up the floor of the loft? If not, it is possible that boards have been laid on top and there may well be insulation underneath the boards. You need to see if this is the case before laying more insulation. Lift one board and measure the depth of insulation you find there. If it is less that 300mm it might be worth topping it up, but if you want to carry on using it as a storage space you may have to raise the boards and raise the level of the joists before adding insulation. This will require a complete measurement of the loft area – including joist length, depth and width, and area of roof to be insulated. If you go down this route, be sure to use a thick plywood (non tropical FSC approved!) or OSB (Orientated Strand Board), long enough to allow you to walk or crawl safely between the joists.

If you don't need the storage space but want to add more insulation you can simply add the required depth in rolls across (in other words at right angles to) the existing insulation – again measuring the roof area.

If you can see the joists you will either be looking at a bare floor or at insulation rolled between the joists. If there is insulation, again measure it and add more as described above. If not you will need to measure the joist height and again make some decisions about how you want to use the loft. If you are going to use your loft as a room at some point in the future then you need to make another set of decisions because the roof (not the floor) of an occupied room will have to be insulated – a process described on pages 88-89.

Decide on the insulation material

Once you have measured your floor area you need to decide on what sort of rolled insulation to buy – natural or mineral wool. The decision comes down to preferences for natural versus man-made materials, and to cost. Mineral wool is generally cheaper.

At the time of writing some rolled insulation was subsidised under the Carbon Emissions Reduction Target (which will be replaced by ECO under the Green Deal, see page 53). Look out for special offers advertised through DIY retailers and other places.

Laying the material

Laying the material is relatively straightforward. Before you start, remove any debris from the roof. It is best for the insulation to lay flat against the ceiling and tight against the joists. Pipes and wires entering the loft space need to be checked to see if previous builders have left any holes between the roof space and other areas of the house. This needs to be done before the insulation is laid. Any holes should be filled with sealant to prevent air leakage. Pipes should also be insulated – again a job best done before the insulation is laid.

Always lay between the joists using your sturdy board (or two preferably) to work on. Insulate up to the top of the joists and then either fit your boards or lay another layer of insulation across the first layer. This is harder to do as the joists become submerged under insulation. Always work back to the loft hatch so you don't have to worry about moving across the whole of the loft to 'get back'. When you get to the end of a roll and need to start with a new one, make sure the two ends butt up against each other tightly. The efficiency of roof insulation deteriorates if there are gaps.

Super insulation and loft storage

If you want a little more insulation than your joists allow but don't want to give up your storage space, one option is to fill up to the top of the joists with rolled insulation and then lay special hard insulation boards across them – remembering not to squash the rolled insulation down (as insulation works better with air spaces). The disadvantage with hard insulation boards is that they are quite easy to lay badly, so you need to make sure they butt up against each other tightly and are firmly fixed in place with no gaps in between.

Electric cabling and loft insulation

If there are any visible electric wires in your loft, do not handle them if there is any doubt that they are safe. If safe to handle, be sure to keep them above your insulation so as to prevent any chance of overheating. When laying the insulation feed it under the cables.

Water tanks

You should also insulate over your water tank (if you can't remove it altogether and place it in a heated part of the house, which is much better as the water is to be heated anyway). Do not insulate under the tank as some hot air getting to the tank is useful anti-freeze.

Loft hatch

Finally, remember to insulate your loft hatch with the same level of insulation you afford the rest of the loft. The insulation has to be attached to the loft hatch and you can do this by building a box on the hatch for the insulation to go in, or wrapping the insulation in material and attaching your insulation 'pillow' using tape or staples. Again, it is best to avoid squashing the insulation if you can. Also lay draughtproofing strips around the edges of your hatch.

Insulating difficult roof spaces – dormers, short sloping ceilings and thatched roofs

Dormers and short sloping roofs that come off the main steep pitch of a roof can weaken the thermal performance of a building if they are badly – or not at all – insulated. These are difficult spaces to insulate well and guidance should be sought for the best results. Quite often they are best tackled when the rest of the roof needs retiling but, if this is impossible for financial reasons or because the roof does not need it, it's worth downloading the relevant guidance notes from English Heritage, CADW or Historic Scotland. The same goes for thatched roofs. Properly maintained thatched roofs have a U-value rated at between 0.23 and $0.29W/m^2/k$ depending on whether the material used is long straw or water reed. This is very close to the 0.20 required by Building Regulations. You can further insulate cold loft spaces as previously described but correct maintenance of the thatch is essential.

Listed buildings, conservation areas and National Parks

If you are responsible for a building which is listed or sits in a conservation area or National Park, check with your local planning authority conservation officer. Installing external insulation or double glazing on a listed building or a building in a conservation area requires permission from the local planning authority under the Planning (Listed Buildings and Conservation Areas) Act 1990. Planning Policy Guidance (PPG) 15, *Planning and the Historic Environment*, can help you with this – see www.planningportal.gov.uk Work of any kind to a Scheduled Monument requires consent from English Heritage, Heritage Scotland or CADW under the Ancient Monuments and Archaeological Areas Act 1979. *Energy conservation in traditional buildings* from English Heritage is a useful guide.

Insulating walls

There are three main types of wall construction: cavity, solid and timber frame.

Cavity wall insulation

A cavity wall has two skins – an inner and an outer. In between the two skins there is usually at least a 50mm air gap. The air in this gap does provide some level of insulation but insulation values can be greatly increased if the cavity is filled with a material with plenty of air pockets in it. These pockets of air reduce the U-value from 1.50 to 0.50W/m^{2}K. In new buildings and extensions (and those built within the last ten years) cavities are insulated during the construction phase, most often with slabs of insulation material. Many super insulated buildings have now been constructed with a 200-300mm fully filled cavity. This super insulation can reduce the U-value to as low as 0.14W/m^{2}K.

Older buildings can be retro-fitted with insulation using an easy and well established technique: small holes are drilled in the outer skin and the insulating material (usually mineral wool plastic beads or perlite) is pumped in until the gap between the two wall skins has been filled. When the work is completed the holes are refilled using a material appropriate to the construction. Installation is carried out by registered installers, details of which can be found from the Energy Saving Trust (0800 512 012). Make sure your installer has signed up to a code of professional practice like those provided by the NIA (National Insulation Association) and that the installation carries a 25 year guarantee by CIGA (Cavity Insulation Guarantee Agency).

A useful online toolkit

Check out the English Heritage Energy Toolkit for easy savings, how well your house performs, draughtproofing and easy insulation, and planning for the long term. www.climatechangeandyourhome.org.uk/live/ saving energy in buildings intro.aspx

Annual cash saving for cavity wall insulation

The Energy Saving Trust estimates that for a three bedroom house the annual saving per year for a standard cavity filling is around £110, with an installed cost of £250 and a payback of around two years (figure includes a 50% subsidy available at the time of writing under the Carbon Emissions Reduction Target (CERT).

Solid wall insulation

Whereas cavity walls are very easy to insulate, existing solid masonry walls (which could be rubble or dress stone, rammed earth, flint, brick or concrete – block or solid) can be hard work. This is because solid wall insulation requires the addition of an extra layer, either internally or externally, and many buildings have been constructed without this addition in mind. They are already tightly packed into their space.

External solid wall insulation

External insulation protects the inner skin from the elements and allows the original wall to act as a heat store. The appearance of the building will change and this may be a problem for the occupant or for the planning authorities (especially if your property is listed or rests within a conservation area or National Park). For listed buildings any form of external insulation will require listed building consent, and for most other buildings planning permission will have to be sought. If in doubt, contact your local planning officer.

Internal solid wall insulation

Internal insulation (known as dry lining) allows the external appearance of the building to stay the same, and it is cheaper and can be carried out on a room by room basis as funds allow. However, it is more disruptive and steals space – which can be a problem in old cottages with their narrow rooms and low ceilings.

Whichever method you choose, solid wall insulation is the most difficult and, in many cases, the least cost-effective building element to insulate. Thus, before considering solid wall insulation it pays to

Cash saving for solid wall insulation

The Energy Saving Trust estimates that around £365 a year can be saved by solid wall insulating an average three bedroom house. But with a total insulation cost of between £5,500 (minimum internal costs) and £14,500 (maximum external costs) the payback time is significantly greater than all other insulation measures. With external insulation saving only an additional £20 and only 0.1 tonnes of CO_2 a year compared to internal insulation, financially and environmentally, internal insulation is the best option. The only reasons to go external will be technical.

What is cold bridging?

Some structural elements, such as beams and joists, especially those situated in places where walls meet roofs or floors, can create cold bridges. These channel the cold from the outside to the inside and heat from inside to outside, reducing the environmental performance of the building. Sometimes external insulation can reduce the impact of cold bridges but the reverse can also be true and so great care should be taken to achieve full wall coverage. Any areas left unprotected – typically around window and door reveals, points where floors meet external walls and the ends of floor joists embedded in external walls, will not only be colder but at increased risk of condensation and decay.

insulate and draughtproof all other areas first. If your house is still losing too much heat and not affording you adequate thermal comfort, then solid wall insulation is the next step.

If you choose to insulate externally, it is worth combining the work with any changes or improvements to the building you have to make anyway, such as re-rendering, reroofing or extending.

As buildings are not generally designed to take an extra layer on the external wall, the addition of one often requires significant changes to other parts of the building – raising and extending the roof, for example. If you choose to insulate internally, doing so when replastering or carrying out other work can also help reduce building costs.

Solid wall insulation – either external or internal – can also affect the way the wall reacts with moisture. Most old solid walls are designed for breathability, which means they allow water to pass into and out of the wall to a certain extent. On a wet day the wall will accept moisture, on a dry day the moisture will pass out again. North facing walls with little sunshine will be more likely to suffer from damp problems. Choosing the right insulation material for the right situation is important, because the wrong material can cause moisture to be trapped in the wall, which then leads to rot and decay. Care must also be taken to avoid the creation of cold bridges, which are structural elements that draw cold into the house.

In any of these cases you should seek the advice of a professional specialising in solid wall insulation. And make sure they can show you examples of their previous work – they will need to know how to bring the U-value down to about 0.35 W/m²K without causing condensation on the walls. Any contractor who can't demonstrate these skills should be avoided as the work is expensive and, if carried out incorrectly, can potentially be very damaging to a building and its occupants. For external walls, contact the Insulated Render and Cladding Association (INCA) (www.inca-ltd.org.uk).

Timber frame wall insulation

The structural load of a building (that is, the weight created by the building, its users and the things its users need (baths, desks, beds and so on) is carried either by the walls (and only the walls) or a frame into which a wall is then built. Frames tend to be made of steel or timber, with timber being the ecological preference.

Insulating new build timber frame buildings

It is easy to super insulate a new timber frame building, which is why they are a popular choice in colder countries like Canada and Sweden; these countries also have lots of trees and not very many people! The spaces between the vertical posts that make up a timber frame (there's usually one every 600mm or so) can be filled with insulation and then walled off using an external panel board and internal plasterboard (all of which must be breathable). The depth of insulation required guides the thickness and construction of these poles. Most timber frame constructions have about 150mm of insulation, but it is possible to build super insulated houses with 250-350mm worth of insulation using spaced, layered or I-stud techniques which all reduce the thermal bridging effect of timber (previously discussed in the loft insulation section).

Insulating existing timber frame buildings

Existing timber frame buildings can be harder to insulate. The type and quality of wall construction vary enormously and if the house is very old the wall could be made from wattle and daub or lath and plaster. Some walls might even have been concealed by masonry or are partly of masonry construction. In many cases it will be more practical to treat some timber frame walls as solid walls.

As we mentioned earlier in the solid wall section, old materials are breathable and modern methods and materials that resist the passage of water vapour are not normally appropriate because they can increase the risk of decay. Instead, use materials that have similar 'performance' characteristics – in other words, that also breathe: wood fibre board, sheep's wool batts, hemp fibre insulation boards, flax fibre batts and cellulose fibre.

Hemp lime composites (based on the remains of the woody stem of the plant mixed with lime based binders) have also been used successfully (including in the WISE building at CAT. These are mixed like concrete to give a light weight, air filled 'hempcrete'. It is blown on to the wall material and finished externally and internally with lime renders, cladding or clay plasters.

Insulating floors

In one way the importance of floor insulation is relatively small when compared to insulation in other parts of a building, partly because the difference between the temperature in a room and the temperature of the ground is relatively small in comparison to the temperature difference between internal and external air. On the other hand an uninsulated floor can wick heat away from the building, in effect acting as a huge cold bridge. For this reason, wherever possible, floor insulation should be added to retrofits; under Building Regulations it must be included in new buildings and new extensions.

Suspended floor insulation

A suspended timber floor – where the floorboards are laid on joists supported by the walls – can be fairly easily insulated simply by lifting the floorboards and laying the insulation material between the joists. Mineral wool or loose fill insulation that is either supported by netting or placed on a low vapour resistant board is usually used.

The Energy Saving Trust estimates that the average DIY payback for mineral wool supported by netting is around two years (on an initial outlay of £100). Other materials and systems could cost more. However, 150mm of insulation can reduce the U-value of a typical non-insulated timber floor from 0.83 to 0.25W/m^2K, and 250mm will bring it down to 0.14W/m^2K.

Care must be taken to avoid gaps and air infiltration points around the skirting boards and between floorboards when fitting the insulation. Insulation

Finding out more about external wall insulation techniques

There isn't space here to explore the technical details of external wall installation. If you want more information about techniques, download *Insulating Solid Walls* from the English Heritage website and visit the Energy Saving Trust website. *The Complete Guide to External Wall Insulation* by Christopher Pearson will be useful for builders, architects and students.

can push cold air into draught spots, which reduces thermal comfort. Gaps can be filled with a silicone sealant (as described in the draughtproofing section). Like any insulation job it is cheaper and more cost effective to do the work during any scheduled renovations or building work.

Solid floor insulation

Solid floors can provide a different set of problems depending on the age and construction of the floor.

Very old constructions were designed with breathability in mind so the addition of modern non-breathable insulation materials can push ground moisture towards the walls of the buildings where the moisture concentrates and influences damp problems. This can lead to severe decay in the wall structure.

It is better in these cases to install an insulation material that allows evaporation to take place across the whole of the floor or insert an impermeable floor covering such as lino or vinyl. For example, one recent method of insulating solid floors in traditional buildings combines natural hydraulic lime binders (NHLs) with insulating aggregates (see English Heritage download *Insulating Solid Ground Floors* for a full description). This technique allows moisture to come freely in and out of the floor whilst still reducing the U-value.

Like many other types of solid floor insulation carried out on existing buildings, NHL insulation normally requires excavation work which can be very difficult and expensive to achieve. This does push up the cost of insulation work and a careful cost analysis would be required to see whether the job is really worth it in terms of energy saved and comfort provided.

The best time to carry out this type of work is when the floor has to be replaced anyway, for example, if there is a plan to fit underfloor heating. It is worth pointing out here that underfloor heating can raise the difference between the floor temperature and the ground temperature below by as much as 10-15°C, which increases the risk of heat loss. Under these conditions insulation becomes more important.

Building Regulations (2010) state that floors in new

buildings must have a U-value of 0.25W/m²K but it is possible to reduce the U-value to 0.15 using super insulation techniques. To set this in context, the U-value of an average uninsulated solid floor is 0.70. In very old buildings 220mm of light weight expanded aggregate loose fill will achieve a U-value of 0.45W/m²K on its own.

It is also worth bearing in mind that heat loss will be significantly greater through areas of the floor near external walls than through the centre of the floor. The total heat loss will depend upon the amount of floor area exposed to the walls (a long thin floor will have much more external 'heat loss edge' than a square one) and the overall thickness and construction of those walls. Extra insulation material should be placed around the edge of the floor, extending vertically to overlap the wall insulation.

Thermal mass and insulation

Solid floors can also provide a useful amount of thermal mass in a building – thermal mass being the ability of a material to absorb excess heat and release it again when the temperature in a room drops. This is particularly useful when there is a great potential for passive solar gain, that is, when the floor lies behind south facing windows. When the room heats up during the day, the solid floor absorbs excess heat, keeping the room relatively cool; at night the reverse is true – it releases the heat and keeps the room relatively warm. When fitting insulation materials it is important not to lose these qualities.

Materials used for solid floor insulation

If you are building a new solid floor then it is more likely that you will put the insulation underneath the floor, in which case it will be necessary to fit an impermeable damp proof membrane before laying the insulation (and probably a radon barrier). The insulation material must be able to stand a great deal of compression because the weight of the floor on top of it will be significant. Suitable materials include; foamed glass, expanded or extruded polystyrene, rigid urethane foam or rigid phenolic foam, cork, perlite or expanded clay beads – these last three are environmentally preferable.

It is also possible to upgrade an existing solid floor using one of two techniques:

- Rigid insulation and a 'floating' finish of boards or sand/cement/lime screed (a thin top layer of concrete poured on top of the structural concrete).
- Natural timber floorboards supported on battens placed above the existing floor with insulation placed in between the battens.

Of course, both of these techniques can cause a room to 'shrink', requiring all the doors to be cut down to size and refitted (or bought new if cutting is impossible) and for skirting boards to be pulled up and refitted. The only alternative to this (a lot more costly) is to excavate the floor and refit it with insulation to the existing floor level.

Improved glazing

Types of improved glazing

Double and triple glazing is another form of insulation. The air gap between multiple layers of glazing slows down the speed at which hot air escapes from a building.

Single glazed windows have the highest U-value of any common building material ($4.80W/m^2K$), which is why Building Regulations state that new buildings must have double glazing with at least a U-value of $2.00W/m^2K$. It is possible to get the U-value of a window down to $1.30W/m^2K$ using double super low E (low emissivity) or triple low E Argon filled windows. These are high quality windows and generally more expensive than the standard. Low E windows have an

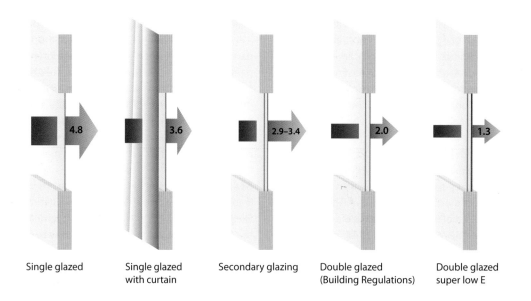

| Single glazed | Single glazed with curtain | Secondary glazing | Double glazed (Building Regulations) | Double glazed super low E |

Fig. 4.4. U-values for different glazing options. The lower the U-value the better.

With careful design it is possible to improve the effectiveness of double glazed windows using passive solar techniques. Taken over the whole heating season, a high performance south facing window should gain as much energy from the sun during the day as it loses at night. So, although it does not have the same low U-value of a well insulated wall (0.35W/m²K), a double glazed window can save more energy. There is more information on passive solar in the next chapter.

unnoticeable covering of metal oxide which allows sunlight and heat to pass into a room but cuts down the amount of heat that can get out again.

To simplify consumer choice, some double glazed windows have a European energy rating, similar to the type most of us will be familiar with on fridges and washing machines – the best windows rated A. The Energy Savings Trust also lends its seal of approval (and logo) to a selection of windows rated B grade or above. Details of these are available on its website.

Choosing frames

UPVC window frames should be avoided. Better choices include: aluminium, steel, or wood (and sometimes a composite of more than one material). Aluminium clad timber windows are also a good option. All of these can be recycled but wood requires a lot less energy in production and, with careful maintenance, can last just as long, if not longer, than some other frame materials. Wooden windows do, however, need to be sanded down, re-painted, touched up, filled in and generally loved (in the experience of this author) at least once every couple of years (especially in areas prone to harsh weather conditions). Wood can not be left to rot.

Frames are generally less well insulated than the glazing so it is better to have less fenestration and/or large areas of glass in fewer openings. Under new Part F Building Regulations (approved in 2010) it is also necessary to choose windows that have some form of trickle ventilation in the frame – even when replacing windows that did not have these – because modern double glazed windows are more air tight than older double glazing.

Alternatives to double glazing

By law all new builds must be fitted with double glazing; there are only three reasons not to double glaze an existing property – because you have a listed building or live in a conservation area, because you rent and you can't make permanent adjustments, or because you can't afford it (either because you haven't got the cash or you consider the payback time too long). The Energy Saving Trust estimate that you can save £135 a year replacing existing windows with double glazing but the payback time will vary enormously depending on the builders you use, the type of windows you choose and the position of the windows in relation to possible passive solar gain (which can further bring down your heating bills).

If you chose to keep your existing windows, there are things you can do to improve their performance – draughtproofing being the first and most important. A thick curtain or insulated shutters drawn at night-time can lower the U-value at these times from 4.80 to 3.60 (keeping more heat in when the temperature is at its lowest).

Secondary glazing can create a permanent U-value reduction (down to between 2.90 and 3.40) but there are limits to the effectiveness of this type of measure; condensation can form on the inner-side of the existing window, frames can be hard to draughtproof, only partial coverage may be possible (leaving weak spots where energy loss continues unabated).

Even so, the Energy Saving Trust estimates an annual cost saving of £85. Whether the payback time is longer or shorter than full double glazing depends on material and labour costs. It is possible to make DIY secondary glazing and low E glass is available. Type in DIY secondary glazing on an internet search engine and various options come up for kits and plans.

Case study

Fintry: a village community making the most of its renewable resource

Pete Skabara

From left: David Howell, Callum Walker and Alan Johnston at the opening of the Fintry wind farm, May, 2008.

Like many rural villages, Fintry in South West Stirlingshire has struggled in recent years. The village shop and the post office closed. There is no longer a regular bus service connecting the village to the outside world. In 2008, a survey found that almost 50% of inhabitants suffered from fuel poverty; half of the 311 households spending more than 10% of their annual income on heating bills.

Luckily, one resource Fintry does have plenty of is wind; a fact that did not go unnoticed by a wind farm developer who scouted the area for good sites and found one close to the village. The developers came up with a plan and brought it to a community council meeting to begin the long consultation process that accompanies every wind farm planning application. What followed next were five years of meetings with developers, planners and the local community to work out the best way for the village to benefit from the new wind farm.

It is standard practice for wind farm developers to offer communities a remuneration package known as community benefit. This guarantees the community a very small percentage of any profits made by a wind farm. Fintry received and rejected an offer of community benefit, opting instead to pursue a proposal that would give the community a better return. Eventually they persuaded the development company to sell the village a share of the wind farm. The village would pay for one of the fifteen turbines in return for a one fifteenth share of the profits.

In an interview recorded by Cornelia Reetz for her Fintry documentary *Wind of Change*, Gordon Cowtan of the Fintry Development Trust describes the agreement that was eventually reached, 'The developers would provide capital for their turbine along with the other 14, build as one site, and we would pay back our capital costs over time, and rather than getting the output from one turbine we would get the output from one fifteenth of the total output of the site.'

To facilitate this, Fintry Development Trust was set up as a company limited by guarantee with charitable status to manage the distribution of revenue for the benefit of the community. The development trust has a trading arm called Fintry Renewable Energy Enterprise that, in turn, manages the relationship with the wind farm developer.

Residents of Fintry celebrate their new turbine with a bit of graffiti.

At the moment the annual income from the turbine amounts to between £30,000 and £50,000, but once the initial capital cost of buying the turbine is paid off this figure should go up to £400,000.

The Development Trust is using this money to make Fintry a zero waste, zero carbon community. This policy brings long term environmental benefits but also helps the village to generate economic activity, employment and stronger social bonds between neighbours.

The first thing the Trust did was to carry out a survey of energy use within the village and then provide free loft and cavity wall insulation to anyone who could benefit from it. As a result, 50% of village households improved their insulation, reducing total energy bills by an estimated £90,000 a year. Now the Trust offers advice and support to anyone looking to install renewable heating alternatives.

The sports club, for example, has replaced its oil-fired heating system with a woodchip boiler.

Money has also been made available for other community activities, including a community orchard and a woodland project for Fintry primary school. Kelly McIntyre is Project Manager for Fintry Development Trust. In *Wind of Change* she explained what the wind farm money means to the community:

'This is a pretty magical place but it can only stay this way if we can make sure the houses are heated with renewables, people can get employment and can afford to live here, and make sure people can get around when they need to. Whilst addressing these key areas we will hit our targets of zero carbon and zero waste because they go hand in hand.'

Fintry shows what a small group of individuals with relatively little specialist knowledge can do with support from key agencies and individuals. In this case the Scottish Council for Voluntary Organisations, Development Trusts Association Scotland, two local Members of the Scottish Parliament, a local renewable energy company and two firms of lawyers.

Fintry is also a great example of what can be achieved if a different financial model is applied to wind farm development. As local opposition to wind farms can kill projects dead, allowing more of the revenue generated from them to flow back into communities through genuine ownership schemes (like Fintry's) is good for both communities and developers. In fact, the 'Fintry Model' of community engagement is now seen as an exemplar by the Scottish Government and the Fintry Development Trust is working with other communities to help them realise their renewable ambitions too.

Chapter Five

Passive solar space heating

Fig. 5.1. Passive solar space heating

The three essential components

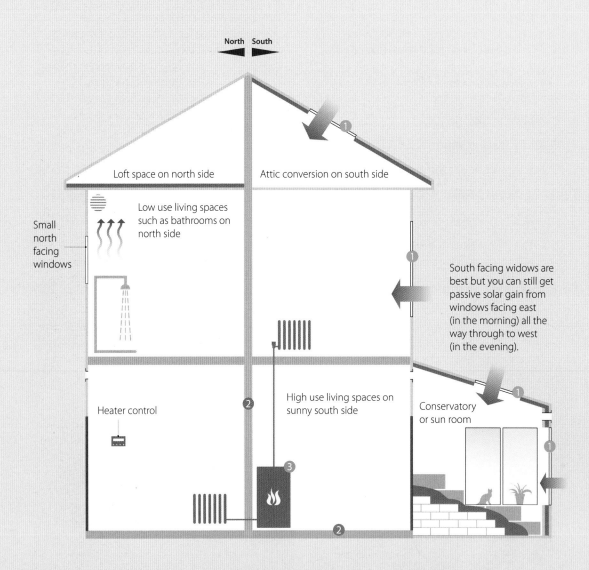

North South

Loft space on north side

Attic conversion on south side

Low use living spaces such as bathrooms on north side

Small north facing windows

South facing widows are best but you can still get passive solar gain from windows facing east (in the morning) all the way through to west (in the evening).

Heater control

High use living spaces on sunny south side

Conservatory or sun room

1. Large amount of south facing double or triple glazing with shading and ventilation to prevent over heating at key times.

2. Walls and floors with a high thermal mass, in other words, an ability to absorb heat. Materials with a high thermal mass include concrete, stone, dark clay tiles and rammed earth. The heat is released from the wall back into the room when the temperature drops.

3. Rapid response heating system that reacts to changes in solar gain.

How much solar energy can we use?

The amount of solar energy falling on the earth in one hour is equal to annual world fossil fuel demand. Solar energy devices can intercept some of this energy and turn it into something we find more useful – organised heat. The amount of potential energy available to us depends on the intensity of the energy when it arrives at any given point on the globe, which in turn is dependent on three things:

- The latitude.
- The time of year.
- The weather conditions.

Solar energy hits earth at a maximum intensity of $1kW/m^2$ but this intensity varies enormously across the globe and across different times of the year (as the angle of the earth in relation to the sun varies). In British latitudes, solar radiation only occasionally reaches this intensity during summer when the sky is clear and dark blue.

How does seasonality, geography and climate affect solar energy?

There is a 47° difference in the angle of the sun at noon mid-summer compared to noon mid-winter – wherever you are in the world; people living on the equator hardly notice the difference, those living on the arctic circle have to change the way they live (the sun's angle varies between 47° and 0° above the horizon so it gets very dark and very light for long periods), and the British moan about the clocks going back.

Britain lies between latitudes 50° and 59° north, so if we take 52° as an example, the sun will be at a minimum horizon angle of 15° at mid-winter noon and 62° in mid-summer noon. This is very useful information if we wish to make the most of winter sun whilst keeping out the worst of the summer sun.

Solar energy arrives direct (as sunshine) or diffuse (as illumination through clouds). The amount of energy available to us is reduced by cloud cover and dust particles. Gibraltar and Scotland receive about the same level of solar radiation in June but the clouds floating over Scotland cut it down to two-thirds.

In the winter, because the angle of the sun in the sky is lower, any solar device used for collecting solar energy must be placed at a steeper angle compared to during the summer. For example, a vertical south facing window is perfect for capturing low angled winter sun but a VELUX captures most of its energy during the summer months and may require shading to prevent overheating on the hottest days.

Variations in latitude and weather patterns can produce some interesting results. For example, although the amount of direct sunshine in North Wales is less than in the Isle of Wight the annual solar energy ends up being the same because the clean winds from the Atlantic result in less particle pollution.

Collecting solar energy

A solar collector is anything that captures and stores energy from the sun, converting it into heat energy that we would otherwise not have or be able to use. So a piece of glazing combined with some thermal mass makes a solar collector, not the glass on its own. The key factors determining the effectiveness of a device are: orientation and tilt; glazing and insulation and; heat storage.

Orientation and tilt

Perfect orientation varies from device to device but all solar collectors perform better when facing south compared to east, west or north. In the northern hemisphere the greatest quantity of solar energy reaches the south face of a building.

However, it is worth pointing out that it is not necessary to achieve perfect orientation to get a reasonable result.

The amount of energy received by a solar collector will rise and fall over the course of the year (to different degrees depending on the tilt of the object in relation to the angle of the sun). A vertical window facing due south will experience peaks of solar irradiance in March and October and will trough through the summer months. This is because sunlight will reflect off glass when the angle is steep. Conversely, an east or west facing window will collect more in the summer as at these orientations the sun is lower in the sky: in fact it is more likely to cause over heating in a well insulated house.

Perfect tilt not only varies between types of devices but also between latitudes. For example, solar water heating systems perform best when they are placed at an angle that relates directly to the latitude, so each 1° latitude change necessitates a 1° change in tilt if perfection is to be maintained. In Britain most of our roofs are coincidently angled in roughly the right position but, as latitudes vary by as much as 10°, performance variations will be inevitable. Perfection is rarely possible if working with existing infrastructure. This doesn't stop us taking advantage of what there is, however.

Glazing and insulation

Glass absorbs infrared heat radiation, warms up, and re-radiates heat both inside and outside, but more to the inside. It also resists the transferal of heat between warm and cold air, or in other words inside and outside. These qualities are improved by taking one or more of the following measures:

- Applying more than one sheet of glass to a window. With each new layer the amount of heat lost is halved, but as we discussed earlier there must be an air gap in between the glass panes to maximise thermal resistance (in other words, to minimise the potential for heat loss). This thermal resistance depends on the width of the gap – up to about 20mm it increases, remains constant between 20mm and 60mm and then, because convection currents become apparent, deteriorates. It is also worth noting that the amount of daylight transmission decreases with each pane added.
- Using Low E coatings. The coating is placed on the inside pane, inside the cavity, and reduces the amount of heat that passes across the gap (the radiant heat transfer). Hard coatings are less efficient than soft coatings.

- Using inert gas-sealed units. Inert gases, such as Argon, conduct less heat than air and are easily placed within the cavity to reduce heat loss.
- Using spacer bars (the strips that keep the glass panes apart) made from stainless steel, polymers and structural foam instead of aluminium. Each of these materials has a much reduced thermal bridging capacity compared to aluminium. In other words they reduce heat loss.

There are other techniques associated with improving thermal performance in windows (including vacuum glazing and translucent insulation) but at the time of writing the measures above are the most common.

Shading and heat storage

Effective use of passive solar heating includes the retention of heat once the sun goes down (through the use of curtains, shutters and blinds – discussed more fully in the previous chapter) and also the minimisation of overheating by incorporating shading and heat storage techniques. Fixed shading devices, such as roof overhangs, are useful to prevent overheating in south facing rooms but are not so effective in those facing east or west where the angle of the sun appears much lower in the sky. These can also block out useful light and reduce spring warmth. Moveable external shutters are more useful, internal shutters and blinds less so (as the energy has to be reflected back out through the glass again – a much harder task).

Vegetation can also be used, though you have to pick plants that are seasonally useful – in other words, that produce leaves when you need the shade they provide and lose them when you could do with a little extra warmth. Runner beans are a classic example but any deciduous plant will work.

It is also possible to do without shading altogether and to allow any excess heat to be absorbed into a material, which later emits the heat as the temperature drops. Common architectural strategies for passive solar heating include elements of shading and heat storage, so a strategic balance can be achieved. The success of this strategy is dependent on:

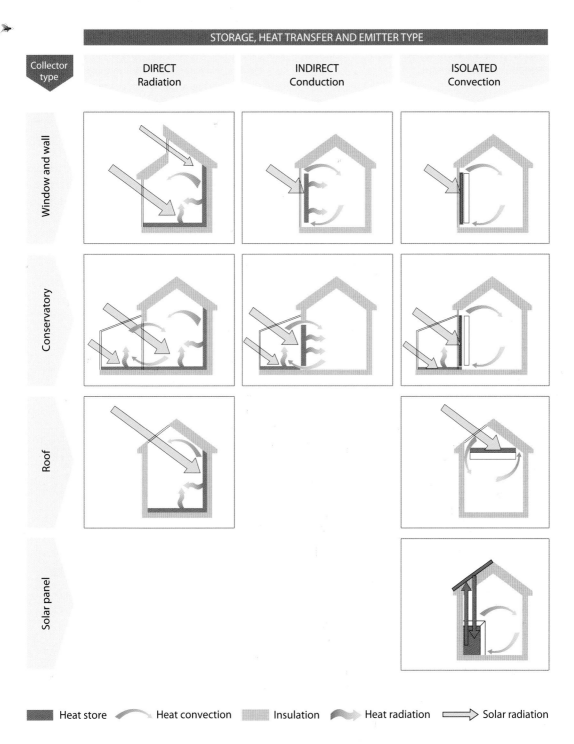

STORAGE, HEAT TRANSFER AND EMITTER TYPE		
DIRECT Radiation	**INDIRECT** Conduction	**ISOLATED** Convection

Collector type

Window and wall

Conservatory

Roof

Solar panel

Heat store ▬▬▬ Heat convection ◠ Insulation ▒▒ Heat radiation ➤ Solar radiation ⇨

Fig. 5.2. Flow of heat using different passive solar techniques. Source: The Whole House Book, Harris and Borer.

- The amount of heat the material is capable of storing.
- The volume of material available.
- How heat gets in and out.

Choosing materials with high heat storage capacity

The amount of heat a material can store depends on its density, insulating value and thermal capacity. By multiplying all these qualities together – and putting time into the equation – we can come up with a material's 'admittance'. The higher the admittance the better the material will be at storing heat. Materials usually absorb and emit heat over a 24 hour cycle so it's common for materials to be given a daily admittance rate. Useful materials include light weight aerated blocks, plasterboard and timber (minimum 50mm thickness); and denser materials such as rammed earth, stone and concrete (150mm). Any greater thickness will not help in storing day-to-day solar gains.
Source: *The Whole House Book*, Cindy Harris and Pat Borer.

Types of passive solar heating systems

There are three main types of solar space heating systems:

- Direct.
- Indirect.
- Isolated.

Let's take a look at each in turn.

Direct gain passive solar heating

This is the simplest form of passive solar heating and the most common. All buildings have it to a certain degree. Energy enters the building through glazing and is absorbed by a wall or floor in the same room which then emits the heat as the temperature drops. The better insulated a building is the longer lasting the effect of passive solar heating will be. The basic requirements are large south facing windows, an exposed thermal mass in the same room and a rapid response central heating system (that is, one that is controllable and can easily adjust as temperature rises and falls).

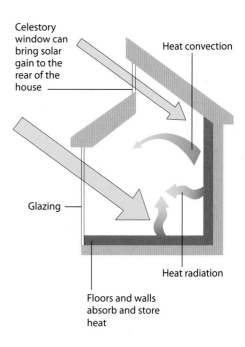

DIRECT Radiation

Celestory window can bring solar gain to the rear of the house

Heat convection

Glazing

Heat radiation

Floors and walls absorb and store heat

Fig. 5.3. Direct heat gain using passive solar techniques. Source: The Whole House Book, Harris and Borer.

Optimum window size and other design issues

The optimum window to wall ratio depends largely on the thermal performance of the glazing and its cost. For normal double glazing about 50% of a southern facade can usefully be window (25% of the house floor area or 30% of floor area for low E or triple glazing is the recommended figure). Windows facing north should be as small as possible and areas such as stores, utility rooms and the garage should also be placed on the north side, leaving the main living areas to face south. For maintaining privacy a courtyard layout is also useful.

Thermal mass requirements

Considerable thermal mass volume is needed to soak up passive solar gains from large south facing windows, for example, a thick concrete floor with a dark clay tiled surface is ideal. Most people prefer carpets to tiles but these isolate the mass from the heat and prevent it from doing useful work. Dense concrete or brick partitions and the inside wall of the external wall skins are the most common form of thermal mass, but stone and rammed earth can also be used.

Combining passive solar heating with a rapid response central heating system

Buildings reliant on passive solar require a central heating system that will respond rapidly to changes in air temperature. For example, a wood burning stove would be less useful than a thermostatically controlled pellet boiler (the heating thermostat should be in the warmest room).

Indirect gain passive solar heating

This sort of system counter-intuitively places a masonry wall between the main living area and the sunshine so the heat can be conducted through the wall to the living areas behind: the time lag is about three hours per 100mm of wall thickness. To supplement this heat, warm air can also be ducted from the space between the wall and the glazing into the house. These systems make more sense in places where bright winter days are followed by very cold nights, for example, in alpine regions. They are not so useful in the British climate where the poorly insulated wall will lose as much heat as it collects.

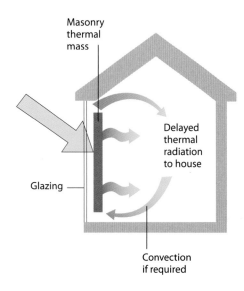

INDIRECT
Conduction

Masonry thermal mass

Glazing

Delayed thermal radiation to house

Convection if required

Fig. 5.4. Indirect heat gain using passive solar techniques. Source: The Whole House Book, Harris and Borer.

Isolated collector

Isolated collectors are a specially designed box – for want of a better word. When warmed, the air inside the box rises, exits via ducts and enters a house to then be replaced by cold air from the house. It is a little more complicated than this – for example, a one-way valve must be inserted into the ductwork to prevent warm air from the house escaping to pass through the collector at night (and thus cooling the house down) – but these are basically quite simple devices. More complex versions direct the air into insulated heat stores which can provide several days worth of heating if correctly designed.

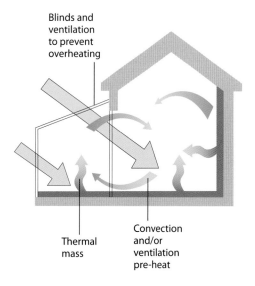

Conservatory

Blinds and
ventilation
to prevent
overheating

Thermal
mass

Convection
and/or
ventilation
pre-heat

Fig. 5.5a. Indirect conduction via a conservatory.
Source: The Whole House Book, Harris and Borer.

Roof

Highly insulated
roof window

Heat radiation
and convection

Thermal
mass

Fig. 5.5b. Direct radiation from a VELUX window.
Source: The Whole House Book, Harris and Borer.

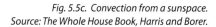

Fig. 5.5c. Convection from a sunspace.
Source: The Whole House Book, Harris and Borer.

Conservatory

Conservatories and sunspaces

A conservatory is almost a separate building, with its
own Building Regulations and standards. For example,
Building Regulations state that any heating appliance
used in a conservatory should be totally separate
from the main heating in the house. This recognises
the fact that a conservatory is not expected to have
the same insulation standards as the main part of the
house and any connected appliance will be a drain on
the rest of the house. In fact better not to heat it at all.

A sunspace, on the other hand, is very much part of
the house and should be treated as such. It will have

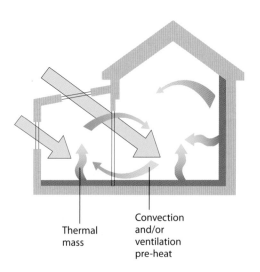

Thermal
mass

Convection
and/or
ventilation
pre-heat

a large amount of glazing (to get the conservatory effect) but will have an insulated floor and roof – the non-glazed roof reducing the problem of summer overheating associated with conservatories (which have glazed roofs). The idea behind sunspaces is that they deliver the benefits of the conservatory without the energy loss. In many cases it is more efficient to incorporate a sunspace rather than build a conservatory.

Having said this, both conservatories and sunspaces can provide one or more of the following principal functions – not counting, of course, the provision of a nice additional living space. They can:

- Provide a buffer effect against the worst weather.
- Facilitate solar ventilation pre-heat.
- Act as a lobby to external doors.
- Bring heat into the house.
- Acclimatize occupants to lower temperatures.

Not all sun spaces and conservatories provide all of these functions, for example, some sunspaces are built into lofts or balconies (in Spain they are called 'galleries'), but the overall aim of both is to raise the air temperature in the main part of the house and keep it warmer for longer. They are effectively another – albeit very nice – layer of insulation.

Tips for getting the most out of your conservatory

- A south east aspect is ideal for a conservatory. Overheating is less likely and you get the benefit of the heat throughout the day.
- Windows between a conservatory and the main living area of a house can be larger than normal because the buffering effect of the conservatory improves their insulating value.
- The better the glazing is in a conservatory the more useful it is as a living space.
- Shutting the conservatory off from the main part of the house with solid doors, or glass doors with thick curtains, will stop heat escaping at the coldest times of the year.
- Beware of trying to heat a highly glazed conservatory to indoor room temperatures on a cold day. Conserevatories are not designed to be heated and a great deal of energy is wasted because people expect to use them as they would an ordinary well insulated room.
- Plenty of 'thermal mass' within the conservatory will store its heat gain for longer. A solid stone or brick floor will soak up heat and then slowly release it as the evening cools.

Case study

Vauban, Germany: Passivhaus, innovative social structures and community building on a city district scale

Daniel Schoenen Fotografie

As far as participatory community projects go they don't come any bigger than Vauban in Freiburg, Germany. This is social and environmental organisation on a city district scale using principles that set people in an enviable landscape of innovative housing designs and open car free spaces. As you can see from the picture of the happy unicycling children, cars have been planned out as much as possible; residents are encouraged by design to walk, cycle, take the tram or share cars.

There are no home garages, no street parking and, if you keep a car, a charge of $30,000 for a space in one of two multi-storey car parks. As one resident reported in a feature by Tristana Moore for *Time* magazine, 'It's like being in the countryside, but I'm living in a big city. I don't have to worry when my child plays on the road because there are no cars.' In fact, Moore reported that, 'Though Vauban is the most densely populated district of Freiburg, you don't notice any pollution.' Vauban is a 'district of short distances', with everything deliberately planned to be within walking or cycling distance.

Renewable energy and ecological design principles have been planned into the development from the start.

What is Passivhaus?

Passivhaus (or Passive house) is the name given to a specific type of building design that can deliver thermal comfort with no active heating system, or with a heat energy consumption under 15kWh per square metre per year. This compares to the low energy standard of 65kWh/m²a for the other houses in Vauban, which in itself was better than the German Building Regulations at the time of construction. In Passivhaus design this massive reduction in heat demand is achieved by combining very good heat insulation, advanced window technology, a mechanical ventilation and heat exchange system and a southerly orientation.

This last contingent had to be planned for at the start of the planning process as houses close by could not be allowed to block out the sunlight to the ground floor of each building on the shortest day of the year, when the sun is at its lowest. The city must also ensure that the street stays as it is for the lifetime of the house, perhaps a hundred years or more. In some ways this is a major challenge for planners because it requires a strategic vision going beyond their lifetime. On the other hand, this is surely something we all now have to do.

Most houses have access to a number of renewable energy technologies including solar water heating, PV and woodchip powered district heating. There are also 270 Passivhaus houses and apartments (see box) and a number of 'plus energy' houses that produce more energy than they need.

The Vauban project began in 1993 when Freiburg City Council acquired the site of an old French army barrack. As owner of the site the city authority was able to use their 'Learning whilst Planning' policy to facilitate extended citizen participation via the citizen's association Forum Vauban, as well as two local authority bodies: Projektgruppe Vauban and Gemeinderatliche AG.

This allowed residents to set the planning agenda for the district, including the no-car policy and a list of other objectives such as: balance of working and living areas and social groups, division of land into small lots, preferential allocation to private and co-operative building projects, conservation of existing 60 year old trees, diversity of building shapes, a very clear low energy policy, primary school and kindergartens, and the construction of a neighbourhood centre.

The emphasis on social housing, co-operative and self-build has created a diverse pattern of development, with houses and workplaces to suit many different ages and social

Daniel Schoenen Fotografie

Daniel Schoenen Fotografie

groups, helping to make the district a truly diverse place. Some commercial property developments were allowed but in total there are approximately 30 co-housing associations and initiatives in Vauban, each with its own flavour.

For example, Genova emphasises young and old living together and encourages participation in decision-making through residents meetings, workshops and a co-operative council. It also builds apartments to rent using this collective process, ensuring that people who are economically disadvantaged have access to affordable homes. Because people are socialised through the planning and construction phases it is easier for them to start other community projects once they have moved in. These have included a co-operative food store, a mother's centre and a farmers' market.

This participation process has been identified as one of the success stories of Vauban but there are many others. You can read about the positive and negative outcomes of the project on the Vauban website, which has been translated into English (www.vauban.de/info/abstract.html). Here you will also find a list of several research studies for deeper understanding.

Chapter Six

Energy efficiency

Fig. 6.1. Energy efficiency

The three main challenges

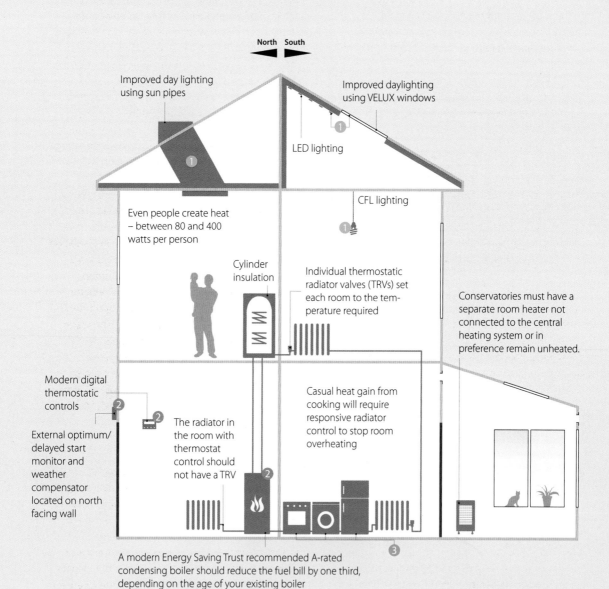

North — South

Improved day lighting using sun pipes

Improved daylighting using VELUX windows

LED lighting

CFL lighting

Even people create heat – between 80 and 400 watts per person

Cylinder insulation

Individual thermostatic radiator valves (TRVs) set each room to the temperature required

Conservatories must have a separate room heater not connected to the central heating system or in preference remain unheated.

Modern digital thermostatic controls

External optimum/delayed start monitor and weather compensator located on north facing wall

The radiator in the room with thermostat control should not have a TRV

Casual heat gain from cooking will require responsive radiator control to stop room overheating

A modern Energy Saving Trust recommended A-rated condensing boiler should reduce the fuel bill by one third, depending on the age of your existing boiler

1. Reduce lighting demand using better day lighting, low energy lights and lighting control techniques such as sensors and timers.

2. Improve heating efficiency with new boilers and better controls.

3. Replace inefficient electrical appliances with Energy Saving Trust recommended A-rated appliances.

Different types of heating systems and fuels

Where as energy conservation is about keeping heat in using insulation and draughtproofing techniques, energy efficiency is about using less energy to do the same amount of work. We can increase energy efficiency by changing habits, switching appliances and establishing better control systems. This chapter covers energy efficiency as it relates to heating, lighting and the use of electrical appliances. Improvements in the energy efficiency of some products mean they now represent some of the easiest and, often, most cost- and environmentally effective changes you can make in a home.

Heating systems

The preferred heating option for most people is central heating combining space and water heating – it is convenient, efficient if controlled properly and easy to run. But central heating might not always be possible, either because of cost or because the infrastructure is not in place to support it. In addition, many people prefer to have additional individual heating appliances to provide extra warmth in one area of the house. For these reasons individual room heaters are very common.

Generally speaking, individual room heaters do not have a facility for heating water (unless they also have a back boiler) and a separate water heater is required.

Heating fuels

The most preferred fuels for heating are currently oil or gas. They are convenient and require no attention from the owner (apart from a bit of thermostat and timer control). Next is electricity (also convenient in certain circumstances but less flexible and more expensive), followed by coal and wood (which both require handling, additional maintenance, regular delivery and additional storage space).

Of these fuels only green electricity and wood are low carbon fuels, although mains gas burns less carbon per kW hour than oil, LPG, coal and non-green electricity (which in terms of carbon emissions is the worst fuel you can use for heating).

Green electricity can be used to heat an element directly or to extract ambient heat that occurs naturally in air, water and the ground using so-called heat pump technologies. Technically speaking, a heat pump is not a renewable fuel but it is a way of delivering a renewable fuel (the naturally occurring heat in air, water and earth). Likewise, solar water heating is a delivery system not a fuel - the fuel here being the sun. The sun can also be used to heat a room directly (as described previously in the passive solar chapter).

The *environmental* logic of heating is to capture as much heat from the sun as possible using passive solar space heating and active solar water heating, and install the most efficient boiler, heating controls and appliances that your situation will allow. Renewables first (wood, heat pumps, green electricity) and, if that is not possible, mains gas, oil, LPG, coal and non green electricity – in that order. Non-green electricity is the fuel of last resort.

Every property is different, with different insulation standards, patterns of use and user requirements. Nevertheless, there are some reliably common themes to consider: improved boiler and radiator controls (using thermostats, timers and optimisers) will reduce costs; lagging of water pipes and water cylinders will save money; modern boilers are far more efficient than old boilers (even if you are replacing like-for-like fuel sources); almost everyone could turn their thermostat down a couple of degrees to achieve the same level of thermal comfort (with or without jumpers and thermals!).

Central heating

Most central heating systems are wet heating systems in which water is used to move heat around a building. It is possible to have dry heating systems (those that do not use water) which are controlled centrally, but generally speaking central heating systems are wet. The water is heated centrally and distributed through standard pipe work to radiators or underfloor heating channels. This is true whatever the fuel. The infrastructure you need to deliver renewable heat around a building is mostly the same as that for conventional heat.

There are, however, some differences.

The two most common types of conventional boiler systems are known as combi and open vent systems. A combi boiler heats water at the time when it is needed – just by turning on a tap or radiator; an open vent system is the technical name used to describe a system that pre-heats water and keeps it in a cylinder until it is needed. We go into the advantages and disadvantages of each of these systems on page 120 but at this stage it is just important to know that one type of heating system – the combi – doesn't have a cylinder and the other one – the open vent – does: a case of tanks or no-tanks.

If you have an existing central heating system it is important to know whether or not you have a tank. This is because almost all renewable heat systems require some sort of hot water storage facility to work effectively. They cannot work with a combi boiler.

If you already have a modern efficient combi boiler that is less than 5 years old, the amount of emission savings you can make for each pound spent will be so small as to make very little economic sense and relatively little environmental sense – in any case it might also be too technically difficult because of space restrictions (you will need to retro-fit your building with additional cylinders and pipe work).

This is not to say that you shouldn't consider it but that you should consider the cost against other environmental improvements you might be able to make to your home or lifestyle. Like any environmental technology, it is good to take an overview of the whole of your life and decide where your spending will be most effective. The big environmental and cost savings come by replacing boilers over 12 years old, those that were not subject to the same stringent Building Regulations control when they were installed.

Room heating

Mostly in this book we talk about central heating systems – where the heating system is linked to a series of underfloor heating elements or radiators in several separate spaces. This is because the technology lends itself to central heating and because, generally, it is more efficient to have one central heating system rather than many individual room heaters – especially if you are able to control temperatures in each room using thermostatic valve controls (see page 122).

But for many users, a central heating system may not be affordable, practical or necessary. In these cases it is possible to install individual room heaters using renewable fuels; the most environmentally efficient being wood (either in pellet or log form) burnt in a stove. It is important here to put emphasis on the word 'stove', meaning an enclosed fire in a metal box. An open fire with a grate is the least efficient way of burning wood or any solid fuel. This is partly because chimneys (as we discussed in chapter three) draw cold air into the house, and also because fuel burnt on an open fire is unlikely to reach the required temperature for fully efficient burning – the chemical process known as pyrolysis (see page 149).

LPG gas and paraffin can be used for single room heaters but these are both costly and environmentally inefficient.

This leaves us with electricity; and it's worth spending a bit of time discussing its use in heating systems. There are some 'wet' central heating systems powered by electricity but it is far more common to use electricity to power room heaters.

Electrical heating

The Energy Saving Trust do not rate the efficiency of electrical heaters because, unlike other heating appliances, they are almost 100% efficient, in that almost all the energy that goes into them comes back out again as heat. This is different to other heating appliances, which have variable efficiencies – in other words, some are better at converting energy into heat than others. However, if you are using non-green electricity to generate heat in your home the efficiency losses occur somewhere else: at the point where the electricity is generated – for example combustion power stations that lose a high percentage of energy to heat (that is not used) when the fuel is burnt to make electricity.

This leaves two questions:

- Is all the heat produced actually needed – that is, can you control the appliance well enough to avoid wasting heat?
- Does it use green or non-green electricity?

Some electrical appliances have faster start up times, some have timer controls, some deliver background heat and some receive energy during the night but deliver the heat back into the room during the day (Economy 7 storage heaters). The box to the right provides a snapshot of considerations if you're trying to minimise energy use.

How much heat do I need?

The answer to this question will be found in the dimensions, fabric and patterns of use of the building. Thermal comfort will be an issue, too, but as we have covered this ground extensively (see chapter two) this section is more about heat.

Loads and losses

The word 'load' has all sorts of meanings, especially in relation to building, energy conservation and renewable energy production. There is the load placed upon a roof by the forces of wind and gravity (which affects the safety of roof mounted renewable energy systems); there is the load placed upon a generator by the blades of a wind turbine and from appliances (which affects the amount of potential energy captured by the blades); and there is heat load.

The heat load is all the space and water heating energy requirements of a building added up over a period of time. This period of time could be an average day, week, year or lifetime. You would think it might be hard to calculate the heat load as an average like this because activity in buildings is not necessarily that regular, however, the figure does not have to be – and cannot be – exactly precise. Having said this, since heat load defines the size and type of heating system you need, the cost of that system, and the measures you can take to reduce that cost, it must be roughly in the right area.

How to choose the right electrical heater

- Heat in one spot for a few minutes – choose a fan heater or a halogen heater.
- Instant heat throughout a room – choose a fan heater (you may need more than one for fast heat up in larger rooms).
- Long term background heating throughout a room – choose a convection heater, panel heater or oil filled radiator. These include Economy 7 storage heaters.
- Heat in one part of a room for an extended period – choose a halogen heater.

Source: Energy Saving Trust.

Calculating the heat load is not necessarily that easy either, and many people prefer to employ a professional heating engineer to do the work for them. Their figures are almost certainly going to be closer to the truth than yours. Sizing is dependent on many complex factors and the final figure varies greatly according to heat loss (see Calculating your loads and losses), which in turn relates to construction materials; a building's exposure to elements such as the wind; the lowest average outside temperature; the desired room temperatures; and room heights.

However, the more you know about your building the better, and even if you only carry out a rough heat load and loss calculation it will help you understand what a consultant is talking about when they create a more precise calculation. It will also help you advise them more precisely about usage patterns and potential heat loss weak spots. If the two calculations turn out to be wildly different there is a focal point for a discussion which might bring more accuracy to the sums.

It is important from the outset to appreciate which type of heating system is going to work best for you. Heat load and heat output (which we talk about next) can be calculated on a room by room basis or for the whole house, but it is important not to try and size a room heater for a building and vice versa. Sounds very obvious, but a mistake like this will be very costly so it's worth ramming the point home.

Calculating your loads and losses

Element	Area m² W/m²K	x	U-value loss	=	Specific heat
Glazing					
North	1.00	x	3.0	=	3.00 W/k
East	2.50	x	3.0	=	7.50 W/k
South	14.00	x	3.0	=	42.00 W/k
West	2.50	x	3.0	=	7.50 W/k
Roof	1.50	x	2.2	=	3.30 W/k
Floor	45.00	x	0.82	=	36.90 W/k

		Less window area	Net area				
Wall	145.00	20.0	125.0	x	0.45	=	56.25 W/k
Roof	45.00	1.5	43.5	x	0.25	=	10.88 W/k

Infiltration	Airchange rate		House volume m²				
	1	x	225	x	0.3333	=	74.99 W/k

Total specific heat loss	=	242.32 W/k
Design temperature difference		22K

Peak heat loss
(Specific heat loss x temperature difference) = 5331 Watts

Approximate annual heating
(Specific heat loss x degree days x 24 hours/1000)

242.32 x 2000 x 24 /	1000 =	11631 kWh per year
Divide by boiler efficiency	0.90 =	12,923 kWh per year
Multiply by fuel cost (gas) in £/kWh	£0.05 =	£646 per year

Carbon dioxide emissions

Annual delivered energy		16616 kWh per year
Carbon dioxide emission factor	x	0.187 kg/kWh
Carbon dioxide emission	=	3107 kg (3.107 Tonnes)

To calculate heat losses you need three sets of figures:

- The areas of all the different construction elements through which heat will pass to the outside (walls, roofs, windows, floors).
- The U-value of each material – from figure 2.6 on page 67
- The volume of the building (floor area times the overall internal height).

Now make the following calculations:

Multiply the area of each construction element (recorded in m²) by its U-value. This gives the specific heat loss for each element.

Calculate the infiltration heat loss by multiplying the volume by 0.33 and then by the number of air changes experienced in the house. This will be approximately 4 for an old, un-draughtproofed house, 1 to 2 for an average modern house and 0.6 for a very tight, super insulated house.

Add all the heat losses together and you have a total which is in the units of watts per K. K refers to the difference between the inside and outdoor temperature in degrees Celsius. As you are trying to find the maximum heat loss, the specific heat loss total you have calculated must then be multiplied by a likely temperature difference. If you want it to be 21°C inside, and the external minimum temperature is normally taken at -1°C, the difference is 22°C. This then gives you a peak heat loss in watts. You should add 10% to this figure (to cover the initial heating up period – that is, heating the house from cold) and divide the answer by 1000 to give the required boiler (or stove) output in kW (multiplying by 3400 to get BTU/hour).

To get an approximation of your annual space heating bill, multiply the specific heat loss by degree days (take as 2000), multiply by 24 (hours in a day), and again divide by 1000 to get kWh per year. Then divide by boiler efficiency and multiply by fuel cost to arrive at your annual space heating fuel bill. The same kWh/year number can be used to estimate the weight of CO_2 given out by your boiler in a year.

Source: *The Whole House Book*, Cindy Harris and Pat Borer.

What is heat output?

Heat output represents the rate at which the system (be it room or central heating) can deliver heat energy. This is different to the heat load, and it's good to be clear about this from the start so that the two things don't get mixed up. Heat output is specified in kilowatts (kW metric) or BTU per hour (Imperial British Thermal Units) and every heating appliance will be rated according to a peak output. This is the maximum amount of heat the appliance will be able to deliver when it is operating at full efficiency and full power. This appears as the 'headline' figure in most promotional material for heating appliances so is fairly easy to spot.

If your appliance is a log boiler for instance, the peak output might rarely be reached because often output depends on the quality of the wood, the way the system is used, the fire skills of the user and so on. But it is also worth pointing out that the required peak output may only be needed very occasionally. In fact, the coldest times of the year and/or the times of highest domestic hot water flow rates, will determine the likely required peak output of a heating appliance.

Sometimes two appliances can look the same but have quite different kW peak outputs depending on internal adjustments. As a rule, heating systems should not be intentionally oversized as the coldest period of the year lasts only ten days on average. Hence for the majority of the year the appliance would work only at a fraction of its potential output and thus at low efficiency. Furthermore, heat storage, multiple heat sources or a few electric heaters can be used to avoid over sizing and still meet short term peaks. Modern, insulated and draughtproofed rooms require more care on sizing as they can easily overheat.

Sizing a room heater to include water heating

Heating appliances can deliver either space or water heating or both. Single room heaters generally do not heat water (unless you count a kettle popped on a hot plate) but some single room heaters (wood stoves mainly) can be fitted with back boilers and these can be connected to an existing water tank or central heating system.

If you are sizing a single room heater with a back

boiler for heating water you will need to calculate the amount of heat that will be lost from the room to the back boiler. If a system is not carefully planned it is possible for almost all of the heat generated by a wood stove to be absorbed through the back boiler and taken away from the room where it is primarily needed. Likewise it is possible to get the balance wrong the other way and have too much hot water with no where for it to go.

Improving the efficiency of an existing system

Replacing an entire heating system is not necessarily the best way of improving its efficiency. Furthermore, it is not always possible or appropriate to replace an existing heating fuel with a renewable alternative. What can you do instead?

Replacing the boiler

When renewable energy is not the right option (for space and water heating) replace your old boiler with a modern A rated condensing boiler combined with heating control improvements to radiators, thermostats and weather compensators. Replacing a fifteen year old boiler with a modern condensing boiler should reduce your fuel bills by one third. If you also install good heating controls, the savings could be around 40%. A new boiler would also reduce your carbon emissions: because of the monetary savings, it will be one of the most cost-effective ways of reducing your emissions.

Before you do anything, check what sort of boiler you have. There are two types of condensing boiler – a combination (or combi) boiler or a system – or open vent – boiler.

Combi boilers take a water feed direct from the mains supply, heat it up and distribute it direct when the heat is needed. There is no need for timers and – as the hot water is not stored – no heat loss during storage. They also save space and are good for situations when the demand for hot water is infrequent. System or open vent boilers take water from a header tank and feed the hot water into a cylinder. These are much more useful when demand

for hot water is high and water pressure low.

It will be fairly obvious which system you have. To find out whether you're existing boiler is a condensing boiler or not you need to take a look outside at the boiler vent and flue pipe. Condensing boilers have plastic flue pipes and when the boiler is running release a visible steam. Non-condensing boilers have metal flues and release hot, invisible gases that would burn plastic.

Domestic gas and oil boilers are covered by an energy label scheme. If your boiler is fifteen years old it is likely to have a G rating. Condensing boilers have been compulsory since 2005 but since October 2010 any new boiler installed must be A rated, or at least 88% efficient. You can check the ratings of particular boilers at the Boiler Efficiency Database website (www.boilers.org.uk). You can also look for 'Energy Saving Recommended' logos awarded by the Energy Saving Trust (the Energy Saving Trust has a whole range of products displayed on their website). A long warranty gives an indication that the manufacturer has faith in their product. Only condensing boilers will get an A rating: they increase efficiency by recovering heat that is normally wasted in the hot flue gases given off by a boiler.

Getting your pipes and radiators flushed out (to remove built up gunge) will cost a few hundred pounds, and should be done while fitting any replacement boiler. Annual servicing will ensure that the boiler keeps operating efficiently. Also remember to 'bleed' the radiators to release any air that may be affecting their efficiency. The heating system should be switched off when you do this so that more air isn't drawn into the system.

All modern boilers are complex pieces of equipment and it is worth spending time choosing the right one for you. Using a good installer will help. If unable to get a personal recommendation from a friend (often the best way), then you could look for a tradesperson who belongs to an association that aims to maintain high standards. For example, the Institute of Domestic Heating and Environmental Engineers, the Chartered Institute of Plumbing and Heating Engineering, or the Association of Plumbing & Heating Contractors. The Energy Saving Trust has a quick and easy 'how to' guide on their website for anyone looking for an installer.

Non-boiler improvements
Cylinder insulation
Considerable savings of energy, money and CO_2 emissions can be made by insulating or increasing the thickness of insulation around a hot water tank.

Reducing plumbing losses
Plumbing losses occur when hot water travels around the system, either because the pipes are poorly lagged or because the hot water has to cover a long distance to reach the user. In new developments the cylinder should be placed as near as possible to the most frequently used taps – for example, in kitchens and washbasins. This reduces the effect of the so called 'dead leg' where hot water drawn from the cylinder is left to go cold in the pipe because the tap is turned off before it reaches the user. Pipe lagging will help to insulate the water so it can be usefully used.

The length of pipe between the boiler and the cylinder should also be kept to a minimum and be well insulated, although the crucial factor is the controller that operates the boiler. Ideally, a system should be fitted with a cylinder thermostat operating a three part motorised valve, and a timer that prevents the boiler firing up just to offset cylinder losses at a time when there is no demand.

And contrary to folklore, it is not good to keep the cylinder hot all the time, it is better to use all the hot water in the morning and heat up what is needed for the evening just before you need it: cold water cannot lose any heat, and boilers work more efficiently heating from cold.

Using heating controls more effectively
Heating controls are designed to maximise thermal comfort and environmental efficiency, and minimise fuel use and so also cost. There are controls for water and space heating, for individual room and central heating systems, and for all forms of heating system and fuels. There are controls for temperature and for timing, and controls that relate to external air temperature and weather conditions. There are also controls that relate to the use of the building at any particular time and to zones within the building so each zone has its own temperature and timing controls.

These controls allow your heating system to be smart and stay connected to patterns of use and weather temperatures (including changes in room temperature created by passive solar techniques (see pages 103-109); to prevent overheating (which is more likely than under-heating and just as uncomfortable); and to deliver the temperatures when and where you need them most. They also save money (although the payback period will vary depending on the level of complexity) and CO_2 emissions.

Adjusting existing heating controls
It sounds obvious, but the first thing to do in any efficiency drive is to check whether you're using your existing heating controls effectively. Do this before you consider replacing them. Your room thermostat should be set to the lowest comfortable temperature – typically between 18°C and 21°C. Try turning your thermostat down a degree or two and seeing if your home maintains an agreeable temperature. Once you've found your comfort zone you can leave the thermostat alone.

Most people have turned their thermostat up on cold days thinking they need more heat than normal. This, of course, isn't true. The comfortable temperature range stays the same whatever the weather outside. The difference is the rate at which heat escapes the building. It will take longer for a room to heat up on a cold day because the starting temperature is likely to be lower. In this case, set the boiler control to turn the heater on slightly earlier. It is a myth that heating should be left on all the time to provide a background heat. It is much more efficient to set it to come on when you need it – and switch off when you don't. And for those people that leave their heating on for their pets: try www.stylisheve.com/modern-indoor-pets-houses instead.

It also pays to study the warm up and cool down times in a building. These will define how far in advance your heating system needs to be switched on and when it can be safely switched off without any subsequent loss of thermal comfort. Try it one average winter evening: turn the heater on and measure the time it takes for the room to reach a comfortable

Quick guide to heating control terminology

- Programmer: allows you to set on and off time periods.
- Room thermostat: switches boiler on when room temperature falls below the required temperature and off again when it exceeds it.
- Programmable room thermostat: both programmer and room thermostat. Choose when you want the heating on and at what temperature.
- Thermostatic Radiator Valve (TRV): fitted directly onto radiators they sense the air temperature and regulate the flow of water into the radiator accordingly. Allows you to set each room at the temperature you require. Must not be covered by curtains or blocked by furniture. The radiator in the room with the thermostat should not have a TRV as well. TRVs cannot turn off the boiler, only the thermostat can do this.
- Cylinder thermostat: controls the heat supply from the boiler to the hot water cylinder. Switches on the water heating when the temperature falls below the thermostat setting, and off again when it reaches the target.
- Boiler thermostat: should be run at 65°C to ensure hot water can be heated to 60°C, to reduce risk of Legionnaires. The radiators can deliver heat more quickly at higher temperatures, but the boiler has a maximum output rating and may not condense anymore, losing 10-20% efficiency.
- Thermostatic mixing valve: extra safety measure to ensure hot water delivered to the hot tap does not scold.
- Optimum/delayed start monitor: external sensor designed to reduce heat up times during mild weather. This should be located on a north facing wall, out of direct sunlight and away from other heat sources.
- Weather compensator: device to allow the boiler flow to drop as the external temperature rises, especially beneficial when used with condensing boilers.

temperature. Then turn the heating off and see how quickly the heat leaves the building. If you have a fairly regular routine, set your timer accordingly. The sooner you can turn the heat off at the end of the evening the better, so if you're cool down time is an hour you can turn the heater off a full hour before bedtime, and probably have a more comfortable sleeping heat too.

Water heating controls All water heaters will have a thermostat to control the temperature of the water. The thermostat can be altered but should be set at only 60°C or 140°F. Any higher is a waste of energy; any lower and there may be a risk of legionella bacteria forming.

Replacing heating controls

There are prescribed standards for heating controls so if you can identify a failing in one of the following areas you should try to upgrade your controls.

TACMA recommend that your heating controls should:

- Automatically turn off heating when not required: time control requiring a programmer.
- Automatically prevent the building getting warmer than it needs to be: temperature control requiring a programmable room thermostat that allows you to set different temperatures for different times of the day.
- Avoid overheating parts of the house that are unoccupied or need lower temperatures: zone control using thermostatic radiator valves (see box), or using separate heating circuits each with their own programmer and room thermostat.
- Prevent stored hot water being hotter than it needs to be: cylinder thermostat separate from the boiler thermostat.

There are also differences between older mechanical thermostats – which often provide a slow response and maintain temperatures higher than those required due to inaccuracy – and newer digital thermostats, which provide a greater degree of accuracy and rarely exceed the target temperature. You can also use optimum or delayed start operation sensors to reduce the heat up time during mild weather and weather compensators which drop the boiler flow temperature as external temperature rises.

Quick guide to electric heating and hot water controls

- Heat input control: determines the amount of electricity going into a storage heater at night. A manual or thermostat control that adjusts charge according to overnight temperatures. The Energy Saving Trust recommends manual users should watch the next day's weather forecast before setting the input control.
- Heat output control: thermostatic and manual control to determine the rate the heat is released back into the room.
- Cylinder thermostat: as described previously.
- Time switch: allows the user to take advantage of off-peak electricity.
- Boost switch: some cylinders have a second smaller heating element at the top. The boost switch allows you to heat a small amount of water using this second element.

Reducing electricity consumption: lighting and appliance use

Lighting

Light bulbs are sold according to the amount of watts they consume whilst switched on. 12, 40, 60 and so on. This information doesn't tell you the amount of light you get from a bulb, just how much power is consumed. Light is actually measured in lumens. An old 60 watt bulb might provide 700 lumens, but so will an energy efficient 12 watt bulb.

Whether retro-fitting or designing a new building, a lighting designer can work with you to decide how many lumens you need in your home and then work out the most energy efficient way of getting them. Of course, good natural daylight will reduce the amount of artificial daytime lighting required. Careful positioning of light fittings will make the most of nocturnal lighting.

Most of us will not be considering a lighting redesign but instead simply want to replace existing

Daylighting

Generally speaking, the more daylight we can get into a home the happier we will be. However, a balance has to be struck between daylighting, heat loss and thermal comfort; big windows let light in but they can also let heat out (at a quicker rate than insulated walls). Increasing daylight is easier if designing from scratch, but it is very much possible in existing homes too.

Factors affecting the amount of daylight entering a room include: window size, type, angle and cleanliness of glazing, how much of the sky is seen (in other words, are there objects blocking the light?). The room depth, height and even the internal decoration can then affect the distribution of daylighting. When designing a room to maximise natural lighting you need to use a measurement technique called 'daylight factors'.

The daylight factor in a room is measured as a percentage of the light found outside on a horizontal surface; you can get a feel for it by taking measurements with a photographic light meter. Divide the internal reading by the external reading and multiply by 100. A good percentage figure is 2% for a kitchen and 1.5% for all other rooms.

Source: *The Whole House Book*, Borer and Harris.

high energy bulbs with their low energy equivalents. Although ultra low energy LED lights are available, most people will currently opt for a CFL or Compact Fluorescent Bulb. These have come along way in the last three years and the Energy Saving Trust provide a very clear photographic guide of recommended products in their free download *A bright idea has got even better.*

Beyond changing the bulbs and the positioning of lights the only other way to save energy is to ensure that bulbs are turned off when they are not needed. This can be achieved through technology: by using lighting sensors that respond to the level of natural lighting available, a designated time period, or to motion. Or we can just remember.

Monitoring electricity consumption

Most electrical appliances have a power rating but these will not accurately predict how much energy they will actually use. Energy use of a particular product varies enormously between households. It is possible to estimate how much you are using by multiplying the power rating on an appliance by the average amount of time you think you use it, but a metering device will give you a truer picture. They will often show that the appliances that are most costly to run are not the ones we expect. Sometimes very small appliances that are left on in some households all the time (for example, wireless internet routers) use as much energy per week as a single large appliance, like a washing machine that is perhaps used only once.

Types of metering device include:

- **Plug in kWh meter**. Each appliance is monitored separately, but only those that can be plugged in. Fixed lighting, heating and cooker circuits can not be monitored using a plug in meter.
- **Whole house electricity meter**. These can be clamped onto the 'meter tails' between your meter and consumer unit. The obvious disadvantage of these monitors is that they read the whole house, not individual appliances.
- **Smart meters**. The first wave of smart meters are likely to be rolled out during 2012 and will carry on being rolled out until every household in England, Wales and Scotland has one by 2020. Not only will they allow consumers data on whole house energy consumption (both gas and electric) they will provide time of use data, historical use data, differential tariffs based on time of use, greater control over peak demand, accurate and timely billing and also net metering for microgeneration.

Source: *Choosing Solar Electricity*, Brian Goss.

Appliances

In Britain we're quite used to buying and using any appliance we want, whenever we want. When you start generating your own energy, however, you tend to rethink your life with appliances, especially if you live off-grid (where the amount of electricity available is limited by generating capacity), or if you are selling electricity to the grid.

Every unit of electricity produced and consumed becomes precious, and has a more significant economic and social value. It pays to analyse your appliance use carefully, to swap your old inefficient appliances for Energy Saving Trust Recommended products, and to rethink how you actually use your appliances. Of course, it pays to do this if you are not generating renewable energy, but as soon as you become a generator you learn the true value of your energy. It's yours and you don't want to waste it.

If you want to replace appliances with more energy efficient versions then the Energy Saving Trust website has a wide range of recommended products across all appliance categories; washing machines, fridges, kettles, home entertainment and so on.

Chapter Seven

The power up home

Fig. 7.1. The power up home

Five renewable options and how they might combine

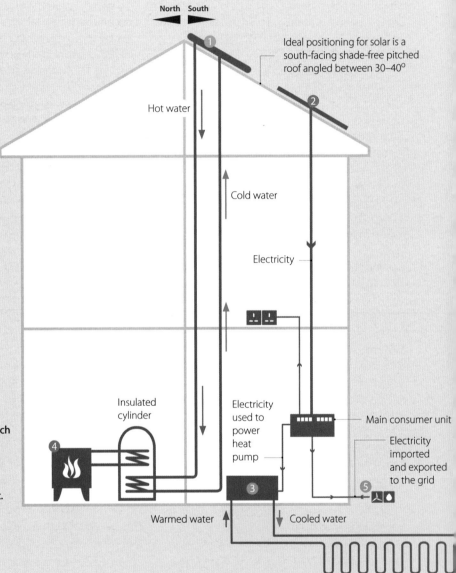

North South

Ideal positioning for solar is a south-facing shade-free pitched roof angled between 30–40°

Hot water

Cold water

Electricity

① Solar water heating will usually be combined with a renewable or conventional fuel system (most commonly wood or gas).

② Solar PV electricity can be used to power heat pumps but most domestic systems will not provide enough electricity to do so especially at the time it is needed.

③ Heat pumps will usually be combined with other heating systems using a buffer tank (see page 155).

④ Wood heating can be used as the main heating system or a back-up combined with other systems.

⑤ Imported renewable electricity such as wind and hydro is essential for most heat pump systems and for supplementing average domestic power consumption, when home power production is not sufficient.

Insulated cylinder

Electricity used to power heat pump

Main consumer unit

Electricity imported and exported to the grid

Warmed water

Cooled water

Why power up?

The illustration opposite shows three steps to power up your home:

- Switch to renewable heat (where possible!).
- Become a renewable electricity generator.
- Scale up to community level energy generation.

Inevitably the power down process can only ever take us so far. Even with the most extensive national retro-fit and zero carbon new build programme we will always need energy. CAT's *ZCB2030* report suggested that energy demand could only be decreased by 50%; the remaining 50% would be generated by renewable energy. Most of this energy however will not come from domestic or community scale generation but from large-scale renewable energy production. This begs the question, why bother with domestic and community scale generation?

There are several good reasons:

- A significant amount of heat demand (the *ZCB2030* report suggests over 50%) can be met using biomass, solar water heating and heat pump technologies. These technologies are all available to install at a domestic and community level and are supported by government subsidies. Space and water heating accounts for 82% of domestic energy consumption and 73% of domestic CO_2 emissions so switching to renewable heat cuts your personal energy use and carbon emissions significantly.
- Although community and individual electricity generation will only ever provide a small percentage of national electricity needs, local renewable energy generation can foster green values in neighbourhoods, provide a direct income through the Feed-in Tariff scheme and meet a significant proportion of individual or community electricity needs, reducing personal emissions once again.
- Powering up your home and community offers personal satisfaction, a sense of community and individual empowerment and greater resilience and resistance to energy price shocks.
- Investing in community renewable energy schemes allows you to keep the profits from power production within your local area.
- Local generation boosts local employment in jobs as diverse as woodland management, plumbing, electrical services and engineering.

Can everyone power up?

Yes, and no, is the real – though complicated – answer. Yes: in the sense that everyone can buy green electricity in one way or another (see box on page 133) or has the potential to be part of a community generation scheme. No: in the sense that all renewable technologies are site specific and cannot be applied universally to every household or community.

As well as the technological restrictions – which we will go through in each of the chapters that follow – there are many social and financial barriers to powering up. It is true to say that most people who currently power up have access to capital; not that they are wealthy necessarily, but that they have money to invest in technologies with higher upfront costs than the current alternatives. Of course, the RHI and FIT payments pay back this capital and cost differential but only after a number of years. The social barriers are perhaps harder to overcome. Powering up will be 'off the radar' for a huge number of people because they do not have access to the numerous drivers that make change possible: education; social networks; technological knowledge and so on.

Nevertheless, if these barriers can be overcome, community generation projects can help to create social cohesion and change the way communities view themselves, instilling a sense of pride through community ownership. Community renewables advisors Jarra Hicks and Nicky Ison discuss some of the ways in which communities can set about creating power up projects in chapter ten.

The power up technologies –

a short portrait of each to help you work out which one might be for you

Heating space and water

Heating systems are either connected to the national gas grid or independent from it. Whether or not you are connected will be a factor in deciding whether you power up your heating supply. Mains gas has the lowest CO_2 emissions of all fossil fuels and is also the cheapest. If you are already connected to mains gas the environmental and cost benefits of switching to a renewable heat source are much lower. Thus installing a more efficient gas boiler (perhaps combined with a solar thermal system) is usually a better bet than switching over to a biomass boiler or heat pump system. It is now even possible to subscribe to a green gas scheme (through Ecotricity). If you are not connected to mains gas then you are likely to be using oil, LPG or electricity, perhaps coal. In this case switching over to renewable heat is a much more cost-effective option. In many cases renewable energy heating systems are combined either with each other or with a fossil fuel system to create a sensible mixed approach that provides a back-up to the primary heating system; the goal being to reduce CO_2 emissions as feasibly as a particular site or situation will allow.

Solar thermal

Solar thermal, or solar water heating as most people know it, is best installed on roofs facing due south, or failing that at a point facing between south east and south west, or in the worst case scenario between east and west. An unshaded roof is best, with a tilt of roughly between 30 and 40 degrees. The amount of useful energy you can get from a solar collector goes down the further away your site is from these ideals, in which case you need to install more panels to get the same amount of energy, raising the cost of installation.

Solar thermal panels can be used to provide space heating but this is very unusual. Most installations provide domestic hot water (DHW) via a cylinder. Generally a solar thermal installation is combined with another heating source and raises the temperature of water in a cylinder before the other heating source kicks in. This is where the energy, CO_2 and financial savings are made – not by eradicating the need for the other heating system but by saving it work.

In June and July a solar water heating system can provide almost all of an average family's DHW requirement. This goes down to 95% in May, then to around 75-80 per cent in April, August and September, and in the winter months – November through to February – to less than 10-20%. This is why solar thermal is generally not used to heat space, but over the course of the year a solar water heating system will be able to provide 50% of the energy needed for DHW. All the payback times for solar thermal are thus based on the cost of the fuel you are saving, as well as the payments. As the cost of fuel goes up the payback time on solar thermal shrinks.

The cost of installation can also depend upon existing plumbing arrangements. Sometimes it is necessary to replace existing pipe and tank work to facilitate installation. It is possible to use solar thermal without a tank (for example to heat a swimming pool or to provide a limited provision of hot water where demand is low) but nearly all household installations will require a cylinder.

Biomass (wood fuel)

We call it biomass but for most domestic applications what we're really talking about is wood fuel. There are some larger scale biomass burners that use materials other than wood (which we talk more about in the biomass chapter) but for most people, for most households, and even for most community projects the most common biomass fuel used is wood.

Wood fuel is delivered in three forms; as logs, pellets or chips. Logs can be manufactured from recycled wood waste (sometimes called briquettes) or come straight from the tree. Pellets are manufactured. Chips come from the tree. Logs and pellets are burnt in stoves or boilers. Chips are only burnt in boilers (and at a larger scale than most individual households require).

There are two ways to burn wood: in continuous feed or in batches. A good example of a continuous feed burner that everyone knows is a wood stove (you keep on having to place logs in the fire) but there are also automated continuous feed pellet and chip boilers which store the fuel in a 'hopper' until it is fed automatically via a delivery system into the fire. This

certainly takes the effort out of wood burning and delivers very good efficiencies of fuel use, as the more sophisticated systems feed fires in a very precise way, keeping the fire at the exact heat required.

The other way of burning wood is to batch burn. Batch burners stay alight for a set period using a set amount of wood and store the resultant heat in water in very well insulated accumulator tanks, until it can be used; a bit like an immersion heater.

The efficiency of wood fuel heating varies enormously between appliance and between wood fuel, with efficiencies and cost more or less rising hand in hand. It is worth spending as much as you can afford on both if they deliver the substantial efficiency improvements they promise. But even if you buy the cheapest wood stove, its efficiency can be raised significantly by ensuring the fuel you burn is well seasoned 'dry' wood; in other words wood with a low moisture content. There is nothing more depressing than the sound of a sizzler on a cold winters evening. I shudder at the thought!

Heat pumps

Heat pumps do not create heat, they move it from one place to another. The heat itself comes from natural outdoor heat stores – the air, the ground, still and running water. The heat is collected from the heat store at low temperatures, raised to a more useful temperature using compression techniques and circulated around the building – most usually using underfloor heating.

Because heat pumps deliver heat at significantly lower temperatures than wood fuel or solar thermal, they are used most effectively in very well insulated buildings – preferably in those that are insulated above the level demanded by current Building Regulations (see the chapters on insulation). They are also more suited to buildings with a high occupancy rate.

They also require a significant amount of additional electrical power both to operate the system and to

provide additional heat. The proportion of electrical power varies depending on the type of heat pump used; it being greater for air source heat pumps than for ground and water source heat pumps. Because of this it is important that your electricity source is green.

Heat pump systems can be combined with solar electric (PV) modules or with a wind turbine, or electricity can be bought from a green energy supplier (see page 133). It is also possible to combine wood heating and solar thermal, as well as more conventional fuel systems, with heat pumps so long as an additional 'buffer' tank is fitted – in other words a hot water cylinder – into which all the systems can be connected.

There are three main types of heat pumps - air, ground and water. Within each of these categories there are various sub-categories. For example, fresh air and exhaust air heat pumps (recovering waste heat from ventilation systems); horizontal and vertical ground source heat pumps (which includes geo-thermal heat); and river, lake, sea, waste and ground water heat pumps (which use water flowing beneath the surface of the ground (in other words aquifers)).

Air heat pumps take up relatively small amounts of space compared to the other systems but deliver poor results by comparison. However, they are more universally applied. Horizontal ground source heat pumps require a substantial amount of land (at least two and a half times the ground area of the building); vertical ground source heat pumps need expensive drilling equipment and deep bore pipes.

Generating electricity

As with heating systems, electrical systems are either grid-connected or off-the-grid (stand-alone as they are often called). Most houses not connected to the gas mains are connected to the national electricity grid; the number of stand-alone properties requiring an independent electricity supply is thus much much smaller. Most readers of this book will be contemplating a grid-connected system, and almost certainly thinking about solar PV over wind and water power. If not then they should be!

The number of useful wind and water power sites connected directly to a grid-connected dwelling are extremely small compared to the number of useful PV sites (see below for the reasons why). Stand alone systems tend to be in very remote places, due to the fact that it has always been (and is still) too expensive to connect them up to the grid. These places are sometimes on windy hilltops or by fast flowing streams and rivers; places where wind and hydro power can reasonably be considered a cost and environmentally effective alternative to grid connection or diesel generation.

The overwhelming advantage of grid-connected systems is the fact that there is no need for a battery store. Electricity is imported from and exported to the grid as required. Batteries are essential to stand-alone systems but they are expensive, environmentally polluting and dangerous to handle. As with heating systems it is possible to combine renewable energy generators. Wind and PV are quite often used in combination in stand-alone systems because one tends to start generating when the other is less active.

Solar PV

As you would expect, the site requirements for solar PV are more or less the same as for solar water heating, with the optimum site being an unshaded south facing roof with a pitch between 30 and 40 degrees. Having an optimum site is not as important as it might sound. Complete system performance does drop the further away you get from the optimum but not enough to rule out less than optimum sites.

For example roofs facing south east to south west will perform at up to 95% of optimal output, whereas east or west facing roofs reduce performance by 15%. Likewise most roofs with a pitch of between 10 degrees and 50 degrees will be above 97% of the optimum. Shading may be a bigger issue, especially in the winter when the sun passes the day lower in the sky. If you think shading might be an issue you can use a sun-path diagram to make a rough assessment (see page 172), but you will probably also have to seek advice from an installer.

It is possible to compensate for a less than perfect site by installing a larger array (the name given for a number of PV modules (panels) connected together) but obviously the cost and the price per unit of electricity produced rises too. Most new solar PV installations are grid-connected (in the first few months of FiT's the number of installations doubled from ten to twenty thousand). As most people are out during the day most of the electricity produced will be sold directly to the grid, unless appliances can be set to run when the modules are generating the most power. Generators receive an extra FiT's payment for each unit of electricity exported to the grid (known as the export tariff), but pay more for electricity they import. Because of this (and because its your electricity!) it makes sense to use as much of the PV generated energy as possible.

Wind power

Wind turbines are iconic symbols of the green energy revolution and many have been purchased and placed in completely the wrong place! Not least by public figures like David Cameron, who, as leader of the opposition, famously attached one to his chimney.

The performance of a wind turbine is determined by average wind speed, the height of the tower (because the turbine needs to be raised above zones of ground level turbulence) and of course the quality of design of the individual machine. Not surprisingly average wind speeds are highest out at sea, in upland areas and in flat places with few obstacles. Most urban, suburban and populated rural areas are completely unsuitable for wind. Wind turbines will produce electricity in these areas but at a rate below (in some cases way below) what is economically viable, the unit cost of the electricity rising beyond what can be reasonably expected.

Poor installations may never even generate the amount of energy it took to make them (known as paying back the embodied energy cost). In these cases they can rightly be described as eco-bling. Vertical axis wind turbines (those that resemble giant egg whisks) are often visible in the urban landscape. Although these can cope better with the turbulence associated with urban areas, low wind-speeds are still the over-whelming problem.

There are exceptions to these rules: for example where no other source of power is available and the wind turbine is still a cheaper and more logical alternative to a diesel generator: for boats, remote dwellings or remote lighting or monitoring stations.

The potential for wind power has to be assessed using wind speed monitoring equipment. This is a process that takes time; to establish useful data perhaps as long as two years. It is possible to get average wind speeds for an area from existing data but not for specific sites. Grid connected community wind projects often make more logistical sense because resources can be combined to pay for monitoring equipment and also to buy a bigger turbine and tower and to purchase access to a suitable site.

Many sympathetic land owners value the potential of wind turbines to bring them a reliable income over time so its not an impossible proposition. Owning and operating a community wind turbine requires the formation of a group with a formal legal structure which gives due consideration to legal, planning and health and safety requirements; not an easy task by any means, but one that can be achieved with the help of relevant support agencies such as Plan Local, Local United and Community Energy Scotland, and perhaps using the services of a dedicated service provider (see page 202).

Connecting wind to the national grid is not as easy as connecting PV. At the time of writing the arrangements for grid connecting wind power were being reviewed so please do check with a relevant advisory body. Wind turbines are eligible for Feed-in Tariff payments using MCS accredited installers and technology. It is worth checking the payment rules in great detail before moving forward with a project as they are more complicated than those for PV.

Water (micro-hydro) power

We use the words micro-hydro power to distinguish small scale water turbines from the kind of large-scale hydro-electricity projects we associate with big dam building. Micro-hydro power is easy on the landscape, has a small ecological footprint and can deliver reliable electrical power year in year out, given some fairly simple criteria based on the average flow rate and head of a water course.

The flow rate is the volume per second passing the catchment point. The head is the difference in height between the point where the water is directed away from the river (via a constructed channel known as the intake) and the point where it passes through the turbine (we illustrate this in more detail in the section on pages 180-181).

Generally, the higher the flow rate and head the greater the generating potential, although some turbines (for example the archimedes turbine featured in our case study on page 207) are designed for low heads. The average available flow depends on the catchment area size and run-off characteristic, the rainfall and evapo-transpiration (water returned to the atmosphere). The rate of flow can vary enormously over the course of a year, from flood to draught, but the head is fairly constant once the system has been set up (changing slightly with river levels).

It can take up to two years to get a micro-hydro project up and running, from initial assessment through flow rate testing and analysis, through planning and construction. It is also necessary to apply for various licences to work in the river and abstract water from it, as well as get the normal Building Regulation and planning permission approval. In some cases it may also be necessary to build a fish ladder! Micro-hydro schemes have proved themselves an effective technology in the right situation and can be operated as stand-alone, grid-connected, household or community schemes.

Combining power up technologies

Power up technologies are often used in combination with each other and/or with conventional fossil fuel systems. Possible combinations include solar thermal and biomass, wind and solar PV, solar PV and heat pumps, or gas and solar thermal. During the planning phase of a power up project its worth assessing the individual and combined merits of each technology to see how they might complement each other. If you're planning an installation of one technology there are definitely economies to be made by installing two at the same time. For example, solar thermal and biomass installations will both require a certain amount of plumbing work, so doing them at the same time will make sense.

Buying green electricity

There are numerous green electricity tariffs available but some are definitely more green than others. There are various websites set up to help you make a decision, including www.greenelectricity.org

The best place to begin your research, however, is with the Energy Saving Trust's guidance at www.energysavingtrust.org.uk/In-your-home/Your-energy-supply/Buying-green-electricity

This explains the differences between green tariffs.

Getting the most out of a system

In the sections above I've tried to give you a quick portrait of each technology to allow you to dismiss or embrace one, more or all of them as being a practical solution for your situation. The next few chapters will help give you a deeper understanding of how each system works so you can start to get a feel of how you might make the most of a system when it is fully operational.

The effectiveness of a renewable energy system depends in part on the level of knowledge and understanding of the user, as well as the user's ability to monitor and assess whether their system is working well. Ownership of renewable energy systems can be challenging at times, so it is worth knowing how these challenges might play out over time.

You will also need to know about maintenance, planning requirements and legal obligations. I cover these in brief in each section but you may need to talk to an installer in more depth about these processes.

I have deliberately not talked in as much depth about wind and hydro power as I have for the other four technologies; this is because I have weighted the book in favour of those technologies I see as being more applicable to the greater majority of readers. For a more in-depth look at wind and hydro I would recommend CAT's other books: *Choosing Wind Power*, *Choosing Water Power (out of print at time of writing but new editions due late 2012)*; *Off the Grid* and *Wind Power Workshop*.

Case study

Gamblesby village hall: crisis hit community centre turned around with power up plan

In 2001, huge swathes of the British countryside went into lockdown because of an outbreak of foot and mouth disease: ten million sheep and cattle destroyed, the movement of people and animals restricted, village life paralysed. Those of us who lived in the countryside at that time will remember how troubled life became.

In Gamblesby in Cumbria, population 150, the foot and mouth outbreak further accelerated a decline in village life that had already seen the closure of the pub, shop and church. The remaining hub of social activity – the village hall – was now under threat. The low point, what Gamblesby's William Mitchell described in conversation with Paul Allen as 'our darkest hour', came when the trustees of the hall were left with a £4,000 architects bill following a failed lottery bid and the hall itself left closed due to wet rot in the floor joists:

'At this point the trustees had the choice of giving up the hall, selling it for development or taking up the fight again. Consultation with the whole village secured wholehearted support for another effort. All residents were consulted and a skills audit carried out.'

The two phase development that proceeded from this consultation process allowed for a largely 'do it yourself' first

Gamblesby's wind turbine supplies power to the village hall and exports surplus to the grid.

phase and then a builder-led second phase that would see the main school room and the old kitchen/toilet extension replaced.

With the backing of the community, the thirteen strong trustee board led the process, attending local 'funding fairs' to work out on what basis a bid should be put together. A 'distinctive' appeal tied to a 'green' agenda led to bids being made on the basis of underfloor heating via a ground source heat pump, use of renewable materials sourced locally and use of the highest possible amount of insulation.

A key part of the funding bid was full community involvement. As William Mitchell describes: 'With great pride, nearly everybody played a part, whether it was attending a fundraising event, painting a wall or wheeling a barrow of ballast. Farmers brought machines, engineering expertise, landscaping, well-developed local contacts and bargaining skills! Incomers offered skills in IT, financial and business planning, public relations and media. There was a good mix of complementary skills that made a well-balanced and effective team. One trustee was a professional fundraiser, another was a banker, one villager was a freelance TV cameraman so made a DVD of the project, another resident a manager at British Gypsum – ideal for getting discounted plasterboard.

'In phase one, budgets from the funds generated were allocated to 'mini managers'; Eric responsible for building works/electrics, George for ground works and heat pump, John for floor heating and covering, Vicki for landscaping. Others were responsible for internal decoration, for internal fundraising, for external fundraising, for publicity and for managing the finances of the project fund. Mini managers brought their recommendations to the trustees for discussion and approval. In general, trustees did not pore over the detail again but trusted their colleagues to have done their homework and moved quickly on. It worked well and the only dissent was over the choice of colour for the walls!'

Key organisational support came from Cumbria and Lancashire Community Renewables (CLAREN), Voluntary Action Cumbria and the District and County Councils, with funding provided by the EU, Northern Rock, Eden District Council, the Big Lottery fund, Defra, Cumbria Community Foundation, community fundraising initiatives and a landfill grant.

Apart from the heat pump, the other key technological component was a wind turbine. As William Mitchell explains, this has not lived up to all that the trustees originally hoped for: 'The plan was to be able to switch the turbine output three ways: a) to supply power to the hall when there was demand, b) next to pre-heat the circulating water in a large storage tank, and c) after the water reached a certain temperature to export electricity to the grid. The installers designed an electronic switching system but it was not able to do everything we wanted so we have settled for the turbine supplying power to the hall on demand and otherwise exporting to the grid.'

As well as these technological difficulties the wind turbine also raised some social issues. Although the turbine successfully passed planning, some vociferous objections led to an unusual compromise: 'We live in a small village and although we lose revenue, the trustees agreed to dismount the turbine during the summer holidays, when it was claimed to be most intrusive by the objectors. This was a compromise – but I am still waiting for the approach to say "it's not as bad as I thought – you might as well keep it running all year".'

Gamblesby village hall illustrates how a community can come together to do something truly remarkable. William Mitchell believes that early community involvement was absolutely crucial and offers this advice to anyone hoping to achieve something similar with their village hall or community centre:

'The process must start with gaining support and commitment from the community. Ways must be found to engage as many people as possible in 'hands on' activity within the project. It has to be "ours" to ensure future use of the hall and future commitment to its maintenance and development. It is also very useful to find out what skills exist within your community and to use them. Where there are shortfalls, seek expert help and advice. Also, make sure that the trustees/committee are representative of the community and keep the social events going to reinforce the bonds of trust, respect and friendship that will be vital to the success of the project.'

Chapter Eight

Renewable heat

How does renewable heat fit with existing heating systems

Making a decision on whether or not to switch to renewable heat will depend as much on your existing heating system as any of the other potential factors outlined in the previous chapter. For example, heat pumps work very well with underfloor heating but not so well with radiators; yet installing underfloor heating from scratch could add hundreds, even thousands, of pounds to the cost of installation.

Likewise, if you decide to install solar water heating you will need a cylinder, but this makes it incompatible with combi boiler systems. If you already have a highly efficient gas condensing boiler, it is not really worth switching to a renewable heat source (at least in financial terms). Furthermore, some biomass boilers require a heat store to work properly and this might also make it incompatible with your existing heating system.

Solar water heating

What is solar water heating?

Put simply, solar water heating is a technique to turn energy from the sun into latent heat that can be used at our convenience. The water in a solar water heating system is effectively a heat store, just as the walls and floors of a building are a heat store in passive solar techniques. The heat is carried from the solar thermal panel (more correctly named a solar thermal collector) and transferred to an insulated cylinder, where it remains until it is needed.

Currently, most of the heat absorbed from the sun by solar thermal collectors around the globe is used to heat water for taps, showers and baths; this is referred to as domestic hot water, or DHW. However, solar thermal power is also used for heating swimming pools and sometimes also for space heating. Most solar water heating collectors contain a heat transfer liquid to take the heat from the collector

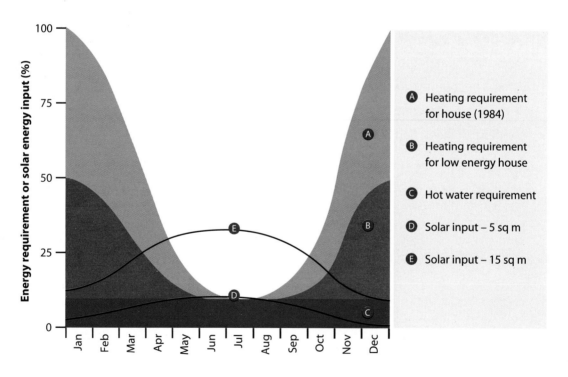

Fig. 8.1. Amount of solar energy available compared to various heating demands throughout the year.

Radiators are the conventional means of distributing hot water for heat around a building but this is largely because it has cost advantages over underfloor heating and is easier to install, particularly in existing properties.

Radiators

The term radiator is slightly misleading because the majority of the heat is given off in air convection currents, not heat radiation. Their heat emission is 1300-2500W/m², depending on the number of fins on the back. Low temperature versions are available to prevent scolding, as the water supply temperature will be about 80°C.

Underfloor heating

Hot water pipes are embedded in concrete or limecrete floor screed, or they run in insulated channels in timber floors. This means the whole of the floor area becomes a radiator, and so with a rating of about 90W/m², the water temperature can be quite low (30-40°C). Because we are more sensitive to radiant heat it is possible to set the temperature 2-3°C lower than with conventional radiator use too. Underfloor heating can be used in conjunction with wood boilers,

and it should be used with heat pump systems – heat pumps are more efficient when delivering heat at low temperatures, so the low temperature required by underfloor heating makes the two technologies an ideal match.

Heat stores

Heat stores allow heat to be kept stored for use at convenient times. Overnight storage heaters and hot water cylinders are the most common examples. Construction materials can also be used as heat stores, particularly when combined with passive solar techniques. They absorb excess heat during the day and release it during the evening and at night when it is needed most.

Some wood heating systems rely on an additional heat store to improve efficiency. Kakkelovn are Swedish ceramic tile stoves designed to be fired up to burn dry timber at high temperatures once or twice a day. They store heat in the high mass walls and release it slowly over several hours. Similarly, log batch boilers (see pages 146-152) require accumulator cylinders – without them the peaks and troughs of temperatures between firings will produce uncomfortable results from the radiators, and inefficient combustion.

to the cylinder. This is usually a glycol mix but it could be water, or it could be water in one part of the system and another liquid (such as alcohol) in a different part of the system.

Types of solar water heating – domestic hot water (DHW), swimming pools and space heating

There are very few solar water *space* heating systems in Britain. One of the main reasons is that we need the heat when the solar resource is least effective. During the middle of the winter, five times less solar energy

is available than at the height of the summer. As you can imagine, this is a serious handicap for any space heating system.

Although a backup fuel source is still needed for DHW, the seasonal variations are not so much of a problem because demand for DHW is fairly constant throughout the year; and while backup fuel use will rise in the winter, a solar water heating system will still be able to provide 50% of the energy needed overall. For an average household over the lifetime of a system, this can amount to a 20 tonne saving in CO_2 emissions.

Swimming pools

There are thought to be over 100,000 swimming pools around the UK, with over 70% in private gardens. Solar water heating could reduce fuel use in many of these, especially as many outdoor pools are not used in winter and water temperatures in swimming pools remain fairly constant throughout the year. Collectors for swimming pools are different to those used for DHW and space heating. Lower temperatures are required so there is no need for glazing or insulation. The heat from the water is fed into the swimming pool indirectly via a heat exchange in order to avoid corrosion caused by chemical cleaning agents used in the pool. As a rule of thumb, the area of of a solar water heating collector should be 25% of the surface area of the swimming pool.

Direct solar water heating
Water in hot water storage cylinder same as water which flows from taps.

Indirect solar water heating
Water in solar water heating pipework does not mix with water in hot water storage cylinder. Heats water in tank through coil(s).

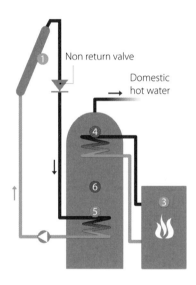

1 Solar panel
2 Hot water storage tank (single coil)
3 Central heating boiler
4 Central heating hot water coil
5 Solar hot water coil
6 Hot water storage tank (dual coil)

a) Solar heating coil (5) always positioned below central heating coil (4).

b) Dual coil hot water storage tank may be larger in dual coil arrangement.

c) Hot water tank and solar heating pipework must be insulated.

Fig. 8.2. Direct and indirect solar water heating systems. Source: Renewable Energy – A users guide, Andy McCrea.

Parts of a DHW solar water heating system

DHW solar water heating systems (as opposed to swimming pool or space systems) generally require:

- One or more solar thermal collectors.
- A hot water storage cylinder connected to an existing boiler or immersion and cold water inlet.
- A heat transfer system to take the heat from the thermal collector to the cylinder.

The way these components are connected together varies depending on whether you are using a direct or indirect system.

Direct and indirect systems

Figure 8.2 shows both a direct and an indirect solar water heating system. The pictures almost look like something from a spot the difference competition but there is only one difference – you'll see it if you focus on the bottom of the cylinder. The direct system on the left takes water for the solar collector directly from the cylinder; the indirect system on the right keeps the heat transfer liquid separate from the cylinder water, transferring the heat by way of a second coil.

The direct system has the advantage that an additional storage cylinder or a new cylinder with an additional coil is not required. In situations where space is tight it might be the only option. However, an indirect system allows you to keep the heat transfer liquid separate from the water in the tank, which ensures that there is no risk of lime scale deposits gradually reducing the efficiency of your collectors. Most of the solar water heating systems currently being installed are indirect systems incorporating a replacement hot water storage cylinder which is larger than the original and has two coils plus better insulation.

You'll also notice that both of the systems above fit together with existing boiler infrastructure quite easily, and

it will be clear from the picture that solar acts as a pre-heat facility which raises the overall temperature of the water inside the cylinder so that the existing conventional boiler has to do less. This will extend the life of your boiler as well as reduce your fuel use. The fuel with the lowest carbon emissions is wood and wood fuel boilers are often used in conjunction with solar systems.

Solar thermal collectors – heating the water

There are three different types of solar thermal collector and a corresponding range of efficiencies. The simplest solar collectors, designed to raise the temperature of water in a swimming pool by a few degrees, are unglazed and uninsulated (you don't want boiling water pouring into a swimming pool). Next are the two most common and most efficient types of manufactured solar thermal collector used when demand for hot water is high: flat plate and evacuated tube collectors. Both of these types of collector are required to meet European standard BS EN 12975:2000, which sets down standards for durability, reliability and recommended performance. You can make a DIY flat plate panel but these will never meet these standards.

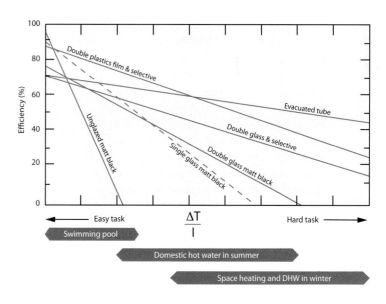

Fig. 8.3. Efficiency variables for different types of solar thermal collector. Source: The Whole House Book, Harris and Borer.

Flat plate vs evacuated tube collectors Both flat plate and evacuated tube collectors are built to maximise efficiencies using glazing, a heat absorbent coating and insulation techniques, however, the evacuated tube collectors are generally considered to be more efficient. Speaking of efficiency with reference to solar water heating can be a bit confusing; the response of the collector constantly varies according to variations between the temperature of the heat transfer fluids and the ambient air temperature outside the collector (the greater the difference the lower the efficiency), and also with the angle of direct sun, cloud cover and so on. UK government funded studies have shown that there is very little difference in total annual energy yield provided that the collecting area of the lower efficiency collectors is oversized.

As a general rule, 0.7m² of evacuated tube collector surface is required for each occupant of a building while 1.0m² of flat plate collector surface is necessary. As such, an average family home will need about 3m² of evacuated tube coverage and 4m² of flat plate collector coverage. Evacuated tubes are more expensive but more fragile than flat plate collectors, which often blend in with roof lines better (looking more like a VELUX window from a distance) or can even be fully integrated with the roof. It is not possible to integrate evacuated tube collectors with the roof or to use them as part of thermosiphoning or direct systems.

Siting the collectors Most solar water heating collectors are roof mounted (pitched or flat) but it is also possible to fix them to a wall or site them on the ground. Indeed, in the famous rotating house in Germany (yes, the whole house rotates!) the collectors double as balcony railings and follow the sun throughout the day to maximise solar potential.

Tilt In the previous chapter we talked a little about the importance of tilt when siting a solar collector. The optimum tilt angle for a solar water heating collector is usually about 20° less than the latitude. In Britain, latitudes range from 50° (Land's End) to 60° (Haroldswick, Shetland Islands) so, in theory, the optimum tilt angle should be between 30° and 40°. In practice, most roofs have not been built to perfectly accommodate solar collectors and are pitched between 20° and 50°. Variations in pitch between these angles produce only minor losses, however – between 2% and 3% – and these losses can be regained by expanding the collector area.

Orientation As with all types of solar collectors, orientation should ideally be south facing with no substantial shading. However, orientations between south east and south west are also good. For example, a solar thermal panel mounted on a south-west facing roof with a 40° tilt would produce only 5% less output than a panel with perfect tilt and orientation. Collectors should never be positioned on north facing roofs; if your roof faces east or west then you will need more collector area for the best result. It is also possible to mount solar collectors on the ground.

Try to avoid significant shading of more than 2 hours per spring or autumn day. Solar shading can be calculated using sun-path diagrams and a compass or a solar horizon estimator. There isn't enough space here to explain how this is done but the information can be found in another CAT book, *Choosing Solar Electricity* by Brian Goss – the technique being the same for Solar PV as for solar thermal. You can download sun-path diagrams free of charge for your latitude from various websites – type 'generate sun-path diagram' into a search engine for a few options. An example site is http://solardat.uoregon.edu/PolarSunChartProgram.html Here you can enter your longitude, latitude and time zone and download the resulting sun-path diagram as a PDF.

Hot water storage cylinder

In the UK, most professional installations involve the removal of an existing water storage cylinder and the replacement of it with a twin coil hot water cylinder like the one shown in figure 8.2. The top coil is connected to a boiler, the bottom coil to the solar collector. This twin coil system allows you to pre-heat a volume of water independently of the boiler. Sizing the pre-heat area correctly is incredibly important because undersizing can lead to overheating in summer, limited domestic hot water availability and a low solar collector performance. In order to get it right you need to size the pre-heat area in proportion to the amount of hot water used every day.

Specially manufactured solar cylinders are designed to be tall (to increase stratification between the cold water at the bottom of the tank and the heated water at the top) with a high level of insulation (at least 50mm of high density polystyrene or fibreglass) and an extra large coil to facilitate heat exchange. It is possible to use existing cylinders, particularly for direct feed systems, but they can hold the system back and even create dangerously high temperatures if undersized in relation to collector area. In most retro-fit installations a standard 100 litre tank will be replaced by one with a capacity between 160 and 220 litres.

An alternative to a twin coil cylinder is to use two or more separate cylinders where one acts as the solar pre-heat area and the other is heated by the boiler. This can be easier to install alongside existing solar thermal installations and allows large storage volumes whilst retaining flexibility. But it can also 'trap' solar heat in the first store if there is no DHW draw off (in other words, if people are not turning the hot water tap on) and, as such, the final store might be heated by an automatic boiler or immersion needlessly.

The heat transfer (or primary) system – getting the hot water from the panel to the cylinder

The components containing the heat transfer fluid, including the solar collector, pipes and heat exchanger, are generally termed the heat transfer or 'primary' system.

Circulation around the primary system In order for heat to flow from collector to cylinder the primary fluid must be able to circulate. In normal operation one pipe will allow the flow of hot fluid from the cylinder and the other pipe return cool, forming a loop that moves heat from one end to the other. Due to the layout of most houses, a pump offers the best flexibility and response to intermittent weather conditions and can permit simple protection from overheating and frost.

In rare cases, natural thermosiphon circulation can be used without a pump – that is, as warm water naturally is more buoyant than cold, the fluid moves upwards in the pipes without assistance. However,

for this to work satisfactorily, the collector must be below the cold water store and the pipes must also continually rise upwards towards it. This arrangement is quite difficult to achieve in practice, hence its rarity.

Direct types of thermosiphon systems are seldom seen in the UK due to the risk of the safety vent freezing. In general, this cannot be reliably prevented. Furthermore, prevention of overheating is difficult with thermosiphoning. Overheating and loss of useful heat are also drawbacks of using pumps that are directly coupled to a solar PV module where there is not also a temperature pump control.

Primary fluid expansion When water is heated it will expand and it is especially important to allow for this in system design. If there is a fault with circulation under hot, sunny conditions, liquid-based collectors can boil and the contents turn to vapour. There are three main methods of accommodating this safely, one of which must be used in the primary system:

- A vent to atmosphere into a header cistern; these are called open vent systems.
- An expansion vessel and safety valve; sealed systems.
- Switch off pump and drain away from collector into a vessel; drainback.

Installers will invariably talk about open vent, sealed or drainback systems. Collectors are normally specifically designed for using one of these systems but some can use either.

Protecting from 'freeze' damage When water freezes it becomes solid and expands, causing not only circulation to cease but also the bursting of metal pipes and other rigid elements, such as joints or pumps. Protection methods include:

Antifreeze. This is the most common method found in the UK. It incorporates a special non-toxic, food grade chemical available from plumbing merchants (not car antifreeze). It cannot be used in a direct system.

Drainback. Also common in the UK, where a temperature/light sensor switches the pump off, permitting the fluid to drain from the collector. This requires careful plumbing to ensure pipes always fall back to a special vessel, which is not always easy to do.

Auto pump control. This is triggered by a collector temperature sensor. It is only recommended if freezing is expected just a few days a year due to electric pump losses each time it switches on. This can be used with direct systems.

Auto drain down. This is a valve controlled by a temperature sensitive lever which opens in order to dump fluid contents when close to freezing. It requires a manual refill and is only suitable in warmer climates with very occasional freezing.

Controls and measurements Without any control devices, a solar water heating system can become dangerous because it is difficult to stop the sun from heating the collector – you can't just unplug a system. In a situation where there is overheating, pipes and fluid can cause pressures to rise to breaking point. A well designed and installed system employing the correct control devices will reduce this risk. The control devices are placed in strategic positions around the primary circuit and controlled centrally through a digital controller. Controllers vary in sophistication but most perform the following functions:

- Measurement. Sometimes built-in, these controllers permit safe commissioning of the system and provide extra user information, such as cylinder temperatures, thermostatic and time-clock control of auxiliary heat (in other words, heat from the boiler), plus error messages.
- Differential thermostat control (DTC). This allows the pump to switch on and off effectively when pump action is needed to maintain circulation within the primary system. It does this by monitoring the temperature in the collector and switching the pump on when it registers a differential of 6°C, when compared to a fixed spot elsewhere in the primary circuit (not in the collector) – and off again when the differential is around 3°C. The DTC can also switch on a pump to prevent freezing.
- Flow indicator and regulator. These set the flow rate for maximum efficiency, ensuring that there

is no air in the system and no vapour locks.
- Non-return valve. This stops unwanted heat flow reversion – in other words, this stops hot water heading back out of the cylinder and into the collector. A non-return valve is often fitted in the pump.
- Thermal mixing valve (TMV). As solar water heating systems create water temperatures well above those normally found in DHW systems, a thermal mixing valve – which mixes cold water with hot before it leaves the tap – is important, if not essential.

Planning, Building Regulations and other legal issues
Planning permission. Planning permission for solar water heating is allowed under permitted development rights. These vary between England and the devolved countries. In England and Scotland, changes to permitted development rights in 2008 and 2009 respectively allowed roof, wall and ground mounted systems to be installed without planning permission as long as they met certain size requirements and were not in conservation areas (including National Parks), World Heritage Sites or on listed buildings. If a building is listed it might still be possible to have solar water heating in the grounds, but you will have to seek permission from your local planning authority. New legislation in Wales and Northern Ireland is expected but, until it happens, contact with the local planning authority is essential.

Building Regulations. Solar water heating panels require a Building Control Certificate, issued following an inspection by the local Building Control Officer. There is a fee for this, which varies from council to council. This inspection ensures that the installation is safe.

RHI installation. To be eligible for the RHI, equipment and installers must be certified under the Microgeneration Certification Scheme (for all systems under 45kW). At the time of writing RHI was only available for the commercial sector. Householders apply for the Renewable Heat Premium Payment via the Energy Saving Trust.

Insurance and mortgage. It might be worth

checking with your insurers and mortgage providers to see whether an installation will affect your existing agreements.

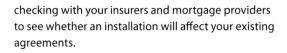

Heating with wood and other biomass

What is biomass heating?

Most of the technologies in this book can be replicated at a community and individual level by scaling up or scaling down to suit.

Biofuel heating is slightly different in that you can scale up wood heating to work at a community level, but you can't very easily scale down some large-scale biofuel processes to the household level. Landfill gas, for example, is never going to be a backyard technology. Who would want it? Similarly, gasification and anaerobic digestion (of which more later) are techniques more suited to community, farm or industrial level heat production – mainly because you need a lot of source material to create the fuel, the technologies are expensive and the quantities of heat generated substantial.

For this reason, most of this section is about wood heating, by which I mean small scale boilers and stoves where the main fuel is wood, be it in log, pellet or chip form.

Nevertheless it is very useful to talk briefly about the other types of biofuel, because chapter ten specifically concentrates on district heating and combined heat and power units which use a wide variety of biofuels as the primary energy source.

Before we get on to this, it is worth clearing up a question that many people ask; why is biomass considered to be a renewable fuel? It's a useful question, particularly as there has been much debate about the environmental cost of some biofuel production – although it's worth pointing out that this debate has focused largely on high impact fuels, such as ethanol and bio-diesel, used as a replacement for petrol, and these fuels are not considered to be renewable because the carbon cost of producing, processing and transporting them is too high. This is not the case with the types of fuels we are talking about in this chapter.

Biomass fuels are different to the other renewable technologies described in this book because they are a managed fuel crop. All other renewables capture energy that would be present on earth whether we were here or not – wind, wave, hydro, tidal, solar. So why is biomass a renewable fuel?

The answer lies in photosynthesis, the natural process by which plants abstract carbon from carbon dioxide to fuel their own growth. The carbon is locked inside the plant as it grows and only released back into the atmosphere when the plant rots, is eaten or burnt. Theoretically, as long as the plant is replaced by another, there is no net addition to carbon dioxide levels because the plant can only ever release into the atmosphere the amount of carbon it extracted during its lifetime. Of course there is always an addition of CO_2 through the use of chain saws, transport and if the wood does not achieve 100% combustion, but these emission figures will be less than similar associated CO_2 costs from other non-renewable fuels. Thus, a biofuel, although a managed part of the earth's natural energy cycle, is still essentially solar power in that the energy used to create it comes from the sun via photosynthesis.

Types of biomass heating systems and fuels

Most biofuels are burnt to produce heat, either as a solid fuel in their original state or via one of two processes which have previously converted the solid fuel into a gas – gasification or anaerobic digestion. Gas is cleaner and easier to use but the process of conversion is more complicated and expensive. The gas produced also burns at a higher temperature (allowing for greater efficiencies) and can be used to generate electricity as well as heat.

Gasification occurs when solid fuel is reacted with steam and air (or oxygen) in a gasifier. Anaerobic digestion occurs when organic materials decompose without the presence of air in a digester.

The fuels – either burnt directly or turned first into gas – are:

- Fire wood (logs or chips cut from timber felled in managed woodlands, individual felled trees, even hedgerow trimmings).

- Manufactured wood fuel products (logs, briquettes or pellets).
- Grown agricultural products, such as short rotation coppice fuel (fast growing tree species like willow) and Miscanthus (a grass). Also known as energy crops.
- Waste agricultural products (mushroom compost, straw, animal and vegetable waste).
- Landfill gas (derived from rotten vegetation buried in landfill).

Wood heating

Types of wood fuel and appliance

The choice of fuel and appliance goes hand in hand, the one informing the other. There are three main types of wood fuel – wood logs (either 'real' or manufactured), pellets and chips. Appliances are generally designed to accept just one of them. You could throw pellets and chips on a log burner but it would be an inefficient use of the fuel. You certainly can't throw logs in anything other than a log burner.

Logs (real or manufactured) are burnt in individual room heaters or in separate batch boilers kept away from the main living space, quite often in an outbuilding. Batch boilers heat water, which is stored in an accumulator vessel and then distributed by a pump around the central heating system. Individual room heaters are often fitted with a back boiler connected to both the domestic hot water supply (via a cylinder) and/or a central heating system. Pellets are burnt directly in pellet burners for room or central heating, or in separate boiler units connected to central heating systems. Chips are generally burnt in separate boiler units connected to central heating systems. You wouldn't really consider a wood chip boiler for an installation less than 40kW so they are more suited to district heating schemes, community projects, educational facilities and commercial operations. The chips themselves are also low cost and readily available, but quality of supply is often a concern.

Logs are fed into a burner by hand, while for pellets and chips it is possible for them to be fed by hand – in the case of single room heaters or small boiler units connected to central heating systems – or via automated auger or vacuum systems which carry the fuel load from a hopper (a large container for storing fuel) to the boiler (usually for larger systems). These hoppers can be conveniently filled direct from the lorry and the user need not touch a single pellet or chip. Wood pellets require less storage volume than chips and logs, are easy to ignite and to handle.

Efficiency of wood fuel systems – getting the most out of your system

The efficiency of wood fuel heating systems is dependent on the following factors:

- The level of moisture content in the wood.
- The performance of the wood stove or boiler.
- The suitability of the heating appliance for the job you want it to perform.

Improving performance by reducing the moisture content of wood Wood with high moisture content – in other words, green wood – will burn ponderously and inefficiently, sometimes using as much energy to expel the moisture as it does generating heat. This is a waste of good wood, an unsatisfactory living experience (who wants to wait for heat on a cold night!) and a costly way to warm a room. All species of wood have a high moisture content when they are first cut and must be left to dry for one or two years. This process of drying out is known as seasoning.

Manufactured logs and pellets are always well seasoned and have a low moisture content. They are a 'dry' fuel, burning to the maximum efficiency and providing the user with a consistent heat. Wood chip should be burned dry, although some wood chip boilers are designed to burn wood with a higher moisture content than others. Cut logs are sold green or seasoned but should never be burned green. Some wood (such as the tree species Ash) will burn better than others green but all wood benefits from a year or two's worth of drying.

Anyone with only a small amount of storage space should buy a seasoned wood fuel product. Many wood sellers prefer to sell their wood green, forcing you to make your own arrangements for drying; a practical impossibility for many people as the amount

Fig. 8.4. Biomass heating

Four options: pick to suit your needs and heating demand

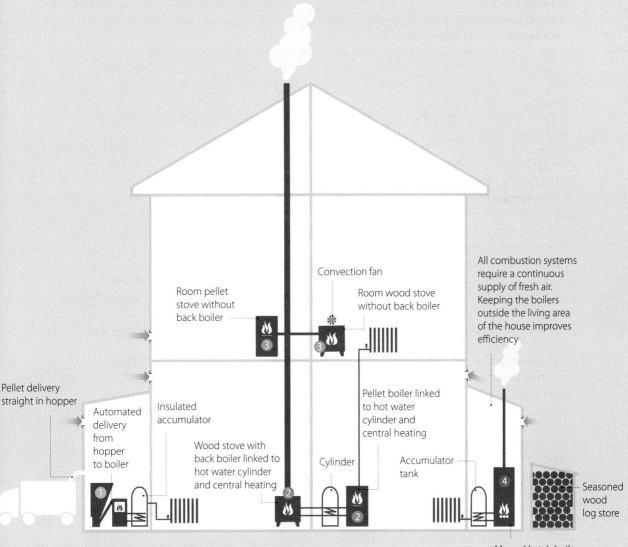

Convection fan

Room pellet stove without back boiler

Room wood stove without back boiler

All combustion systems require a continuous supply of fresh air. Keeping the boilers outside the living area of the house improves efficiency

Pellet delivery straight in hopper

Automated delivery from hopper to boiler

Insulated accumulator

Pellet boiler linked to hot water cylinder and central heating

Wood stove with back boiler linked to hot water cylinder and central heating

Cylinder

Accumulator tank

Seasoned wood log store

Manual batch boiler using logs

① Automated pellet boiler linked to central heating and DHW.

② Manual feed pellet or log burner with back boilers for central heating and DHW.

③ Individual room heaters without back boilers.

④ Batch boiler, linked to central heating and DHW.

	Density	Moisture content	Calorific value	Calorific value	Calorific value
	Kg per solid m³	%	MWhrs per solid m³	MWhrs per stacked or piled m³	KWhrs per kg
Unseasoned beech logs	1000	50	2.1	1.5	2.1
2-year air-dried beech logs	650	18–25	2.6	1.9	4.0
Unseasoned conifer logs	1000	60	2.3	1.6	2.3
2-year air-dried conifer logs	450	18–25	1.9	1.4	4.1
Pellets	800	8–10	3.8	3.1	4.7
Chips	375	20–30	2.3	1.0	3.6
Briquettes	800	8–10	3.8	3.8–3.1	4.7

Fig. 8.5. Comparisons of different energy values and moisture content for different types of wood fuels. Source: Home Heating with Wood (to be published in late 2012 as Choosing Wood Heating), Laughton.

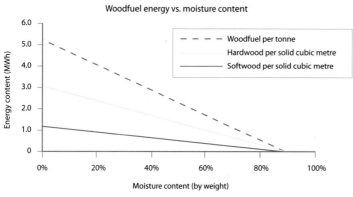

Fig. 8.6. The energy value of wood increases as the moisture content decreases. Source: Home Heating with Wood (to be published in late 2012 as Choosing Wood Heating), Laughton.

Fig. 8.7. Effective heat energy per kilogram of wood at various stages of seasoning. Source: Home Heating with Wood (to be published in late 2012 as Choosing Wood Heating), Laughton.

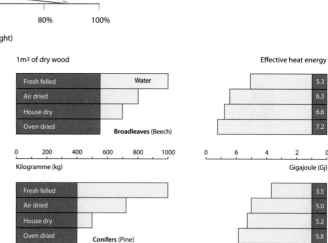

of room required to season two years' worth of cut logs may exceed 40m^3 for larger houses.

As a rule, logs and chips are bought by volume (logs often by the 'load'), whereas pellets or briquettes tend to be bought simply by weight and with a given moisture content due to consistent processing methods. With years of experience it becomes possible to 'see' the moisture content in cut logs because you become familiar with the look and weight of seasoned and green wood. But to be doubly sure, use a moisture reader. If you're using a supplier you don't know, ask to test the wood before it is unloaded. Turn back wood that doesn't make the grade. Freshly cut timber has only approximately half the calorific value by weight of well-seasoned wood.

Appliance performance – the six stages of thermal degradation Once a wood is seasoned and ready for burning its effectiveness as a wood fuel is dependent on the appliance it is fed into. To perform successfully as a fuel, wood must go through six stages of thermal degradation when it is burnt (thermal degradation involving a series of complicated chemical reactions that reduces the solid wood to combustible gases). The first three stages are endothermic, which means they involve heat being sucked from the existing fire. Only as the fire passes through stages 4 and onwards – the flash point being 230°C – will there be a net heat gain.

If a wood is green (or, indeed, very damp from rainwater), the time spent in the first three phases will be longer. The quicker the wood can pass through the first three stages the quicker and longer the heat will be delivered to the room and not used by the fire itself. It is also important to maintain a high area of 'reaction' surface, which means allowing as much of the wood as possible to be exposed to the fire. Consequently, logs should be split so that they are no more than 10cm in diameter. With pellets, briquettes and chips a high area of reaction surface is automatically assured.

Modern stoves are designed to bring the wood efficiently through to stages 4 and beyond by controlling the flow of air into the fire in an effective way. The worst type of wood fire is an open grate. The air is uncontrollable and it is quite possible that the

fire never goes beyond stage 3. This brings all sorts of problems, as incomplete combustion also leads to higher levels of pollutants escaping up the chimney. If phase 6 is not reached, the unwanted chimney emissions can increase tenfold, the risk of carbon monoxide poisoning goes up and the efficiency of combustion drops by over 10%.

To get the most out of wood fuel it is important to invest in a modern stove or boiler that maximises the potential for complete thermal degradation through the use of controllable air vents and in some cases, internal pipes and motorised dampers linked to electronic sensors. Although these types of stoves and boilers are more expensive, the running costs will be less (unless you have a never ending supply of free wood of course), the gain in thermal comfort greater and the environmental performance far superior.

The source of air supply Burning wood requires oxygen. For every kilogram of dry biomass used, several m^3 of air has to be supplied. If a wood burning appliance uses warm air from inside a building, then cold air from outside is sucked into the building to replace it – not a good idea if heating the building is the purpose of burning wood in the first place! Also, modern energy efficient houses are built to high levels of air tightness which won't let enough cold air into the building.

One way around this is to use a 'room sealed' appliance which is directly connected to an external air supply, although it should be noted that Building Regulations still specifies that air flow into the room should be the same with or without a direct external air supply. The other solution is to use a boiler designed for installation outside the heated part of your house. Modern log and pellet boilers are well insulated and almost all the heat energy is used for heating water and not the room they are in. Therefore, they can be placed outside, for example, in a (ventilated) utility shed attached to a house.

The suitability of the heating appliance There are a huge range of wood heating appliances to choose from (see http://guide.hetas.co.uk/guide.html) and beyond the question of efficient thermal degradation there are a number of important issues to think about before a decision is made. These issues are both technical and, for want of a better phrase, personal. Unlike most of the other technologies discussed in this book, there is a strong aesthetic charm to wood stoves which sometimes overrides more logical considerations, as well as a number of personal considerations to take account of; wind and water turbines are rarely picked for pleasure, wood stoves are.

Let's break down these issues into a series of questions. We haven't got space here to answer all of them but they will help you formulate a plan. In the questions below I have used 'I' instead of 'we' throughout, but in reality most people are making a decision with someone else, be it their spouse, other members of a committee, business partners, council officials and so on. It's worth bearing these questions in mind with the plural firmly fixed in the consciousness. It's also worth looking ahead too – especially if you are responsible for a community building. At some point you may have to pass on the operation of your system to someone else. What will they think of the decisions you made?

Technical considerations

- Do I need my appliance to heat one room, the whole building, or to supply hot water?
- Do I want to use my wood heating in addition to an existing heating system, or as a replacement?
- How much heat do I need? What is the maximum heat loss of the whole building? We've discussed in detail (on pages 117-119) how to go about calculating the heat load of a building. Like any other source of heat, under- or oversizing a wood burning stove or boiler can lead to inefficiencies, either because the boiler does not heat the building quickly enough or it delivers too much heat, requiring the unhappy tradition of opening the windows to let the heat out.
- How often do I need heat? This is a fundamental question. Is your building occupied all the time or only infrequently? Wood burning boilers are more expensive than conventional boilers so the frequency of use is important – especially since the introduction of RHI. Some wood burning stoves are more suited to regular sustained use than others. If you only need heat for the evenings when you happen to be home, a wood burning stove is perhaps a more cost-effective option than a boiler. Spend a little time jotting down occupancy times (both present and potential future).

- Where will the air come from? Ideally, your wood burning appliance is either located outside your building and supplying heat to the inside through service pipes, or connected to a direct external air supply. Whether or not air has to be taken from the inside of the building it is important to ensure there is enough ventilation. Building Regulations have very strict rules about the amount of air that must be allowed to flow into a building to compensate for the loss of air in a space as it is sucked into a fire, and for good reason these rules are the same whether you have a direct external air supply or not. A professional heating engineer will ensure that the Regulations are met, but its worth asking before any work is done what additional ventilation is needed.
- Is it more efficient to keep a boiler in an outbuilding where the delivery of wood fuel is more convenient and the ventilation can be controlled without reducing the heat of the building?
- What is the peak heat output required for the room the appliance is situated in – in other words the maximum amount of heat needed to raise the room temperature to an acceptable standard on the coldest day of the year? Boilers kept in an outbuilding are designed to keep as much of their heat as possible. Room stoves give as much of their heat as possible to the room, unless they are fitted with a back boiler, in which case a proportion of the heat goes into the hot water in the boiler and is then distributed via radiators to other rooms in the house and/or the hot water cylinder. The heat output is measured in kW; 1kW is equal to around 3400 BTU (British Thermal Units). All stoves and boilers state a peak heat output.
- Will my wood heating system combine with a solar water heating system? The simple answer is yes, in most cases, but you will almost certainly need to make adjustments to existing pipe work and cylinder storage.
- Will my heating system require a heat leak radiator? This is a safety measure used in central heating

systems, allowing hot water to be dumped into a specific radiator in case the pump fails or the electricity is turned off. The radiator is commonly sized at between 10-20% of the stove's heat output to water volume. The appliance manufacturer should specify size requirement.

- How much storage space do I have and how much do I need? Pellets take up less space than chips and logs and can be stored easily inside the house in bags.
- Can I keep my fuel dry? Felled logs should be kept in an open sided shelter with a roof. The wind and air does the seasoning. Pellets are already seasoned and need to be kept in a totally dry environment, just as if you were keeping them inside. Any damp ingress will soften the wood and slow down their burn rate. Wood chips are

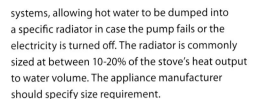

	Quantity per annum	Units
2-year air air-dried logs	8–18	Stacked m³
Pellets	4–9	Tonnes
Chips at 25% moisture content	40–100	Loose m³
Briquettes	4–9	Tonnes

Fig. 8.8. Wood quantities for full central heating from a boiler at 70% efficiency. Source: National Energy Foundation/Logpile http://www.nef.org.uk/logpile/faqs.htm

kept either in a hopper, protected bunker or wood shed with sides.

- Do I have a reliable supply of fuel? See the 'Where to buy wood' box on page 153.

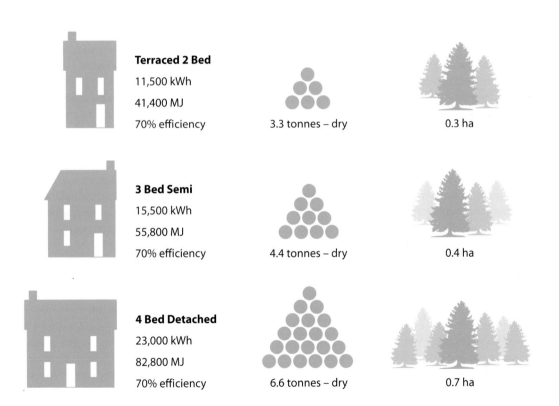

Terraced 2 Bed
11,500 kWh
41,400 MJ
70% efficiency

3.3 tonnes – dry

0.3 ha

3 Bed Semi
15,500 kWh
55,800 MJ
70% efficiency

4.4 tonnes – dry

0.4 ha

4 Bed Detached
23,000 kWh
82,800 MJ
70% efficiency

6.6 tonnes – dry

0.7 ha

Fig. 8.9. Estimated annual wood fuel consumption for different types of houses.
Source: National Energy Foundation/Logpile http://www.nef.org.uk/logpile/faqs.htm

- Do I want an automatic fuel mechanism?
- Do I want auto or manual ignition, thermostatic controls and automatic burn control? Some stoves and boilers include a range of control devices to maximise efficiencies and give the convenience associated with more conventional fuels.
- Is my hearth big enough? Building Regulations specify hearth size and type.
- Do I need to make any alterations to my chimney? Building Regulations are now much stricter regarding the installation of new wood fired stoves and boilers. Any work that affects an existing chimney – including fitting a new stove or liner or creating a new chimney – now comes under Building Control.
- Do I need to store heat for use later? Some boiler systems use water accumulators (heat stores or cylinders) to give greater control over the flow of heat to radiators and underfloor systems, and to enable integration with other heat sources (for example, solar thermal, heat pump or conventional backup boilers). Accumulators store (or accumulate) heat for later use – just the same as any hot water cylinder. They are the hub of a sophisticated heating system; all heat enters the accumulator and leaves when it is needed to do the various jobs required. Separating the heat from the load in this way improves efficiency. They are always used in association with batch boilers that burn a large amount of wood very quickly and efficiently. Other kinds of heat stores include Swedish style 'Kakkelovns', which store the heat in ceramic tiles placed around the stove.
- Have I made a price comparison with other boilers and fuels? Is this the most cost effective solution for my situation? Calculating fuel use and average cost is very difficult with logs (because of variations in quality and quantity) but easier with wood chip and pellets. There is a comparison chart on www.stovesonline.co.uk/doc-l-fuel-prices.html. Logs are the cheapest fuel, electricity the most expensive.

- Do I live in a smokeless zone? Can I still burn wood if I do? See page 153.

http://www.nef.org.uk/logpile/faqs.htm is an excellent resource to follow up on many of these questions.

Personal considerations

- Do I care more about romantic aesthetics or about energy efficiency and the environment? More often than not, pretty stoves with glass are significantly less efficient than more industrial looking boilers. Choosing a less efficient appliance means you waste wood and produce more smoke, which contains substances that are harmful to both humans and the climate.
- Do I value convenience? Some systems require more manual effort and planning. See 'Light my fire' box.
- Am I confident dealing with wood fuel suppliers and checking for moisture content? Whereas gas is gas and oil is oil, wood quality varies enormously according to the supplier.
- Am I physically fit? In other words, can I chop, stack and move wood and will I be able to do so in 25 years time? Anyone suffering from repeat illness or a back problem that might make it impossible to keep their heating system going when it is needed most should think carefully about how they can manage any disruptions. This might mean having a backup plan or choosing a system that requires less manual handling.
- How much time do I have or am prepared to set aside for stacking and cutting wood and loading and cleaning my appliance?
- Which fuel is going to fit my lifestyle and the use of the building?
- Do I want to use my appliance for cooking? There are several cooking 'ranges' on the market but also smaller stoves and boilers that allow a limited cooking facility. Be wary though, the fact that in the hands of most a wood fired cooking range is an inefficient unruly beast of heat doesn't stop many people desiring them simply because they are beautiful.

Where to buy wood

- Under the 'Firewood' or 'Coal and Solid Fuel' section in telephone listings.
- Tree surgeons, local landowners and farmers.
- Joinery machine shops and builders' merchants. My sister and her husband get all their wood supply as offcuts from a builders' merchant – the company would otherwise have to pay to dispose of this waste wood.
- National databases of suppliers, such as those held at www.nef.org.uk/logpile and www. stovesonline.co.uk/services/wood-suppliers.html.
- An internet search on 'wood', 'firewood' or 'fuel'.
- Wood burning appliance suppliers.

Wood prices

When asking for wood prices, it is useful to be clear from the outset about the following:

- The moisture content (dry basis) and for how long it has been seasoned.
- The species of wood.
- The price per volume or weight.
- The average length and diameter (will it fit in the stove or will you have to chop it yourself).
- Delivery costs and whether delivery includes a tail lift or crane.
- Packaging; whether loose, wire cage, pallet and/ or big bags.
- Whether VAT is chargeable at 5% or 20%.
- Whether the wood is from a 'sustainable' source.

Planning, Building Regulations and finance

- Planning permission. Planning permission is not normally necessary for most existing domestic and community buildings but could well be for listed buildings, or those in conservation areas or National Parks. Additional storage facilities and boiler houses may need planning permission. If you are planning a substantial new community

Light my fire

www.stovesonline.co.uk/how-to-burn-wood.html is a good website if you want some advice about the basics of wood stove management – even down to showing you how to light a fire.

sized power plant you will of course need planning permission.

- Building Regulations. Building Regulations concerning all wood fired heating appliances are covered by Approved Document J. This can be downloaded at www.planningportal.gov. uk/uploads/br/BR_PDF_ADJ_2010.pdf For a brief summary, visit www.stovesonline.co.uk/ stove_building_regulations.html Since 2010 any work that affects an existing chimney – including fitting a new stove or liner – or creating a new chimney must be passed through Building Control. Boilers are covered by Water Regulation (G). Systems will need to be signed off by Building Control or a competant person (HETAS approved installer).
- Clean Air Act. The Clean Air Act created smokeless zones in populated areas. Wood can be burned in a smokeless zone if the appliance has an exemption certificate or the fuel is authorised. To see if you live in a smokeless zone or whether your appliance or fuel is exempt or authorised visit http://smokecontrol.defra.gov.uk
- RHI installation. To be eligible for commercial RHI all equipment and installers must be certified under the Microgeneration Certification Scheme (for all systems under 45kW). Householders can apply for the Renewable Heat Premium Payment via the Energy Saving Trust. Log burning wood stoves are not eligible.
- SAP calculations. These are used to determine the efficiency of a new or refurbished building. The Standard Assessment Procedure (SAP) helps to reduce CO_2 emissions associated with new builds. Fitting a wood burning stove can provide

a 9.8% emissions saving – nearly half of the saving needed.

- Water Regulations. These apply to all fittings in contact with the water utility's supply. Responsibility for compliance lies with the householder and installer. See www.wras.co.uk
- Pressure Equipment Directive. The manufacturer or the commissioning engineer is responsible for compliance.

Cost of wood fuel heating

The capital cost of installing a wood fuel central heating system is higher than conventional oil and gas systems, but the fuel costs are lower. To calculate the payback period – that is, when the fuel price savings equal the additional capital costs – you will need to know how much fuel you expect to burn each year, the cost of this fuel compared to other fuels, the capital cost and expected maintenance costs (which at potentially £200 per year are presumed to be higher than those for other heating systems). www.nef.org.uk/logpile/pellets/cost.htm and www.biomassenergycentre.org.uk are good places to get comparison costs. On the Biomass Energy Centre

Comparable costs of boilers

Estimates for a three bedroom semi-detached house (around 15kW). Prices will vary depending on size, efficiency, make and model. In addition, there is the cost of the flue and installation (£1,000 to £1,500, plus VAT).

Boiler type	Estimated cost
Condensing gas or LPG boiler	£500–£600
Condensing oil boiler	£1000–£1100
Solid fuel (coal) boiler	£1400
Coal- or wood stove (or inset) with back boiler to run 10 radiators	£600–700
Pellet stove (without back boiler)	£1500
Log/pellet boiler	£3500

Source: National Energy Foundation (NEF).

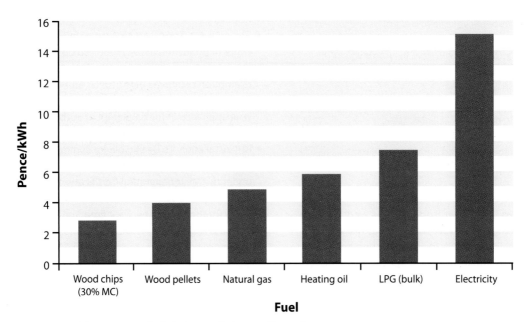

Fig. 8.10. Typical domestic prices for fuels. Source: The Biomass Energy Centre
http://www.biomassenergycentre.org.uk/portal/page?_pageid=75,59188&_dad=portal&_schema=PORTAL

website go to reference library, then facts and figures, then costs. Obviously, additional storage space, chimney alterations, boiler houses and so on will add to the cost. Payback time will be considerably improved if you can successfully apply for the Renewable Heat Premium Payment or RHI (though log burning stoves are not eligible).

Heat pumps

How do heat pumps work?
As the name suggests, a heat pump 'pumps' heat energy from a source – typically ground, air or water – to a target or 'sink', the fluid in your heating system for instance. It is important to understand that there is heat energy even in things we consider to be cold, even air at temperatures well below freezing point still has heat energy!

Normally heat energy only flows from higher to lower temperatures – for example, from a warm house to the cold outside. To make it flow in the opposite direction, energy (typically electricity) is needed – just like pumping water uphill. In this way, it is possible to extract heat energy from, say, the

ground at 5°C and use it to heat water to 40°C. Heat pump systems use a collector, for example, a series of pipes buried in the ground, to collect heat energy from a low temperature heat source.

Inside the heat pump, heat energy from the collector is extracted and pumped 'uphill' to a higher temperature, through expansion and compression of a refrigerant fluid or gas. The refrigerant 'soaks up' heat as it expands and vaporises (think of a camping gas container getting cold when you release gas as you're cooking), and releases heat when it is compressed and condensed (ever noticed your pump getting hot when inflating a bike tyre?). This released heat can then be used to raise the temperature of the fluid in your heating system, typically to temperatures around 30-45°C.

The heat source
The heat sources of heat pumps (stores of solar energy (not geothermal)) do not themselves maintain a constant temperature, although ground and water source temperatures are more constant than air temperatures, which can change hour by hour as well as through the day and night or through the

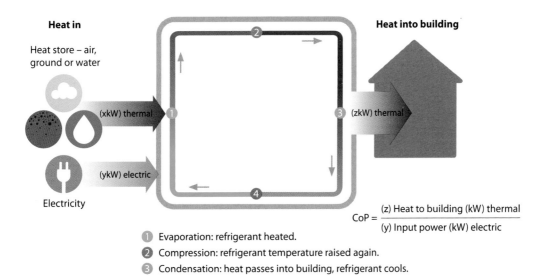

$$CoP = \frac{(z)\ \text{Heat to building (kW) thermal}}{(y)\ \text{Input power (kW) electric}}$$

1. Evaporation: refrigerant heated.
2. Compression: refrigerant temperature raised again.
3. Condensation: heat passes into building, refrigerant cools.
4. Expansion: refrigerant expanded, ready to be re-heated.

Fig. 8.11. How heat pumps work.

Fig. 8.12. Heat pumps

Four options: pick to suit your site

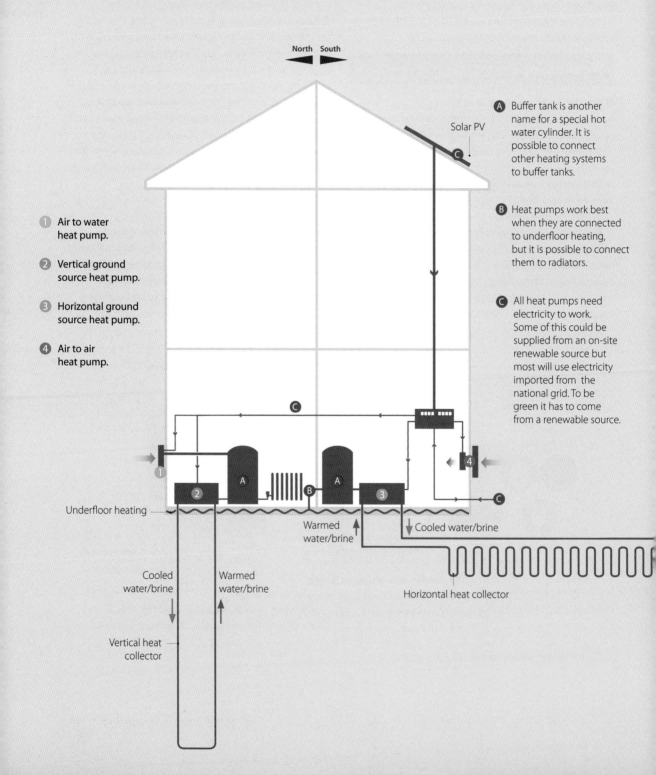

North   South

Solar PV

A Buffer tank is another name for a special hot water cylinder. It is possible to connect other heating systems to buffer tanks.

B Heat pumps work best when they are connected to underfloor heating, but it is possible to connect them to radiators.

C All heat pumps need electricity to work. Some of this could be supplied from an on-site renewable source but most will use electricity imported from the national grid. To be green it has to come from a renewable source.

1. Air to water heat pump.

2. Vertical ground source heat pump.

3. Horizontal ground source heat pump.

4. Air to air heat pump.

Underfloor heating

Warmed water/brine

Cooled water/brine

Horizontal heat collector

Cooled water/brine

Warmed water/brine

Vertical heat collector

seasons. Water temperatures in aquifers are more constant than those found in rivers and lakes, which can obviously freeze, and ground temperatures are the most constant of all – deep ground temperatures (from vertical bore holes) more so than shallow temperatures (where horizontal pipes are used).

Heat pumps need electricity to move heat energy from a low temperature source to a higher, more useful target temperature. A bigger difference between source and target means more electricity is needed to move a unit of heat energy and, therefore, the heat pump is more expensive to run and environmentally less beneficial.

Measuring heat pump performance

The performance of heat pumps can be assessed using two measures – the (more useful) seasonal performance factor (SPF) and the coefficient of performance (CoP). Both compare the amount of energy that a system outputs to the amount of energy that goes in to make it work. But whereas the CoP is tested to one set of conditions the SPF takes into account weather patterns and use of the heat at a higher temperature than that at which it was tested.

The CoP is the ratio between how many units of heat energy a heat pump delivers and how many units of electrical energy it consumes. It depends on the temperature difference and so, as temperatures of source and target change over the season, so will the CoP. The seasonal performance factor (SPF) expresses the performance over a year, and also includes electricity consumption of components, such as pumps and auxiliary heaters.

Installed in a suitable building, a ground source heat pump should achieve a SPF between 3 and 5 and an air source heat pump a SPF between 2 and 3. For example, if over a year a heat pump system delivered 12,000kWh of heat energy and consumed 4,000kWh of electricity, then the SPF would be 3. Since air temperatures are generally lower than ground temperatures during the coldest months when the heat demand is highest, SPFs for air source heat pumps are generally lower than those for ground or water based systems.

Air source heat pumps are generally cheaper to install and more universally applicable, requiring no land access and no complicated ground or pipe works. However, whether you use ground, water or air source heat, it is important to understand that the system will only bring environmental and economic benefits if a sufficiently high SPF is achieved.

Electricity is currently predominantly produced in power stations which are only 30% efficient. As a result, a unit of electricity costs four times as much as a unit of heat from mains gas, and has three times the CO_2 footprint. So you would need an SPF of three or four to 'break even' against a good gas boiler! As a result, heat pumps – especially air source – are currently most suitable if the alternative would not be mains gas but a more expensive and carbon-heavy form of heating, for example, oil or electricity.

The main factors affecting the SPF are the temperature difference between the source and the target. There is not much you can do to change the temperature of ground, water and air, but it is important to use a big enough collector. Try to extract too much heat from too small a piece of ground and in very badly designed systems the ground will 'permafrost'!

On the delivery side, you can reduce the target temperature by choosing the right heat delivery system and with good insulation. If you insulate as much as possible and choose the right delivery system (underfloor heating, for example), the temperature required to heat the fluid in the system will be much lower – which in turn means a higher SPF.

Sizing a heat pump

Having already read most of this book, by now you will know that there is always a logical way of approaching heating design:

- Reduce demand through insulation and efficient control.
- Choose the most effective delivery system – for example, air vent, radiator, underfloor heating.
- Size the collector or heat source so that it delivers the temperatures you need in the most efficient way.

In all cases, under- and oversizing the heating system can lead to excessive amounts of waste. In the case of heat pumps it can lead to disastrously high electricity bills. Oversizing increases capital costs (why pay for a bigger system than you actually need?) and leads to system malfunction; undersizing creates a heating shortfall, which means that the system will automatically compensate by drawing heat from a backup heating source, an electric immersion heater for instance. This is not a good way of heating a building!

The supply temperature to a building should be kept as low as possible, always below 50°C. This is fine for central heating systems provided an underfloor heating system is used. If underfloor heating is not possible, radiators will need to be oversized by at least 30-40% to compensate for the lower temperatures (radiators are normally designed to run closer to 70°C). Note that there are now heat pumps on the market that can theoretically deliver at high temperatures of 65°C and more, but heat pumps will always run much more efficiently at lower temperatures.

Heat pumps can be used exclusively for central heating systems and not connected to a domestic hot water (DHW) system, but many systems combine both through a buffer cylinder – this uses a standard immersion to raise the temperature to the 60°C required by law to prevent legionnaires. Some heat pump systems are able to supply water in this higher range (often using an off-peak tariff and large water storage facility), but most do not. The reason for this is that high flow temperatures cause low CoP.

A ground source heat pump has the potential to provide most of the heat you need in spring and autumn and any you might need in summer. It will probably provide most of your heating in winter if you have a very well insulated house, the ground conditions are right, the system has been sized correctly (according to the Carbon Trust many existing heat pump systems have ended up costing their owners more in fuel because they were sized incorrectly) and you don't mind a bit of chilliness. It wont provide for your DHW needs, unless you are prepared to pay higher electricity bills. Most heat pump systems are fitted in combination with some

sort of back-up or even primary heating source. Air source heat pumps are not likely to meet your heating needs.

Since the cost of getting your sizing calculations wrong are so high, a professional heat pump installer should calculate the following for you:

- Your heat load and load profile (when the heat is needed).
- The infiltration rate (see pages 76-78).
- The heating requirements for each room (don't trust existing radiator sizing – they are usually wrong).
- The heat pump collector size (this will depend on the first three things in this list but also on external factors to do with the site, weather patterns, seasonal temperature changes and so on).

Heat pumps – are they for me?

Heat pumps are an impressive solution for highly insulated, constantly occupied buildings that love to receive a constant circulation of low temperature heat. They are no good in draughty old homes, or even in places where the occupants are hardly ever there, for example, village halls that are only occasionally used. In these cases, a heat pump becomes an expensive heat source that doesn't really provide any environmental benefits.

So bear the following questions in mind when making a decision:

- Is it technically possible to fit a heat pump system? This is not just about access to land or water but also the way your building is constructed. The best scenario for a heat pump installation is a new building where both the building and the heating system are designed by the same architects and engineers, and in tandem. This does not mean you can't retro-fit a heat pump system but, if you do, it might require substantial additional floor work for the underfloor heating, either raising or digging out your existing floor. In many cases this is a practical impossibility.

- Is my land the right land? This does not apply to air source heat pumps, which are more universal, but water and ground source heat pumps, which are site specific. Rocky or well drained soils do not suit ground source heat pumps, a better CoP is achieved in damp or marshy ground. This is because water is a better conductor than air, so heat stored in the the soil is able to get into the collector easier. If too much heat is drained from the land too quickly the heat pump will not function and in cold weather it can lead to the ground freezing. One rule of thumb suggests that a heat collector area of at least two and a half times the ground area of the building is required to provide enough heat. However, you should never use rule of thumbs to make a proper assessment about suitability; instead, get a quote from three different installers. If you want to do your own maths, a list of relevant calculations that can give a good estimate of the size of ground loop and heat output required is available from the IEA Heat Pump Centre (see Resources).
- If my building is badly insulated can the insulation levels be improved to the point where heat pumps are a good idea? Some buildings are built in such a way that super insulation is practically or financially impossible. It may also be wise to arrange a pressure test to check for infiltration rates.
- Will a heat pump fit? The size of the heat pump unit will vary depending on the output but will be larger than a gas boiler of the same capacity. Typically, a 12kW single packaged unit will be about 1000 x 600 x 600mm and weigh between 150kg and 220kg. Products with integral DHW storage can weigh double this when full. Heat pumps can be installed inside a building, mounted on the side of a building or kept in a separate outbuilding.
- How often is my building occupied? If your building has a low occupancy with low conventional fuel use, a heat pump is never likely to deliver the fuel cost savings you are looking for long term.
- What is the alternative to using a heat pump? If your other option is mains gas with a modern condensing boiler then heat pumps are often a bad choice. If the alternative is electric radiators then heat pumps are an option worth considering.
- Would choosing a cheaper heating option allow you to deliver an environmental solution that saves more CO_2 in another area?
- Do I need quick bursts of heat? Heat pumps are not good at providing quick bursts of heat when a room is cold; they are a slow response heating system.
- Do I love shag pile carpets? If you are using underfloor heating you are advised not to have carpets (they interrupt the transfer of heat from the floor to the room), so heat pumps will affect the cosmetic decisions you make inside a building. This will also affect the cost of interior finishes. Wooden floors can be used with underfloor heating, but there are some issues as wood can dry out and crack. In all cases, it is worth checking with your underfloor heating supplier.

Planning, Building Regulations and finance

Planning permission. Installing a ground or water source heat pump does not normally require planning permission. Installation is allowed under permitted development rights. However, if you live in a listed building or conservation area you should contact your local council to check. Air source heat pumps currently require planning permission but the law may change within the lifetime of this book so please check. Additional buildings built for the purpose of housing heat pump technology may need planning permission.

Building Regulations. Installation of heat pumps will have to comply with Building Regulations. Your installer will tell you what you need to do.

RHI installation. To be eligible for commercial RHI all equipment and installers must be certified under the Microgeneration Certification Scheme (for all systems under 45kW). Householders can apply for the Renewable Heat Premium Payment via the Energy Saving Trust.

System type	Ground coil costs (£kW)	Heat pump costs (£kW)	Total system (£kW)
Horizontal	250–350	350–650	600–1000
Vertical	450–600	350–650	800–1250

Fig. 8.13. Estimated costs per kW of installed capacity. Source: The Building Research Establishment.

SAP calculations. These are used to determine the efficiency of a new or refurbished building. Heat pumps are defined as a controlled heat source. For specific ratings, see SAP guidelines.

Water Regulations. Permission may have to be sought for some water source heat pump installations. Check with your local water control authority.

Electrical connections. Most domestic properties are connected with a 'single phase' electricity supply (see chapter nine). This is usually fine if the maximum output is 12kW (sufficient to heat a well insulated property of around 200m^2). Anything bigger than this may require a 'three phase' supply. Some single phase supplies are inadequate, and require a transformer up-grade; especially in remote areas. So, before you do anything, check the adequacy of your single-phase supply.

Your installer will almost certaninly need to talk to the distribution network operator (DNO) before connection.

Access issues and surveys. Because ground and water source heat pumps involve some disruption to sites, a check should be made as to the legal implications of such disruptions. Is your site connected to an SSSI? Is there a danger of unearthing archaeological remains?

How much will a heat pump cost?

The cost areas for a heat pump can be broken down roughly into:

- Capital costs.
- Running costs (fuel).
- Maintenance/service costs.

On top of this there is the cost of any additional insulation and of installing underfloor heating if none exists already.

Capital costs

It is risky to give definitive capital cost guidelines because capital costs depend on so many variables. However, the Energy Saving Trust estimates typical system costs range from between £9,000 and £17,000. The Building Research Establishment (BRE) does provide the example in figure 8.13 above for ground source heat pumps.

The capital costs of an installation fall if one system can be constructed to supply several buildings at the same time. For example, a ground source system supplying five houses could save up to 15% for each house compared to the cost of making a system for just one house. This is because the costs of design, land clearance and commissioning make up a substantial part of the capital costs – worth bearing in mind for community projects.

Running costs

The unit cost of electricity and the SPF of your system are the key factors in determining running costs. Signing up to special heat pump tariffs or Economy 7 or 10 can reduce the average unit cost. Having your own renewable electricity supply may also reduce the unit cost of electricity (partly because you will be paid to produce the electricity through the Feed-in Tariff scheme). In terms of estimating the value of a heat pump system it is also important to compare the unit cost of the electricity needed to power your heat pump to the cost of other heating fuels.

Inspiration is global. This is the message to take from Nigel and Karen Lowthrop's community project, ECONS. Marrying a natural resource with the needs of their local community, they have turned the 34 acre woodland they own in the West Lincolnshire village of Disney into a social enterprise which offers potential support to over 10,000 people. The idea originally came from a conference they attended in Canada where they heard about a Costa Rican project run by the Pro Iguana Verde Foundation. You never know when inspiration will strike, or where it might take you.

ECONS – Economic Community Opportunity Natural and Sustainable – is not as directly related to energy conservation or energy production as some of the other case studies in this book, but it does show how communities can effectively change the lives of their members by making use of a natural resource in a sensible, pro-active and environmentally friendly way. It has four principal aims: to maintain the woodland for use by the public; to teach and help young people develop so they can realise their potential; to create products and services valuable to the community; and to promote the cause of environmentalism and sustainability.

How do they do this? Hill Holt Wood educates and trains young people excluded from school and the long term unemployed, giving them the lasting benefits of education, practical skills, the ability to work in a team, increased confidence and time spent outdoors. Whilst working in the woodland, the programme participants (which include Solution 4, Entry 2 Employment, Future Jobs Fund and Knowledge Transfer Partnerships) learn eco-construction techniques, wooden furniture manufacture, conservation principles and the installation of reed bed water purification systems.

The most recent Ofsted report gave Hill Holt Wood an outstanding Grade 1 in achievements and standards. It stated that learners 'often have a very low starting point but make huge progress in a short period', that Hill Holt

Community space built with materials from the woodland.

at which point they became a charity, making it possible to drive profits back into the work.

They have also been careful to make the most of ongoing funding opportunities as well as one-off grants, but also to develop self-sustaining commercial operations alongside. Now their income comes from a mix of woodland product manufacture, environmental consultancy, training and Service Level Agreements with local district councils (for the provision of ranger services). They have also cleverly tapped into free resources when they became available. For example 41% of the costs of a recently constructed woodland community hall came from staff and timber resources from within the wood itself, or from nearby woodlands owned by the Wildlife and Woodland Trusts.

Wood is developing 'work of exceptional quality' and has 'an outstanding work ethic'. Hill Holt Wood also has the third highest level of 'positive outcomes' in its region.

It's a remarkable achievement for an organisation that started off in the Lowthrop's living room with an informal meeting of interested people who came together because Nigel Lowthrop had started writing articles about the woodland in five parish magazines. The progress of Hill Holt Wood could almost be described as textbook community development; from the initial meeting came a woodland management committee that evolved over ten years into a Community Controlled Membership Organisation Not for Profit Ltd by Guarantee, a Social Enterprise Limited by Guarantee and, finally (due to an increase in size), a charity. The board now has seven individual members, three corporate members, two staff members, one funder and a faith director.

The success of the organisation can be put down in part to the understanding that the project should not be dependent on two people alone, and would be better able to deal with expansion if a diverse pool of talent could be relied upon. Also, the ownership of the land has been transferred over time from the Lowthrop's to the business (initially the business rented the building and woodland using a £100,000 loan). They were also careful to set up structures that would maximise the return on investment (ROI) for their community. As a Social Enterprise Limited by Guarantee Hill Holt Wood was exempt from tax for the first three years

In addition, the local architecture firm drew up the plans for no cost, the turf roof was fitted for no cost and a large number of discounts were secured from sympathetic companies.

But all of this success would have been impossible without the support of the local planning authorities which, as it happens, was hard won through the support of the local community. As Hill Holt Wood is based in an ancient woodland any development was initially rejected out of hand. Following this, Nigel and Karen contacted the local authorities and the Director of Planning and invited them out to see and hear for themselves the work and the plans.

Their relationship with the two district authorities is now fantastic – they are exemplars of a true working partnership. Both Nigel and Karen work hard at this – they are members of local community groups, the Local Service Partnership and various working groups. Karen is also a Social Enterprise Ambassador, mentoring other social entrepreneurs. They speak at and attend corporate events and know all the senior councillors.

Based on his experience with planning and local authorities, Nigel's key observation and advice is that the planning law needs to change. At the moment it does not recognise the applicant, just the application. But the applicant is relevant – if the owner is the community then it should be assessed differently, based on social considerations. If the government wants to see more successful projects like Hill Holt Wood developing, this is a key change.

Chapter Nine

Renewable electricity

Fig. 9.1. Renewable electricity

Two scenarios (mainly PV): grid-connected and stand alone

House number 1: Grid-connected, generating own electricity and buying and selling to the grid

House number 2: Remote cottage using wind or hydro and PV combined in an off-grid system

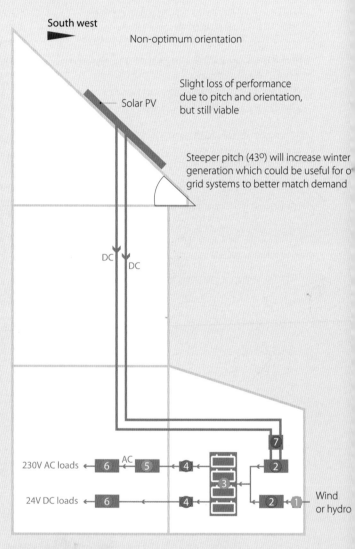

South — Optimum orientation / Unshaded

Solar PV

Optimum angle 30°– 40°

DC   DC

Renewable electricity imported and exported via the grid

South west — Non-optimum orientation

Solar PV — Slight loss of performance due to pitch and orientation, but still viable

Steeper pitch (43°) will increase winter generation which could be useful for o⁤ grid systems to better match demand

DC   DC

230V AC loads ← 6 ← AC 5 ← 4
24V DC loads ← 6 ← 4

7
2
3
2   1 ← Wind or hydro

House number 1 key:

1 Grid-link inverter
2 DC isolator
3 Generation meter for FITs calculation
4 Consumer unit
5 Import meter
6 Appliance

House number 2 key:

1 Dump load
2 Charge regulator or controller
3 Battery set
4 Low volt disconnect
5 Off-grid inverter
6 Consumer unit/distribution board
7 DC isolator

Understanding renewable electricity

Before we talk about generating renewable electricity, it's important to understand the basic concepts of energy and power and the units we use to measure them.

Perhaps most fundamental is energy. When we talk about how much electricity has been generated or produced *over a period of time* we talk about **energy**, and the most common unit for measuring energy is the *kilowatt-hour* (kWh). Often 1kWh of electrical energy is simply called a 'unit', and you will find kWh units on your household energy bills. When we talk about the *rate* at which energy is consumed or produced *at any one moment* then we talk about **power.** Power is measured in watts (W), a thousand watts makes a kilowatt (kW).

Devices for producing or consuming electricity typically come with a power rating. For example, you can buy a 20W light bulb or a 5kW wind turbine. When the power consumption or production is constant, we can calculate energy by simply multiplying the rated power with time. For example, if a 20W (0.02kW) light bulb is switched on for 100 hours then it consumes 2kWh of electricity.

But with generators of renewable electricity things are usually not so easy.

The rated output of a wind turbine or a solar PV module only tells us how much it can produce under specific rated conditions – for example, for wind speeds of 12 metres per second (m/s) or a solar radiation level of 1000W/m². A wind turbine that produces 5000W at 12m/s might only produce 1200W when the wind speed is 6m/s. Usually these rated conditions are close to optimal conditions and so the rated output can be thought of as a maximum output.

This figure does not tell you the amount of energy that you will actually be able to use because this is determined over a period of time, time in which all sorts of things can occur to prevent the maximum power output being reached; most usually the wrong kind of weather, but also a mechanical or electrical failure, or the existence or arrival of physical obstacles and natural realities that get in the way of generation

(for example, in the case of solar PV clouds or of course, night-time).

It is important to know this because expecting any renewable technology to perform at the rated power output all of the time is likely to lead to disappointment, unrealistic financial planning and power shortages if you are off-grid. Any installer selling you a system must assess realistic performance over its lifetime, which means taking into account all the things that are likely to stop a machine performing at its rated output.

Your installer should then be able to provide a figure for the amount of electrical energy a system can realistically be expected to provide over a period of time, measured in kilowatt-hours. This figure will then have to be balanced against the expected demand, which is also measured in kWh. It is possible for anyone with patience to calculate these figures – and for each of the technologies we outline the basic details of how it is done – but (for systems under 50kW) a qualified engineer accredited by the Microgeneration Certification Scheme (MCS) should be employed to create the final assessment. In fact, with wind turbines there is an MCS document that states the expected kWh per month, or similar figure, for each of a range of average windspeeds. These figures are much more important than the rated power. The hard part is knowing what your average windspeed actually is: beware of over-optimistic predictions by installers!

Grid connection and off-grid systems

Off-grid systems are often called stand-alone. This means that the electricity is produced and consumed within a closed power system. The key components of almost any stand-alone system is the generator (wind turbine, solar PV module(s), micro-hydro turbine), a set of batteries (known also as a 'battery' or battery bank) and a number of electrical components that allow the power generated to be used in a safe and sensible way (of which more later).

Not all stand-alone systems use batteries but they are useful for balancing loads over time and

Other useful technical terms: current, voltage, AC/DC

For the purposes of this book it is not really necessary to understand current, voltage and AC/DC. Indeed, if your sole goal is to employ an installer to connect a small renewable energy system to the grid you can probably get away without knowing or needing to understand current, voltage and AC/DC at all. However, knowledge of these terms is essential for stand-alone systems and can be useful for everyone else.

Photovoltaic (solar PV) panels and some forms of wind turbines produce electricity in a way such that the current – the flow of electricity measured in amps (A) – is always in the same direction, and this is known as direct current (DC). Many electrical appliances can be run using direct current, but only in stand-alone systems. In grid-connected systems all appliances are run using alternating current (AC).

DC is changed to AC when the electricity is passed through an inverter. A little bit of energy is lost when this conversion takes place but it is only significant for very small loads. The conversion allows us to use renewable energy in a wider range of appliances. This is why most stand-alone systems will also have an inverter, allowing the user to use both AC and DC appliances.

It is important not to confuse amps with 'amp-hours'. In the context of stand-alone systems, amp-hours describe battery capacity. For example, a 200 amp-hour battery will give 20A of current for 10 hours, or 10A of current for 20 hours. This is important to know when sizing a battery bank because it will tell the user how long a battery will provide power, without a charge.

Stand-alone users will also need to know about voltage. Voltage is the driving force, the pressure that drives the current through cabling to reach its target: driven from A to B. Some appliances are designed to run off 24 volts (V), some off 12V. Voltage can be selected through system design and electronic controllers to reduce losses and keep cable sizes practical.

for providing an extended power supply. However, batteries are difficult to work with and the cost of replacing them can wipe out the environmental and economic benefits of having renewable electricity (see box below). Even with a battery bank, you might still need a backup power source to supplement your primary provider – either another renewable technology or a diesel generator. For example, combined wind and PV systems work well together because the PV produces more power in the summer when average wind speeds are at their lowest.

Connection to the national grid completely does away with the need for batteries and these days a grid connection is the most likely scenario for a renewable energy system. There are no financial or environmental merits in using a stand-alone system if you could be connected to the electricity grid. Only the remotest sites will not benefit from grid-connection, and this is only because the cost of connection is prohibitively expensive. There is certainly no merit to being off-grid for the sake of being off-grid.

The grid effectively acts as a giant battery, allowing you to buy and sell electricity at will. When the renewable energy system is generating electricity any surplus beyond demand is sold to the grid. When the system isn't generating electricity, or isn't generating enough, the required power is received from the national grid.

Assault on batteries

This is what small-scale wind power guru Hugh Piggott says about batteries in his book *Wind Power Workshop*, 'I hate batteries. They are the worst feature of stand-alone systems. They are heavy enough to damage your spine, full of corrosive sulphuric acid, could give you a nasty burn if you short-circuit them and they give off explosive gases. It has been calculated that the cost of replacing the batteries (perhaps once every seven years) can be roughly the same as the cost of buying the same amount of power as the system produces in this period from the mains supply.'

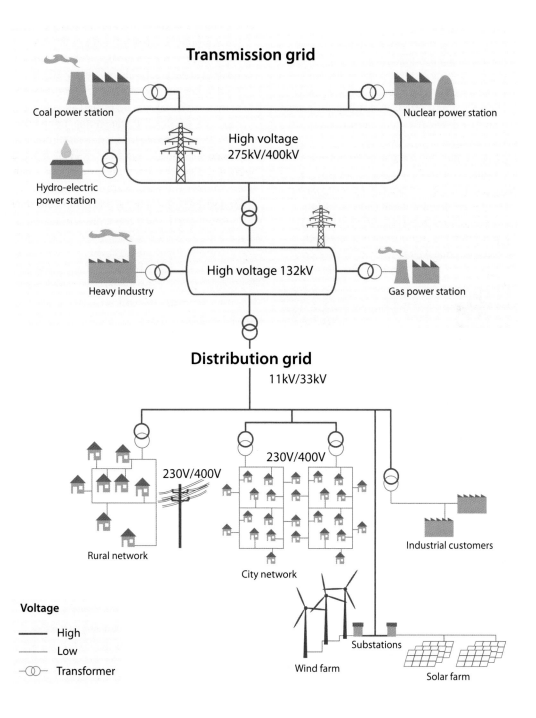

Transmission grid

Coal power station

Nuclear power station

High voltage
275kV/400kV

Hydro-electric
power station

High voltage 132kV

Heavy industry

Gas power station

Distribution grid
11kV/33kV

230V/400V

230V/400V

Rural network

City network

Industrial customers

Voltage

High

Low

Transformer

Wind farm

Substations

Solar farm

*Fig. 9.2. The network hierachy of the national grid. Local distribution grids feed into the bigger transmission grid.
Source: Choosing Solar Electricity, Goss.*

You would always have a meter to see how much electricity your house buys from the grid, and under FITs a separate generation meter to count the units your renewable energy system produces. Currently, the amount of electricity sold to the grid from small renewable generators is often not metered, instead it is estimated or 'deemed' as a fraction of how much has been produced.

It is also worth pointing out that grid-connected systems do not carry on working when the grid 'goes down', so they will not provide a backup power supply when there is a power cut. This is for safety reasons, to stop power being fed into the grid. Loss of mains protection will automatically disconnect a system if there is a major electrical disturbance on the line.

What do renewable electricity systems have in common?

All wind, solar PV and hydro systems have the following two things in common:

- They are site specific, meaning that they will only perform at their best if sited in places that suit them. They might still produce acceptable amounts of power in sites that are less than optimum but the benefits of the technologies will diminish the further they get from the ideal, to the point where a system will not perform at all. The rated output of any technology is the most power the device can ever produce. The resource varies. The same system could be installed in two separate places and yet produce wildly different amounts of electricity.
- They do not produce constant power. The amount of electricity a system is capable of producing is entirely dependent on weather conditions, which vary continuously, from hour to hour, day to day and throughout the seasons. The sun doesn't always shine, the wind doesn't always blow, water doesn't always flow. This creates problems for remote sites where a continuous power supply is essential but no grid connection available. It can also create a tension between

supply and demand in grid-connected systems. For example, PV modules generate all their electricity during the day but in most domestic settings in Britain the electricity is most often used during the evening and at night. Owners of PV systems can end up buying and selling most of their electricity rather than using their own. This is different in countries with a high air conditioning load. Here PV is a good match to the load profile.

Bear both of these things in mind whenever you are making decisions. Is the technology right for the site? What are my estimates for energy yields based on?

Financing

Since there is no fuel, the cost of renewable electricity is borne mainly in advance of use (that is, during the installation phase) and in any maintenance costs that might occur over the lifetime of the system. This means that the financial performance of all systems will be assessed by the length of time it takes to payback both the initial investment and any expected maintenance costs (see section on operation and maintenance on page 169) compared to the comparable costs of alternative fuel sources. A renewable energy system in an off-grid location compares favourably to the alternatives (diesel generator or grid connection) because over the lifetime of a system the alternatives are usually more expensive. This is not the case with a grid-connected system.

Without any grant or subsidy, most small-scale renewable electricity would currently still be more expensive than mains electricity. But incentive programmes such as the Feed-in Tariffs make renewable electricity generation very attractive. And as prices for renewable energy generators fall while electricity prices rise, small-scale renewable electricity gets closer to 'grid parity', where it pays for itself without subsidy.

Payback periods vary enormously between technologies and between individual installations. It is essential for an installer to estimate a payback time based on the individual site; the variables are so many that it is difficult to give anything but very rough estimates in a book like this.

Some sites undergo months or years of assessment before a final plan is agreed, particularly in the case of wind, where wind speeds must be monitored over long periods before a project gets the go ahead. Solar PV is easier to estimate because the position of the sun in the sky at any given time can be calculated and long-term averages for air pollution and clouds can be obtained from satellite data for a specific location.

Even if a careful calculation is made, it is possible that the installation will still be unable to deliver on promise. On the other hand, some systems will do better than expected. Much of it depends on the weather, which may turn out to be different from long-term averages. That is the nature of renewables.

Legal issues

At the domestic level the legal considerations for renewable energy systems are similar to those for heat installations – the key issues being planning permission, Building Regulations, health and safety legislation, MCS accreditation and electrical compliance certification. For grid-connected systems permissions might also need to be sought from the Distribution Network Operator (DNO) which will insist that the installation complies with Engineering Recommendation G83/1, G83/2 or G59/1 (depending on the size of the system).

MCS accredited installers will handle these permissions but it is useful to know what legal responsibilities you have as an owner of a power system, both during the installation phase and throughout its use. It will also be worth finding out whether any installation will contravene or affect an insurance or mortgage policy in any way.

Community level projects will also need a legal structure within which any power generation might operate – be this social enterprise, charity or small business. This requires familiarity with and adherence to public liability insurance, employment law, tax and accountancy procedures, health and safety at work practices (such as risk assessments), perhaps the payment of share dividends, as well as much stronger links with and responsibilities towards the DNO (if the power system is grid-connected) and, usually, a green electricity supplier. The bigger the system gets the more potential danger there is of serious injury and the more rigorous the need for maintenance checks. Nicky Ison and Jarra Hicks talk more about community systems on pages 191-206.

Operation and maintenance

Operation and maintenance duties and costs for renewable energy systems vary enormously between systems. Grid-connected systems require less maintenance than stand-alone systems (as there are no batteries) but require more rigorous electrical checks and safety measures to prevent individual systems being a danger to other users of the grid. Solar PV systems, usually with no moving parts (unless they have sun tracker devices) and fewer electrical components, require the least amount of regular attention.

Wind and micro-hydro power, with some moving mechanical parts and a more complex set of electrical requirements, are more demanding. Wind and micro-hydro power are also more likely to suffer from 'acts of nature' – storm damage being more likely in the case of wind and pipe blockage in the case of micro-hydro (owners sometimes have to dislodge the most gruesome decomposing objects from inlet pipes!).

Of course, it is possible in the design phase to guard against these things, but it is not possible to guarantee that safeguards will always work. Owners of systems need to be prepared for events, especially if their systems are not connected to the grid. A backup power supply (either another form of renewable energy or diesel generator) will often be essential. We can't go into detail about all operation and maintenance duties here – it is something you should discuss in detail with your installer. Never be fobbed off with a cheap sales talk or 'nothing can go wrong' attitude.

Sizing a renewable energy system

Introduction

Sizing is something an installer will do, though with bigger schemes it may be worthwhile to get a second opinion from an independent consultant. It is worth pointing out that when we use the word 'size' in this context we are not describing a physical size but the amount of power a system is capable of producing – although it is true that in general the more power you require the more space you will need.

Sizing a stand-alone system

This will apply to very few readers of this book, but for a stand-alone system, the basis for sizing a system is the expected load (or power demand) over time. The installer will also need to know the maximum amount of power that will ever be needed at any one time – the peak demand – and the number of days the user needs the battery to carry on delivering power if no renewable power is generated – known as the 'days of autonomy'. If the system is required to run 24/7, a larger battery store will be necessary to see the users through any long periods when the weather doesn't work in the system's favour, and to ensure a larger generating capacity (which could include a backup renewable energy source or a diesel generator).

There is a balance to be found between increasing the size of the battery store indefinitely (remembering the extra expense and health and safety hazards described previously) and finding an alternative energy source that will provide the required amount of electricity. Combining wind and solar PV is a popular option but other mixes include hydro and/or a diesel generator. If you can accept some periods without electricity then your renewable energy system can be much smaller (and hence much cheaper). For more information read CAT Publication's *Off the Grid* by Duncan Kerridge.

Sizing a grid-connected system

With grid-connected systems, it is usually much less important to match supply and demand. Under the Feed-in Tariff the primary factor is the total amount of electricity generated, not how much was exported. More often than not, financial rather than technical considerations tend to determine the size of a system, although there are technical limits to the size of some grid-connected installations – for example, the size of a south facing roof for solar PV, or, the type of electrical connection between the system and the grid.

Most homes (but not all so it's worth checking) are connected to the grid using single phase connections, but larger buildings and industrial units are sometimes connected via three phase connections. The size of the system can usually be no larger than 3.68kW if you are connected with single phase, and 11.04kW on a three phase connection, but your DNO may use their discretion to allow a little bit more.

Solar PV

The illustration on page 164 shows the components of an average grid-connected PV installation: the modules generate electricity, which is then fed via an

Inverters: what do they do and how long do they last?

In a grid-connected PV system, the inverter performs three functions:

- It converts the DC electricity produced by the PV modules into the 230V AC, 50Hz electricity required to feed into the grid.

- It ensures that the system complies with standards set out for generators supplying electricity to the grid (small generators need to conform to the G83 standard).

- It optimizes the operation of the PV modules by tracking the 'maximum power point' (MPP), where voltage and current are optimal for maximum power output. Please note that you should use inverters with two separate MPPT units for modules facing in different directions; or micro-inverters or individual module MPPT systems.

Inverters have a shorter life expectancy than the modules themselves. Expect them to last maybe 10-15 years. Replacing the inverter should be included in any system costing.

inverter into the main consumer unit (the box in your house containing all the trip switches, circuit breakers and fuses). From here the electricity is fed directly to household appliances or, if not used as it is generated, sold to an electricity company (also known as a public electricity supplier (PES)), via the grid.

A 'total generation meter' records every unit your PV system has produced – whether you used it yourself or sold it to the grid. This allows the electricity company to work out the generation tariff part of the Feed-in Tariff payments. Currently with small PV schemes, the amount of electricity you sell to the grid is often not actually measured. Instead it is estimated or 'deemed' as 50% of the total amount generated – this will change as more houses are connected to smart meters which measure electricity flows both from and to the grid. The meters and inverters take up very little space.

Is your site right for solar PV?

You can calculate whether or not your roof is suitable for solar PV using tools and techniques described in CAT's book *Choosing Solar Electricity* by Brian Goss, or by using CAT's Solar Calculator (http://info.cat.org.uk/solarcalculator), but an installer will also do the job for you. The three main considerations are:

- Orientation.
- Roof tilt.
- Shading.

The optimum solar PV site is an unshaded south facing roof with a tilt angle of between 30° and 40°. The further you stray away from the optimum, the less confident you can be that your system will deliver affordable electricity; although, unless your roof is north facing, shaded for large parts of the day or year, or at a very steep pitch (something like a Mansard Dutch style roof seen in the photograph here) the productivity losses are not severe and can be made up by increasing the size of the PV array – the system will produce a bit less but it might still be viable. The Energy Saving Trust produces a useful *Buyers guide to solar electricity panels* which includes a comparison table of efficiency losses.

Taking all the above into consideration, an installer may measure potential output using computer software based around a system with a specified maximum rated output, measured in kWp (kilowatt peak – the amount of power it can produce under standardised conditions), and give you a figure for average annual energy production (measured in kWh). They will also work out a cost and a payback time, which will include an estimate of expected Feed-in Tariff payments.

All these initial assessments are very important because without them you can't know whether or not your system is performing as it should be once it has been installed. Although, it is worth noting you can't know this properly without measuring the irradiance and temperature. Bear in mind that over time the weather varies enormously. It's only after years that you'd expect to get results similar to the predictions.

The installer should also give you an indication of what maintenance costs there will be and provide instructions on how you can monitor your system. As Feed-in Tariff payments are based on the amount

What does the rated capacity actually mean?

When we talk about the size of a PV module or roof, we typically talk about the *rated capacity*. This figure describes the output of the component at a particular level of sunshine ($1000W/m^2$) and temperature (25°C). So when I say "4kW PV roof", what I mean is "a PV roof with modules which would produce 4000 Watts if the solar radiation was $1000W/m^2$ and the temperature 25°C." Of course, at any given moment the actual conditions will be different from these standard conditions – when it is cloudy a 4kW roof may only produce 400W. Under identical conditions, the energy output is directly proportional to the rated capacity – a 4kW roof will produce twice as much as a 2kW roof – and two systems rated at 4kW should produce pretty much the same amount of energy, even if they use different modules.

Fig. 9.4 (left). Various slopes and pitches on traditional and modern British roofs and energy losses caused by pitch variations.

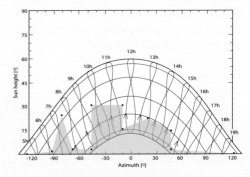

Fig. 9.5. Sun path diagram with shading included.

Fig. 9.5a. Diagram showing effect of array azimuth on performance reduction due to reflection (PV arrays on roof pitch facing away from street).

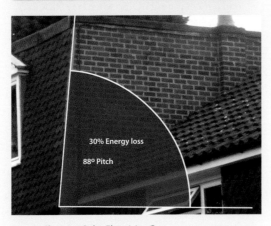

Fig. 9.5b. 100% corresponds to the tilt and orientation which gives the maximum total annual solar radiation (1093kWh/ m²/y on a surface orientated due south at a tilt of 34°) on a fixed surface in Cambridge (52°13'N,0°06'W).

Source: Choosing Solar Electricity, Goss.

of electricity produced, it pays to ensure that any interruptions in supply are kept to a minimum, whatever the reason.

Renewable energy production is not an exact science though and the amount of generating capacity with any PV system also depends on cloud cover and air mass (in other words, particulate pollution) – a particularly cloudy summer will cause generating capacity to fall and you might not hit your expected targets, although over the course of a twenty five year period this should balance out!

Size and cost of installation

Most domestic systems have a maximum rated output of between 1 and 4kWp and carry an average cost of about £3,000 per kWp (though this is coming down and does vary depending on contractor, component costs, local competition, whether the installation can be combined with other work and, of course, on precise system size); if you increase generating capacity beyond 4kW (strictly speaking 3.68 kWp, after inverter losses) there are added complications regarding the connection to the grid and the way that connection is regulated (complications which carry an additional cost).

Providing you can overcome the technical issues with higher load grid connections, the size of array is really only restricted by the amount of money you can afford to invest and the size of your site. Note, however, that there are different tariff bands for the Feed-in Tariffs (4kW, 10kW, 50kW and so on) and it is always economically beneficial to be just below, rather than above, a tariff boundary.

Module choices

Currently, most PV modules installed in the UK use thin slices of crystalline silicon. Within this group, we distinguish between polycrystalline and monocrystalline modules. The former typically have a shiny blue appearance with visible sparkly silicon crystals and are slightly less efficient, whereas the more efficient polycrystalline modules have a more homogenous dark blue or black appearance.

It may surprise you to hear that the efficiency of the PV modules is often not very important. Efficiency primarily determines the area the modules require.

A sample costing

The sample costing below is meant only as a rough guide. It does not factor in potential rises in electricity prices or decreases in module efficiency, and it assumes that the household will use 50% of the power it produces. It could use a lot less than this if the occupants are out at work most of the generating day. Having said this, 85% of the annual income is made from the Feed-in Tariff payments. Since the Feed-in Tariff payments are paid over twenty five years this household could earn £1,500 a year tax free for ten years after the initial cost of the system is paid off.

Rated power output: 3.6kW
Annual energy output: around 3000kWh (based on an annual production of 850kWh per 1 kW of rated PV capacity – a typical value for a south facing, unshaded roof in central England).
Use of electricity: 50% used by the householder at the time when it is produced; 50% sold to the grid.
System cost: £11,000 fully installed, plus £3,000 for inverter replacements over lifetime.
Annual income: around £900 (based on Feed-in Tariff payments of £700 and savings on electricity of £200).
Payback time: 16 years.

Over the full 25 years the (inflation-adjusted) net-income is around £8,000.

Please note that at the time of writing the cost of installations were coming down because of increased competitiveness within the industry and the FIT's cut: the system cost of £11,000 may well now be less, which means the payback time is lower and net-income higher. Shop around for the best quality and value.

A PV module rated at 1kW will take up around 7m^2 of roof area if it is 14% efficient and only 5m^2 at 19% module efficiency. But the less efficient 7m^2 module will produce the same amount of energy as the more efficient 5m^2 module. This is because energy yields are determined by the total rated capacity.

If the size of your PV system is limited by your roof area then you could consider high efficiency modules. But if it is your wallet and not the roof size that limits your ambitions then you might be able to get more energy for your money if you use lower efficiency modules.

Type of installation

When carrying out an initial assessment of your site, installers will also take you through the various options for mounting your PV array. These are:

- Integrated arrays – where the PV modules become part of the roof material (replacing the tiles or slates).
- Non-integrated arrays – where the PV modules are fixed on top of the existing roofing material.
- Flat roof arrays – where the PV modules are fixed to a flat roof but angled to give the array the desired tilt and orientation.

Integrated arrays might be the only option in a conservation area where planning permission may not otherwise be given. They are best fitted when the roof has to be replaced anyway but they can be less cost-effective than non-integrated arrays, which tend to be the most common type of solar array on retro-fitted property.

An installer will also make sure your roof is strong enough: not only to carry the weight of the panels but also to resist any potential uplift caused by winds, or downward pressure caused by the accumulation of snow on or around the modules. Where there is any doubt the installer will consult a structural surveyor.

Up until now I've talked exclusively about roof mounted systems, but PV systems can also be wall mounted on the facade of a building (though there will be a loss of yield due to the absence of tilt), and rack or pole mounted on the ground (in which case they can be angled precisely to choose yield profile required). This might be a solution if you are not permitted to fix an array onto your building. So long as they do not suffer from shading, these systems are just as viable (if not more so) than roof mounted systems.

Performance monitoring and maintenance

PV systems are reliable and not prone to breakdown but monitoring equipment will quickly enable the user to spot a problem and get it rectified promptly without significant loss of generation. You should be able to get a reading for how much energy your PV modules have produced, either from the inverter or from the generation meter. A daily check is not really necessary but most owners love to know what's going on with their system so doing so can become a pleasurable habit; otherwise at least once a week is recommended.

PV yields and seasonal variation

Websites such as the CAT Solar Calculator (http://info.cat.org.uk/solarcalculator) or PVGIS (http://re.jrc.ec.europa.eu/pvgis/) provide very useful tools for predicting how much energy your PV roof can produce in a typical year. However, do keep in mind that some years are sunnier than others, and, more importantly, that some months are *much* sunnier than others! The graph opposite, based on PVGIS, shows typical seasonal distribution of solar yields in a location with a total annual yield of 850kWh per kW installed capacity. As you see, yields can be more than five times as high in summer than in winter.

Grid-connected systems are usually fairly maintenance free. Most pitched roof arrays are steep enough to be self cleaning (by rain, hail, snow). A thin film of dirt will build up at times but this will only reduce output by a few per cent and access to the roof will usually be too expensive to justify cleaning. If you can access your array without specialist equipment, an annual clean is recommended; otherwise (for example if you need to hire a cherry picker or scaffold tower) once every five years is cost-effective. Cleaning should be done with a bucket of warm water with mild soap and a soft cloth.

Annual routine check

- Check array not excessively shaded.
- Check for nests and remove if a problem.
- Check for cracks, discoloration or other degradation of PV modules.
- Check inverter hasn't become hot, dusty, covered.
- Check wiring and fittings for damage or discoloration.
- Check handover documentation is still present and that all parts are accessible and clearly labeled.

How long do PV modules last?

As PV modules have no moving parts they can last a very long time. Most modules that exist in the world today were manufactured in the last 10 years, although some PV roofs installed in the 1980s are still operating, confirming that PV modules can last 30 years or more. However, there is a decrease in output over time, around 0.5%–1% per year. MCS approved modules conform to a standard that sets down a permitted efficiency loss. Check MCS for details.

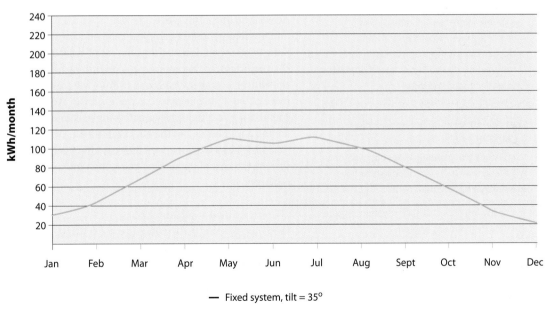

PV estimate: 52°20'23" North, 1°53'22" West

— Fixed system, tilt = 35°

Fig. 9.5c. Seasonal variation in PV energy generation.

Approval - planning permission and Building Regulations

More comprehensive details are available in *Choosing Solar Electricity* but here's a quick round-up.

Most small-scale solar PV systems installed on existing buildings do not require planning permission. The modules however do have to be less than 20cm from the plane of the roof and are recommended to be no closer than 30cm from the edges of the roof. If your property falls within one of the following categories you would definitely need to apply for planning permission or listed building consent and convince the planning officer of the aesthetic merits of your system:

- In a conservation area and your property is visible from a public right of way.
- In a designated area: National Park; Norfolk Broads; Area of Outstanding Natural Beauty (AONB); or Site of Special Scientific Interest (SSSI).
- Is within the curtilage of a listed building.

These permissions do not necessarily prohibit PV systems but the onus is on you to convince the planners that your system will blend in with its surroundings or have exemplary architectural merit.

The following aspects of a PV system require Building Regulations approval:

- Spread of fire to adjacent properties – Part B.
- Wind uplift and structural strength – Part A and BS 6399 Part Three.
- Electrical wiring installation – Part P.
- Accessibility (for example to controls) – Part M.

The installer will also have to seek DNO approval under regulation G83/1.

Wind power

Capturing the energy in wind and turning it into useful power is exhilarating, complicated and on a small-scale potentially expensive. We tend to measure the cost-effectiveness of a particular generating technology by comparing the cost of each unit of electricity produced with other methods. The unit cost of wind power can vary enormously depending on where the turbine is placed; site selection is crucial.

Although wind is a free source of energy it behaves in a completely random way, changing from moment to moment. The amount of power available is constantly changing so it is important to find a site where the wind conditions are consistent enough to produce power economically.

Wind turbine performance – choosing a good site for wind

The economic and system productivity of a wind turbine is dependent on average wind speed – measured in metres per second (m/s). This is average wind speed, so will take into account periods of complete calm and absolute fury. If the wind speed doubles, the amount of available power rises eightfold, so theoretically a wind turbine placed in a site with an average wind speed of 8m/s will create 8 times more power than one placed in a site with an average wind speed of 4 m/s, although in practice the maximum power is limited and this reduces the effect quite a bit. Even so this obviously has a big impact on the cost-effectiveness of the system; the cost of the turbine being the same wherever it is placed.

Cut-in speed – when the turbine starts generating electricity

Every wind turbine also has a cut-in wind speed, the point at which it is able to start generating power. If, for example, the cut-in speed is 3m/s (which it quite often is) the turbine will not start producing any power until the wind speed reaches that point. If your site has an average wind speed which is less than the cut-in speed of a wind turbine, there is very little point having one. OK, there will be some days when the wind is strong enough to generate power, but on the whole the turbine won't do anything (in fact a minimum viable annual windspeed should be approximately 5.5-6m/s, although windspeed alone will not determine viability).

This might be acceptable in some situations (for example, on a boat or caravan) where a little power delivered occasionally is enough to charge an essential battery, but not for a normal domestic or community wind power system. Wind turbines also have a rated wind speed (at which point the wind turbine produces its rated power). You can see what this 'looks like' in the typical power curve below; the crucial thing to see is that the power in watts goes up as the wind speed increases.

Rotor diameter – choosing the right blade length for your power requirements

To capture all this power wind turbines have to be able to sweep through a significant amount of air with each rotation; the greater the swept area the more power they are able to capture. Figure 9.7 on page 178 shows the amount of energy generated in kWh per week for five sizes of wind turbine at different annual mean wind speeds.

You'll see that a small wind turbine with a 2m diameter swept area will be just over 10 times more effective at wind speeds of 7m/s compared to those

of 3m/s, but at 3m/s a turbine sweeping through a 4m diameter will be 14 times more effective than one with a swept area of 1m. You can also see in this table that increasing the diameter of the blades and positioning a turbine in a place with a much higher wind speed can increase energy production by 220 times.

It's worth pointing out that whilst this is good information to know (and essential if you are making your own wind turbine) most people will buy an MCS accredited wind turbine, and these will all be sold not according to blade length, but to a power rating – for example 2.5, 5 or 6kW – which describes the wind turbine output at a particular reference wind speed. However the most important figure to get from the MCS rating is not the power in kW but the energy production per month for a given site's mean windspeed.

Avoiding turbulence

The quality of wind is also important. Wind turbines hate being in zones of turbulence. When wind encounters obstacles, it is not simply slowed down but parcels of air become separated from each other

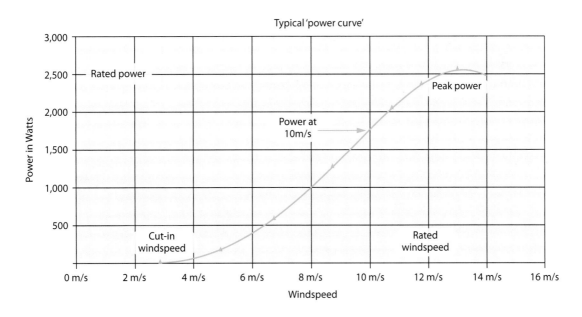

Fig. 9.6. Typical wind turbine power curve showing the amount of power generated at different windspeeds.
Source: Choosing Wind Power, Piggott.

Swept area	3m/s	4m/s	5m/s	6m/s	7m/s
1m diameter	1	2	4	7	9
2m diameter	3.5	9	17	26	36
3m diameter	8	20	40	60	80
4m diameter	14	35	70	100	140
5m diameter	22	56	106	164	220

Fig. 9.7. Energy in kWh per week for five sizes of wind turbine at different annual mean windspeeds. Source: Choosing Wind Power, Piggott.

and swirl off in different directions. This causes the turbine to chase air; it faces the wrong direction or runs at the wrong speed to make best use of sudden gusts of wind, the result being a reduction in the amount of energy captured as well as in the life of the machine and some of its parts.

Sites for small wind turbines are nearly always near to some sort of obstacle so the best advice is to place the wind turbine as high as possible – 10 metres higher than anything else within 200 metres (although the planning process makes this difficult in many areas). Here it will experience higher wind speeds and stand a better chance of avoiding

turbulence (figure 9.8). Increasing the tower height in sheltered places from 10 to 20 metres can mean a rise in wind speed of 20-30% and an increase in yields of 1.5-2.0.

All this information is vitally important when planning a wind power project. With such dramatic increases in energy production at stake you need to get everything right, but especially the siting. This is why a grid-connected community project will always work out better value than trying to connect the equivalent number of homes with individual generators. The issues are different for homes not connected to the grid, but bringing resources

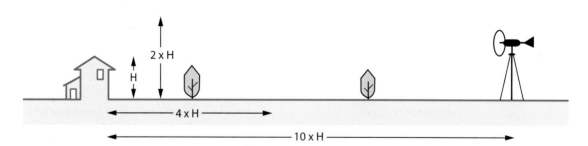

Fig. 9.8. Windflow over an obstacle. The zone of turbulence actually rises as the flow progresses downstream. If the obstacle is a building, then it should not block the prevailing wind. If you have a block of trees near the site, then you may find less turbulent wind above the trees than away from them. Source: Choosing Wind Power, Piggott.

together can allow people to build to a scale and on a site that enables them to maximise return on investment. This is not to say that community wind projects are not without their difficulties, as our case study on page 183 shows.

Gathering data

No commercial wind system will go ahead without site specific wind speed and turbulence intensity monitoring. This is done over one or more years using an anemometer and other data logging equipment. Professional anemometers (wind speed loggers) can be very expensive, but there are now products such as the PowerPredictor (www.bettergeneration.com/power-predictor) which are very affordable and make it easy to interpret the data, even for non-experts.

Just remember; you should always measure wind speeds in the location and at the same height as you plan to mount your turbine. So you will need to put a mast of the right height in the proposed location and measure wind speeds for at least a few months.

There are internet tools which aim to provide average wind speeds for locations (see box) but these have been found to be extremely unreliable and should only ever be used as the very first step – to decide whether it's worth spending a few hundred pounds on wind measuring equipment. It would be foolish to spend thousands or tens of thousands installing a wind turbine without having a very good idea about how windy it is.

Costing a wind system

CAT's *Choosing Wind Power* by Hugh Piggott takes you through all the separate component requirements for wind power generation (at the time of writing a new edition was set to be published in late 2012, the old edition being out of print). This will give you a good idea of how system costs vary depending on whether or not you connect to the grid. Off-grid systems will be more expensive because of the cost of batteries and other components.

A 2.5kW wind turbine (around 3.5m rotor diameter, typically mounted on a 10-15m mast) will cost at least £15,000 including installation. In a good, windy location it can easily produce 4,000kWh per year,

giving an annual Feed-in Tariff income of £1,300. A 6kW wind turbine system costing £28-30,000 can produce 10,000kWh annually, paying £3,100 – although this does depend on average wind speeds. Wind systems are eligible for the Feed-in Tariff as long as they are installed by an MCS accredited installer, using MCS accredited criteria and technology.

Planning issues

Wind power installations require planning permission as set out in Planning Policy Statement 22 (PPS22); you will also have to consult with other stakeholders, including neighbours. Hugh Piggott (www.scoraigwind.com) believes that current UK planning attitudes make it impossible to site wind turbines on tall enough towers to allow them to work at their best. Putting them at the level of treetops (as is the norm) is a severe handicap that impacts hugely on the payback and increases the wear and tear due to turbulence. A briefing sheet is available via the website of RenewableUK, formerly the British Wind Energy Association (www.bwea.com). It is not easy to get planning permission for wind; it might take some time before approval is given, or you might not get it at all. Always apply and make sure you receive planning before ordering parts!

The UK Wind Speed Database and other useful resources

Rough estimates of average wind speeds for any OS grid square in the country are available from the UK Wind Speed Database for the following three heights: 10m, 25m and 45m above ground. The database is housed on the DECC website. You should exercise caution when using this tool though because it TAKES NO ACCOUNT OF LOCAL OBSTRUCTIONS, trees, buildings and so on, all of which can have a calamatous effect on wind speed and quality. Get hold of the Centre for Sustainable Energy's 'Estimating Wind Speed' factsheet from the Plan Local website.

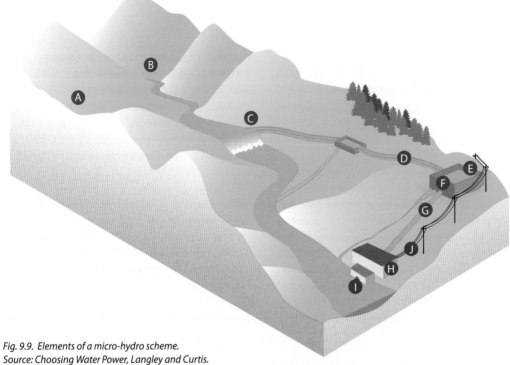

Fig. 9.9. Elements of a micro-hydro scheme.
Source: Choosing Water Power, Langley and Curtis.

Key to illustration: a) catchment area b) watercourse c) intake. At this point a controlled flow of water is diverted from the stream down d) the channel (also known as the head race canal) and into e) the settling tank. The settling tank slows down the water to allow debris to settle out prior to the water's entry, via f) the trash rack (which stops debris), into g) the penstock. The penstock is the pipe that finally carries the water to the turbine, which is housed in h) the powerhouse. The powerhouse will contain the turbine and generator, as well as a device known as the governor, which keeps the speed of the turbine and generator constant. Finally, i) the tailrace delivers the water back into the stream and j) the transmission cable carries the electricity to wherever it will be used.

Micro-hydro power

Figure 9.9 shows one type of micro-hydro installation (there are several others). This style of 'high-head' micro-hydro installation has, to a large extent, been replaced in Britain with a simpler system that does away with the channel and the settling tank. Never-the-less it is worth including it in full because many older systems are built like this. There are also 'low-head' systems which do not look like this at all! An example of a low-head system is the Torrs community scheme featured on page 207.

Will water power work for me?

As I've already mentioned, the success of any water power project depends on the head and the flow rate; the head being the difference in height between the point where the water is directed away from the river and the point where it passes through the turbine, and the flow rate being the total volume of water flowing down the penstock in a given period of time divided by the number of seconds in that period (litres per second usually). These two things determine how much power there will be in the water as it heads down the penstock (g) and into the turbine (housed in the powerhouse (f)). The turbine itself does not create electrical power. It is connected via a shaft to a generator; when the water pushes the turbine round, the mechanical energy in the shaft is converted to electrical energy by the generator, which is then carried to the point of use by transmission cables (j).

The flow rate depends to a certain extent on the size and topography of the catchment area (a) and the type of watercourse (b). If the water course has a big catchment area it is more likely to carry on delivering water through the turbine during drier spells. Even so, flow rate will vary throughout the year and between years as rainfall rises and falls; there is no getting away from this basic fact!

The variable nature of water power affects different projects in different ways. An off-grid residence reliant on water power for its electricity will have to be prepared to live without it at certain times of the year or have a backup power source such as a diesel generator, a wind turbine or a PV array. (There will have to be a compensation flow by-passing the scheme at all times, hence nearly all hydro schemes will not operate for between a minimum of 5 to 10% each year). A community scheme such as Torrs, featured in the case study on page 207, may suffer loss of income, which could have a knock on effect on loan or dividend payments. This all has to be factored into project planning. It isn't easy!

CAT's *Choosing Water Power* by Billy Langley and Dan Curtis (published late 2012) shows how to carry out a desktop study, followed by an on-site evaluation. The desktop study (using existing information, such as topography and predicted flow rates) will allow you to carry out an initial assessment but the on-site evaluation (using new information harvested from monitoring equipment) will be essential to help you get your plans to the point where permission for the final go ahead can be given, or not, as the case may be. As water flow has huge seasonal variations, a site evaluation will last at least a year; for a commercial project it may be longer.

Although it is possible to carry out these assessments yourself you will not be able to claim Feed-in Tariffs unless your scheme is fulfilled by a registered MCS installer (unless it is over 50kW). Thus it is more likely that your installer will carry out these evaluations on your behalf and give you the information you need to make a decision: most importantly, but not solely, whether the scheme will generate enough energy over it's lifetime to justify the cost of building it.

High-head and low-head schemes

The illustration on the previous page shows what a high-head scheme might look like. High-head schemes are typically found in very rural locations in steep sided valleys where the stream or river is not very wide. By contrast low-head schemes tend to be found in more open river plains, where the rivers are wider and also, potentially, closer to urban areas. One example is the Ham Hydro community project: at the time of writing under development on the River Thames at Teddington Weir.

Types of turbines

All turbines are built to match a particular head and flow rate. The Ham Hydro and Torrs projects use a relatively new type of turbine called a Reverse Archimedes Screw. These require large flow rates but a low head. The more traditional Pelton turbine can be used in situations where the flow rate is much lower, but the head higher. Your installer will suggest the turbine that will deliver the most energy based on their analysis of the flow rate and head. Other types of turbines include Turgo, Crossflow, Francis and Kaplan.

Construction

Any water power project requires the construction of several major and potentially expensive civil works (such as the power house, the penstock and so on); the cost of the turbine itself may only be 20% of the entire cost. Once the structures are all built, it is very difficult to change your mind or even add extra generating capacity. Everything is planned and sized in advance to work with the topography of the site and the power generation required.

What can go wrong?

Rivers can run dry, great storms can block the scheme with rocks and other debris, small animals can get stuck in the pipework, water flow can be hit by unusual weather events. You have to be prepared for the times when the weather just doesn't do as you would want, and also for carrying out maintenance tasks at moments of great inconvenience.

Financing

The economics of micro-hydro power used to be fairly straightforward; it would usually make financial sense for a property not connected to the grid (where the alternative was an expensive grid connection or the use of a lot of diesel), but not for one that was grid-connected (where mains electricity was considerably cheaper). This has changed with the Feed-in Tariff, as the costs of both grid-connected and off-grid systems are paid back over time. Micro-hydro schemes can take several years to complete, which could have implications for financing if the government decides to change the level or terms of payment for Feed-in Tariffs half way through the project development process.

For example, the government now insists that houses must have an Energy Performance Certificate (EPC) level D or better to qualify for FITs, a standard which may be harder to reach if you live in an older property.

As with other renewable energy systems the capital cost of micro-hydro is very big – a 5kW project could cost between £25,000 and £50,000 (see box) – and the running costs very small (ask your installer to give you an estimate of maintenance costs). Bear in mind that a typical yield from a 5kW hydro system will be larger than that of a 5kW wind or PV system, so although the upfront cost may be higher the energy cost may also be lower. Read the chapter on community renewables to get a sense of how you might plan the financial element of your project, even if you are only installing a domestic scheme.

Planning permission and approvals

Of all the renewable energy projects, water power is probably the most complex in terms of getting the right permissions. Not only will you have to apply for planning permission and get Building Regulations approval from your local authority, you will need to apply for an abstraction license and works in river permission from the Environment Agency. To protect wildlife in the watercourse, the Environment Agency will often put strict conditions on how much water you can take out, to make sure there is always enough left in the stream. You will need an abstraction license, if you take out more than 20 metres per day. This encompasses all but the very tiniest of hydro schemes. You may also need an environmental impact assessment and a wildlife survey.

You might also need special consents for construction on common land or near ancient monuments, and National Park permissions from the planning authority. Finally, you will need to be responsible for the protection and free movement of fish (which might require the construction of a fish pass or ladder).

It is recommended to start consulting with the relevant authorities early on as these processes can take many months, and will influence your technical design choices.

Case study

The North Harris Trust community wind farm project: when the technology doesn't work out

In a place like North Harris community is everything. Isolated from mainland Scotland, on an island of staggering beauty and empty loneliness, half the population of 700 live in the small town of Tarbert; the rest inhabit small crofting townships scattered along the coastline.

In 2003, the community bought 55,000 acres of land and formed the North Harris Trust to manage its interests; its aim: to increase employment opportunities, to address local housing needs and to protect and enhance the cultural and natural heritage of North Harris. This area of Scotland has the best wind resource in Britain, so it was only natural that the Trust looked to wind power to deliver a long term sustainable income for the community.

Supported by Community Energy Scotland (formerly the Highlands and Islands Community Energy Company) and Highland and Islands Enterprise (HIE), the Trust recruited West Coast Energy and independent consultant Colin Anderson to carry out an Energy Audit and provide technical support. After also considering wave and water power, a wind

power project (with three 850kW turbines) was considered the best option, partly because it was the most advanced technology at the time the project began.

A trading company was set up to pursue the project. Registered for VAT and as a limited company, the North Harris Trading Company Limited is run by five directors (including a local business owner, an ex banker, a fish farm manager and a deputy head teacher). Strong links were formed with the local council, HIE and, of course, the community. As a result there were no planning objections to the wind farm project. In fact, the community were balloted and voted unanimously to proceed.

There was an objection from Scottish Natural Heritage (SNH) – because the site is adjacent to a Special Protection Area (SPA) for Golden Eagles – but this was withdrawn after vigorous lobbying from the community. However, the objection did delay the project by involving the Scottish Executive and necessitating a more detailed Environmental Impact Assessment (EIA). Finally, planning was approved in

2008 – four years after the project was initially conceived.

At the same time as dealing with the planning process the company also started investigating the technical and earning capacity of the turbines, erecting a meteorological mast to monitor wind speed and turbulence. A consistently strong mean wind speed of 8.8m/s at a height of 50 metres was identified, which was considered good enough to make the project work. In 2008, the company applied for, and won, a Big Lottery grant of £900,000, which funded 45% of the project build cost. The rest was paid for by a commercial loan.

With the community on board, the planning permission approved and the finances secured everything looked good, apart from one technical detail – turbulence. Turbulence can cause problems by putting undue stress on a wind turbine and its components, thus undermining overall efficiency and performance. During the first three months of monitoring a small turbulence problem was noted, but not flagged as critical. However, as the monitoring continued (over an 18 month period) it was clear that the turbulence issue could put the whole project at risk.

The intensity of turbulence exceeded the Class A limit set by wind turbine manufacturers to maintain the integrity of their machines. It is possible to maintain a wind turbine even in such intense turbulence, but the only way to do so is to instigate a technical process known as sector management. This closes a turbine down when the wind comes from certain directions, that is, those identified as being the most 'disturbed'.

Only one turbine manufacturer said they could supply a turbine to work in such turbulent conditions, but their insistence on sector management reduced the capacity factor – the ratio of actual output of a power plant over a period of time and its output if it had operated at full capacity over that

period of time – to 22%. Wind farms tends to have a capacity factor of approximately 30%, although some have capacity factors in excess of 40%. In any case, a capacity factor of 22% severely reduced the earning capacity of the North Harris project and made it unfeasible. At this stage the wind project was cancelled and – because an alternative scheme could not be created within a two year window – the Lottery offer of £900,000 was handed back.

The experience at North Harris shows a truth about many renewables projects managed by private companies, communities and individuals – the technical and planning processes have to run hand in hand as one can often unseat the other. It is quite possible to put years of work into a project and for it never to come to anything, despite spectacular successes along the way. The North Harris project did employ a development officer for the last six months before the project ended (supported by external funding) but much of the work was carried out by volunteers working towards what they regarded as an aim that would be critical to the economic success of their community. With only limited resources (both human and financial) available to any community, the North Harris experience shows how important it is to get detailed and critical technical information correct as early as possible.

The happy ending to this story is that it has inspired six other community groups in the Western Isles with consented projects that, when commissioned will have wind turbines injecting £2.5 million a year into community regeneration projects. As far as North Harris goes, technology has moved forward and turbines are coming to the market that can handle turbulent conditions. It is hoped that the community can still benefit from the huge investment made in the site over the years.

Chapter Ten

Community energy generation

Introduction

Allan Shepherd

Introduction

For this chapter we have enlisted the assistance of two more writers – Jarra Hicks and Nicky Ison – both of whom have spent several years visiting and working with community renewable groups around the world and who now run a community renewables company in Australia.

Their specialism is electricity (rather than heat) so they have written one section on community renewable electricity generation as well as a more general section that can be applied to all community schemes, focusing on the nuts and bolt details of making them happen. They will be answering important questions like: how do community energy schemes work? Where does the money come from to make them work? Do the schemes require special legal structures? Is there help available to make them happen?

Electricity generation

Electricity generation at a community scale can be achieved using wind, hydro, solar PV and biomass CHP (combined heat and power). Large urban roof tops lend themselves well to community PV (Harveys Brewery, Lewes, for example), whereas wind and hydro are usually found on rural sites where the wind and hydro resource is most effective, although there are exceptions that prove the rule (Ham Hydro at Teddington Weir, for example).

There are many advantages to scaling up electricity generation to a community level:

- Resources can be pooled to facilitate greater amounts of energy generation. Economies of scale offer communities a multiplier effect, making each pound spent more valuable.
- Cost per kW of installed capacity is lower because bigger schemes are generally more efficient.
- More people – those, for example, who can't install renewables at home – can be included through participation events, share offers or membership schemes.
- The number of sites available to use increases, especially with wind and hydro.
- There are usually subsidiary benefits for the community. For example, income from the sale of electricity can be spent on community projects that bring long term benefit to the community itself and individual members of that community (Fintry on page 98).
- Community projects can attract funding support that domestic projects cannot.
- Energy generation projects at a community level are a shared experience. The value in this is often unseen at first but evolves over time, creating strength between neighbours, which leads to other co-operative ventures.

Heating schemes

Before Nicky and Jarra's sections there is a third section, on community heat, which I have written in collaboration with renewables engineer and lecturer, David Hood, and with valuable advice from CAT Information Officer, Tobi Kellner.

Community heating tends to focus on biomass, particularly woodchip, wood pellet and anaerobic digestion, but there are community heating schemes that also include solar water heating (Cloughjordon on page 189) and heatpumps (Gamblesby Village Hall on page 134). In this chapter we have focused on district heating networks (DHN), which facilitate the delivery of heat to several or many different properties, rather than single property community heating schemes, which are more or less covered in previous chapters.

DHNs allow for the use of fuels and technologies that can't be used at a domestic scale: like woodchip combustion and anaerobic digestion. In the right situation they represent the most efficient way to use biomass heating technology, offering economies of scale, convenience and environmental efficiency compared to individual property biomass heating systems.

Fig. 10.1. District heating

Two common scenario's for community biomass heating

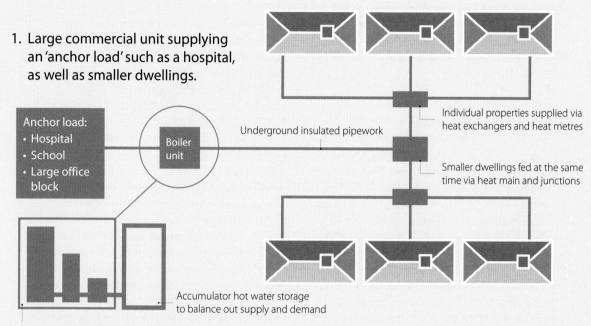

1. Large commercial unit supplying an 'anchor load' such as a hospital, as well as smaller dwellings.

Anchor load:
- Hospital
- School
- Large office block

Boiler unit

Underground insulated pipework

Individual properties supplied via heat exchangers and heat metres

Smaller dwellings fed at the same time via heat main and junctions

Accumulator hot water storage to balance out supply and demand

District heating systems will often have three boilers (each sized to deliver different amounts of heat) that kick in at different times of the year and during periods of higher demands. This is more effective than having one big boiler.

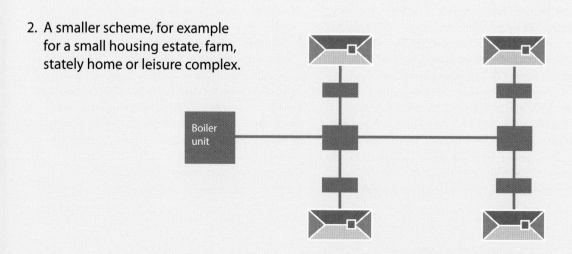

2. A smaller scheme, for example for a small housing estate, farm, stately home or leisure complex.

Boiler unit

Community heating and combined heat and power

Allan Shepherd

District heating

Community – or district – heating schemes distribute heat from a centralised location to two or more properties via a heat main (a set of pipes designed to carry hot water between residences). Any of the heating technologies mentioned in this book can be connected to a heat main.

How district heating varies between countries

Britain is not a very communal country when it comes to heating. Only about 1-2% of all heating required is supplied via a district heating system. In Denmark the figure is over 60%, Finland 50%, Iceland 95%. These differences are largely a fact of history (and of natural resources). Each country chose its own individual path several decades ago and stuck to it. Iceland has a huge geothermal resource so it made (and still makes) economic and environmental sense to have district heating systems. Likewise, Finland has lots of biomass.

Britain didn't have these resources, but it did have access to natural gas. Rather than create lots of separate district heating systems, Britain chose to build a national gas network to supply individual boilers in each property, rather like it had done for its national electricity grid. This national gas grid now supplies somewhere in the region of 75% of all buildings. It is effective, cheap and clean: a 'triple-threat' that effectively stifles district heating in the UK. Furthermore, natural gas delivered through a pipeline and burnt in an efficient condensing boiler has the lowest carbon intensity of all the fossil fuels.

However, the CO_2 emissions are still not as low as community heating using biomass boilers – the direct emissions of natural gas being $0.198 kgCO_2/kWh$ compared to 0.008 for logs, 0.009 for wood chip and $0.028 kgCO_2/kWh$ for pellets. Over the lifetime of a heating system this could amount to a considerable carbon saving.

It is useful to know this history because building on an existing heating culture is a lot easier that starting one more or less from scratch. In the long term it may make more sense to utilise the existing gas infrastructure in a green way, as we do when we feed renewably generated electricity into the national grid (it is already possible to buy a greener gas product through the national gas network (via Ecotricity)).

How district heating systems work

The starting point for any district heating system, as with any other heating system, is a heat load calculation. This suggests how much heat is needed and when it is needed. District heating systems work more efficiently when the heat load is constant. This allows the boiler to run continuously. There is rarely any point in setting up a DHN (District Heating Network) for a few houses with a low and unpredictable heat demand. These houses are better served by individual, fast response heating systems.

Of course, in the winter, heat demand will be bigger than in autumn and spring and district heating systems cope with these fluctuations by operating a multiple boiler system, drawing heat from additional boilers as the weather gets colder. In this way one large boiler can be effectively sized (and costed) to provide the base load for the heating system whilst the smaller boilers deliver the additional heat when it is needed. Those district heating systems where security of supply is absolutely essential will usually add supplementary backup boilers to be sure that the supply is maintained in the event of boiler failure. Some existing European systems use multiple fuels (biomass, oil, gas) and multiple boilers, ensuring security of supply and allowing the operators to switch boilers on and off to take advantage of price fluctuations.

Many systems have at their heart what is known as an anchor load (see figure 10.1). This load usually comes from a single, large building with a continuous demand for a large amount of heat. Hospitals are a classic example. Because the district heating system operator knows that this load will always be there, they can think about supplying other consumers through direct heat mains – schools, community buildings, houses and so on. The high cost of the

infrastructure can be offset by selling heat to multiple consumers, safe in the knowledge that the one big customer will always be there to foot the lion's share of the bill.

As the cost of installing heat mains can be as much as £100 per metre or more, and because there is always heat loss in pipework, the most cost and environmentally effective DHNs are built in places where there are a lot of people living very close together. These areas are referred to as high energy density areas. The London heat map (http://www.londonheatmap.org.uk) is a good example of how people can look at the heat loads of an area to establish the viability of a DHN.

Case study: the Village

The Village is a cluster of eco-houses situated on the edge of a small Tipperary town called Cloughjordan. It's an intentional eco-village project with a participative approach to planning and development and strong environmental credentials. As a new-build project the Village has been able to plan for environmental efficiency in advance of construction and has created a district heating system to provide all space-heating and hot water. Two high-efficiency 500kW woodchip boilers provide the main heat source but these are backed up by 500m² of ground mounted solar thermal panels. In the summer the boilers will rarely be needed as the solar thermal panels will meet demand for hot water. Both boilers and the solar thermal panels feed hot water into 2.2km of well-lagged distribution pipes. The hot water is then fed into individual 800 litre heat storage tanks situated in each home. This tank gives the householder complete control over the distribution of heat within the house. Each household has to pay a community development charge to pay for the capital costs of the district heating system but this is much cheaper than paying for individual wood pellet boiler systems.

The practicalities of heating your home using district heating

Planned community housing schemes such as the one at Cloughjordan (see box to left) and at Vauban (see page 110) lend themselves very well to district heating schemes because advanced planning reduces the infrastructure costs. Biomass also works out cheaper and more efficient on a community scale. There may well also be advantages under the RHI scheme too, because any heating system connecting more than one household is considered to be non-domestic and therefore eligible for payments (although this may have changed since the time of writing). Living with district heating is straightforward. Each house can control its needs using individual control systems and be billed using heat or water meters. Because deliveries and maintenance are centralized, the costs per household are much cheaper and there is none of the hassle associated with getting someone out to fix your own boiler. In fact, because most DHNs have more than one boiler you are less likely to experience a total loss of heat at critical times. The DHN is managed by a central company with its own engineers. Your contract with them will include a payment towards maintenance.

Combined heat and power

One way of increasing the cost-effectiveness of a district heating system is to install a combined heat and power (CHP) system. As the name suggests, combined heat and power boilers generate heat and electricity at the same time.

Most CHP units generate heat as a by-product of electricity production but it can work the other way round, too, with electricity generation being a by-product of a substantial heat load. In all cases, CHP units are always rated according to the amount of heat they produce – in kWt (the 't' standing for thermal) – and the amount of electricity they generate – recorded as kWe.

Most of Britain's electricity is generated using a combustion process, where the fuel (coal, oil, gas or biofuel) is burned to create steam to drive a steam turbine. During the combustion process 50-70% of all the energy produced is lost as heat, so it makes sense to capture this heat wherever possible and deliver it to a place where it is needed. Unfortunately, most older power stations can not easily be linked to district heat mains because they are often situated away from built-up areas. Smaller, newer systems can be more easily integrated with new housing developments but retro-fitting existing housing areas with heat mains is much more expensive.

Biomass CHP

The principles of biomass CHP are not very different to conventionally fuelled CHP but the fuels used vary, as do the techniques for generating the heat and power. Fuels include: miscanthus, wood pellets, wood chip, straw bales, agricultural and domestic biomass waste. Techniques include: Stirling engine, steam turbine, gasification compression ignition engine, hot air turbine and Organic Rankin Cycle system (which uses an intermediate heat transfer fluid). There is not enough space here to go into the benefits of each one but, as a general rule, biomass CHP is currently only feasible at a fairly large-scale – with at least a few hundred kW of heat demand.

Criteria for making a decision about district heating

There are very few district heating schemes in the UK, with very few powered by biomass, and fewer still run as community projects. What is clear is that they only ever work when a number of circumstances collide. Generating this collision is not quite as difficult as making particles collide in the Hadron accelerator, but it is still a pretty rare occurrence.

These circumstances are:

- Location and density of housing (as described already).
- High heat load (with potential anchor).
- Financial resources. There are long term fuel savings to be made using DHN (especially with the RHI) but capital expenditure is high. Of

course, this is less of an issue if the alternative is the cost for every house to have its own heating system. As such, DHN is usually most attractive for new developments where individual heating systems aren't in place yet. Drawing the resources together from multiple sources will be difficult. If it is a community venture it will be necessary to create an operational structure which will allow people to get a return from their investment and to sell on their 'share' should they move.

- Strength of community feeling coupled with realism about the benefits of district heating. There's not much point getting excited about DHN if you can't convince your neighbours. There are some very good examples of small-scale DHN supplying a few dwellings (see the Yard case study on page 69), but these quite often occur when existing large properties have been split into separate units (perhaps as part of a housing co-op). Being part of a DHN is a long term commitment and many people may lack confidence to make that commitment. There has to be strong financial and environmental incentives as well as convenience and sense of security to allow people to feel confident about being part of a DHN. Most people (perhaps particularly in Britain) fear reliance on community resources – even though an individual household boiler can break just as easily.
- The existence of leaders with technological knowledge, business skills and good sense. DHNs have to be run as well organised businesses, including those owned by communities. Someone has to run it and be prepared to take responsibility if something goes wrong. Some community schemes recruit a service provider known as an energy service company (ESCo) to do this for them (see page 202) but, as we are not a country with a huge skills base in this area, these are quite rare. The service providers themselves prefer to operate a number of systems together to save on administration and operation costs. ESCos own the heat plant, the distribution network and heat main; they supply the fuel, give you the heat – and you pay for it.

Community renewable electricity generation

Nicky Ison & Jarra Hicks, Community Power Agency

Communities have played a surprising and significant role in the development of the modern wind industry. In the late 1970s and early 80s, it was not big business and government funding that helped establish what is now Denmark's world leading wind industry, but rather small groups of farmers and townsfolk. At this time, it was common for a few people from a village to form 'wind guilds' and collectively chip in to purchase and install a wind turbine on the edge of town.

This not only provided communities with access to clean energy and an income generating asset, it also provided an early market and testing ground for what is now a sophisticated global technology, crucial to our clean energy future. By 2001 there were 150,000 families involved in over 2,100 wind co-operatives; together they owned 50% of all turbines in Denmark and supplied 3.5% of national electricity needs (DWTOA 2009a:2. References for this chapter can be found on page 216). That's an amazing testament to the power of community owned renewable energy.

Across the UK, and indeed the world, people are increasingly coming together to develop community renewable energy projects. These projects come in many shapes and sizes, growing from the diverse needs and available resources of the local community. They might be anything from PV on a school roof to a four turbine wind farm on the edge of town, to a small hydro system owned by two neighbouring villages.

Community renewable energy (CRE) projects allow you to go beyond the bounds of your own home and in so doing bring a range of benefits and opportunities both for your household and for the wider community. They enable you to collectively achieve power up options that simply aren't available to you on your own.

What is community renewable energy?

A 'community' renewable energy (CRE) project is founded on at least one of the following elements:

- Ownership and/or decision making power involving local individuals and stakeholders.
- Project development and design driven by local individuals and stakeholders.
- Benefits from the project go to local individuals and stakeholders.
- The amount of energy produced matches local energy needs.

The more of these elements that are incorporated into a CRE project, the more strongly embedded it will be in the community. Local individuals usually play a strong role in project ownership and development, but other stakeholders and co-owners can include non-local individuals, small business, government, institutions and so on. Every group's idea of what is and isn't included in a 'community' approach is a bit different, but this is part of the diversity and flexibility that makes CRE so appealing to so many people in so many different circumstances.

Given the sheer diversity of CRE projects across the world, it can be hard to singularly define CRE. Projects vary by technology, size, structure, governance and funding options (Jeong et al, in press). Even people's motivations for setting such a project up vary: some want to reduce their town's carbon footprint, some want local energy security, some want to support renewable energy education and deployment. But there are some common features to all CRE projects that we call the Three D's (Ison (2009)): decarbonisation, decentralisation and democratisation.

The Three D's of CRE projects:

- **Decarbonise** our energy supply by using renewable energy or low carbon technologies.
- **Decentralise** and localise our energy supply.
- **Democratise** our energy governance through community ownership and participation.

CRE projects use different processes and produce different outcomes than other forms of renewable energy development. Walker and Devine-Wright (2008) identify that the processes used involve local people to a greater degree and that the outcome benefits local people more. These unique processes are what help to differentiate CRE projects from industrial and corporate projects

Process – who is the project developed and run by?
Good questions to ask include:

- Who is involved and included in planning and decision-making?
- Who has power and influence?
- How open, inclusive and extensive is the community engagement process?

If done in a locally focused way, a CRE project has the potential to build local resilience and empowerment. It is also likely to increase acceptance and support for renewable energy projects as well as creating greater general understanding and support for other environmental and social change ideas.

Outcome – who is the project for?
Questions you could think about include:

- Who benefits from the project: socially? Economically? Spatially?
- Are profits shared with the local community?

If done in a locally focused way, a CRE project can bring income to a community by way of shareholder dividends or through a community fund. It can also contribute local jobs, support local businesses and provide education, training and tourism opportunities.

The process and outcome dimensions are closely related, of course, because a project that has a majority local ownership is likely to make decisions that bring greater community benefit.

The CRE sector: what's out there?
Community ownership of renewable energy is most well-established and common in the UK and Europe where such projects have been up and running since the 1980s. Wind power is the most common CRE technology, but there are also many examples of other technologies being used: hydropower, anaerobic digestion combined with district heating and electricity generation, biomass boilers and solar PV.

Countries such as Denmark, Germany and the UK (particularly Scotland) are seen as 'pioneers in renewable energy and in policy approaches that encourage genuine opportunities for democratic control, community engagement and economic participation' (Gipe, 2003).

In Germany, for example, 7% of electricity needs are met through wind power, with over 25,700MW of installed capacity and over 200,000 people owning a share of a nearby wind turbine (Gipe 2010). Furthermore, of Germany's 9,000MW of installed solar PV, 7,200MW is community or household owned rooftop systems of 100kW or less (ibid.).

In the past 8 years we have also seen CRE projects popping up in the US, Canada, Australia and Japan. Although the sector is quite new in these countries, it is attracting a lot of interest and emerging quickly.

There are also many community owned renewable energy projects throughout the majority (developing) world, particularly in regions of Africa, South America, India and China. These projects use solar photovoltaic, small hydropower, wind and modern biomass. They also, however, incorporate a range of much more simple, smaller scale and inexpensive technologies, such as solar cooking, solar food driers and simple biogas (using unprocessed agricultural and food waste and animal dung). Over 25 million households meet their cooking and lighting needs from household or village scale biogas plants using simple anaerobic digester technology (REN21 2007: 6). A further 2.5 million households in the majority world use solar PV lighting (ibid.).

Since in these contexts CRE often provides energy needs for some of the poorest people in the world, such projects have a different scale and nature to those in the minority (developed) world. These projects are often funded through government or international aid organisation support, then handed over to the community. Projects are usually focused

CRE projects come in many shapes and sizes. Here's just a few to give you a taste

- **Middelgrunden Wind Farm**
A 20MW offshore wind farm that is a joint venture between a co-operative of 8,500 Copenhagen and wider Danish residents and the municipal utility.

- **Hepburn Wind**
A co-operative-run 4MW wind farm in Australia that is owned by local residents and contributes AU$30,000 a year to a local Community Sustainability Fund.

- **Ellensburg Community Solar**
A 58kW (and growing!) solar installation organised and run by the municipal utility, a local university and a local environment group in Washington, USA. Local residents are investors and receive reductions on their energy bills according to the productivity of the portion they own.

- **Min Wind I-IX**
Nine separate corporations running 1-2 turbine wind farms, each owned by 33 local farmer-investors in Minnesota, USA.

- **Baywind Wind Co-operative**
Initially a joint venture between a wind developer and a co-operative of Cumbrian and wider UK residents. It has a small community fund for energy efficiency projects in the Cumbrian community.

- **Westray**
A one-turbine wind development owned by the Westray Development Trust, whose membership is open to any adult on the island of Westray, UK.

- **Dardesheim Wind Farm**
A large wind farm, predominantly owned by a developer, with shareholding opened up to local community members, a small percentage of the wind farm revenue also goes to the town council, in Germany.

- **Isle of Eigg**
A mini-grid powered by hydro, wind and electric, providing electricity to the residents of the Isle of Eigg. Owned by Eigg Electric, a subsidiary of the Eigg Development Trust.

on providing for basic cooking and lighting needs, rather than supplying electricity in the amounts needed to run a modern Western house.

The three models of CRE development

There are three main organisational models for developing CRE: 'community organisations', 'community investor co-operatives or companies' and 'developer and community partnerships'.

Community organisation

The CRE project is initiated, led and owned by a community organisation, such as a local development trust, school, village hall, or an association. These organisations are made up of local members and are usually not-for-profit or profit-for-purpose (for example Westray and Isle of Eigg).

Community investor co-operative or company

The CRE project is initiated, led and owned by a co-operative or a company whose members and owners are community investors. These investors can be local individuals, organisations, small businesses and so on (for example Heburn and Min Wind).

Developer and community partnership

Either the community or a renewable energy developer initiates a renewable energy project and both parties agree to partner. The community often leads the consultation and the developer leads the technical studies. Both the developer and community members own and invest in the project, to varying degrees (Dardesheim and Middelgrunden).

Why CRE? The benefits

Different groups choose to set up community renewable energy projects for different reasons. There are almost as many reasons to do CRE projects as there are types of projects. Each group setting out on the journey to set up a project will have specific driving motivations and values that will frame their choices and outcomes. These will produce a range of benefits, not all of which will be important to or present in every CRE project.

Having visited and had contact with over 40 CRE projects across four continents, we have seen a huge range of projects and their many possible benefits.

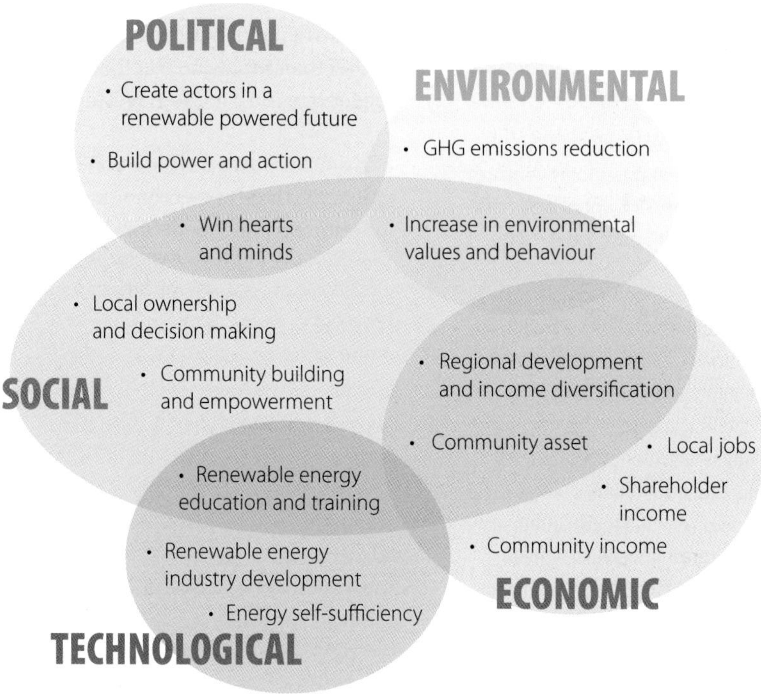

POLITICAL

- Create actors in a renewable powered future
- Build power and action

ENVIRONMENTAL

- GHG emissions reduction

- Win hearts and minds

- Increase in environmental values and behaviour

- Local ownership and decision making

SOCIAL

- Community building and empowerment

- Regional development and income diversification

- Community asset
- Local jobs

- Renewable energy education and training

- Shareholder income

- Renewable energy industry development

- Community income

ECONOMIC

- Energy self-sufficiency

TECHNOLOGICAL

Fig. 10.2. The benefits of community renewable energy projects.

These can be easily categorised into five broad areas: political, economic, environmental, social and technological. These are summarised in figure 10.2 above.

In essence, the particular advantages of a community approach to renewable energy development are:

- Building community resilience and empowerment.
- Building a strong and practical movement of action on climate change.
- Supporting regional communities and fostering local economic development.
- Helping develop renewable energy industries, technology, jobs and training.

CRE challenges

Let's not kid ourselves, CRE projects are not easy to do and we're sure you can come up with many barriers and reasons not to even begin. CRE projects take a long time, they require sustained passion and dedication and they cost a lot of money. It is also likely that there will be opposition to the project within your community; some people won't like it because you can't please everyone all of the time. You will have to negotiate with the institutions and regulations of the mainstream electricity and planning system, neither of which are particularly well designed for small community orientated renewable energy projects. In the next section of this chapter we will take you through some of the key challenges and offer strategies to overcome them.

So why bother? Why go any further? Hopefully all you've read in this book to date will provide multiple answers to those questions, and if you can come up with just one good reason for doing a CRE project, that puts a fire in your belly or a hope in your mind, then it is worth doing. In case you need more inspiration than that, we'll give you a couple of our reasons for doing what we do:

- These projects work! We've visited over 40 community renewable energy projects across four continents that are making real differences in communities and there are hundreds if not thousands more out there. A few of our favourites that we suggest you look up are the Isle of Eigg in Scotland, Jühnde in central Germany and Hepburn Wind in Australia.
- We get to work with and meet the most dedicated and inspiring people we've ever met.
- When we read the paper or watch the news it feels like the world is going to hell in a hand basket, it's nice to know that we're not sitting idly by; instead we're building something new and positive that is making a difference.
- Collectively, communities are able to build renewable energy generation that can meet their town or shire's needs, that saves tonnes of greenhouse gas emissions and builds understanding and support for renewable energy.
- It's great to see communities able to fund important local projects, like energy efficiency programmes or a new playground, with the new source of income their project provides. Hepburn Wind, for example, donates AUD$30,000 a year to a locally run Community Sustainability Fund as well as providing 'better than bank' return on investment to their shareholders.

Those who say it can't be done should get out the way of those already doing it.

Chinese proverb

When developers own your renewable resource

The alternative to community renewable generation is developer led generation. In this scenario a company selects a site, negotiates with the land owner directly and carries out a limited community consultation process to smooth out the planning approval process. This type of development is not necessarily without benefit to the community as, for example, the community living around a wind farm site almost always receives a payment based on the amount of electricity generated (between £750-£3,000 per MW generated is common). This is known as 'community benefit'. It is an annual payment and goes straight to a representative community body, leaving the communities involved with the nice headache of figuring out how to spend their windfall.

However, this 'no ownership' option has also been called community light (as in, without weight), because the community never fully realises the benefit that could be had from its own resource. Some estimates have suggested that communities that own their renewable project outright can earn between 25 and 50 times more money than if they just received community benefit.

Occasionally developers have chosen a more direct engagement process, offering communities the chance to own part of a larger project (see the Fintry case study on page 98). As it is rare for communities to have the financial clout to be able to afford more than a single generator, owning a share in a larger development makes a lot of sense (especially if it is probably going to happen anyway). This idea of owning a turbine or stake in a larger renewable energy project fits in with the community developer partnership organisational model described on page 193.

Community renewables: making it happen

Nicky Ison and Jarra Hicks, Community Power Agency

Making a community renewable energy project happen is exciting. While definitely a big challenge – there will no doubt be moments of tearing your hair out along the way – every person we have ever spoken to who has been involved in a CRE project talks about the sense of satisfaction they felt, not only once it had started operating, but also following the many small achievements and milestones along the way.

The people

So where to start? The very essence of a community project is a group of people. Perhaps you already have a community group that you're part of, or you and some friends have been talking about what you can do for a while and it's time to bite the bullet and turn those ideas into practice. Perhaps there are a number of organisations and individuals in your community that would be interested in being involved and you could create a consortium. Or maybe you need to find people who would also be interested; you could do this by organising an event, holding stalls or placing an ad in the local shop, paper or community website.

Over the past few years we've visited over 40 CRE projects. Typically, these projects have had a core team of five to six people, with a wider group being involved in carrying out smaller tasks flowing in and out as required.

The CRE development framework

Once you've got a group, the next step is to organise a series of meetings. But what needs to be discussed at those meetings? What needs to be done and how are you going to structure the work? Based on our experience, the Community Power Agency (see resources) has developed a framework (figure 10.3) to help groups think through the complex but achievable process of developing a CRE project.

There are many motivations and values that underpin community renewable energy projects.

For example, the motivation behind Hepburn Wind, Australia's first wind co-operative, was to find a tangible and empowering community approach to tackling climate change. For the Isle of Eigg mini-grid in Scotland, however, the primary motivation was a need for an affordable twenty-four hour power supply on the island.

We suggest that at your initial meeting you start by talking about your motivations and together synthesise what you aim to achieve through the project. Questions you could ask include:

- Why are you here?
- What would you personally like to achieve through this project?
- What would you like the project to achieve? Contribute to? Transform?
- How could these different aims and motivations work together?
- Which aims and motivations do you want to prioritise as a group?

In going through this process it is important to recognise that things will evolve and emerge over the course of the project, but that a starting vision is inspiring and motivating for all involved. Having clear motivations and aims will help attract new people to the project too. For inspiration and ideas about how to conceptualise CRE project outcomes see figure 10.2.

Once you've worked out your project aims, consider establishing working groups to tackle important areas such as community engagement, organisational structure and governance, fundraising, and technical project development. Keep in mind that decisions in one area or working group will affect the others, so 'all in' coordination meetings are essential.

What we've just described is one possible approach and there are many others, so you should in no way feel bound to this suggestion. Seeking out and/or developing good group facilitation skills will enable your group to develop processes and structures that work best for you. There are some very useful toolkits listed in the resources section that will guide you through this process.

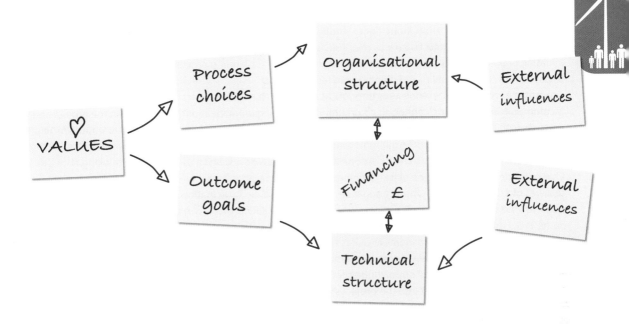

Fig. 10.3. Community Renewable Energy Development Framework (Community Power Agency, 2011).

The six stages of development

Generally, the development of a CRE project can be thought about in terms of six technical stages.

- **Stage 1** – Project initiation; where the group comes together, sets its aims and starts to develop the project.
- **Stage 2** – Social feasibility; to gauge the level of support for the project within the community, as well as scoping at a high level what is technically and financially possible and desirable.
- **Stage 3** – Technical feasibility and planning; where a site is secured and a full technical study is undertaken to design the technical side of the project, an organisational structure is established, planning approval is sought and, if appropriate, negotiations are initiated: in the case of electricity generation both with the local distribution network operator regarding grid connection and one or more national electricity supply companies regarding the sale of electricity. This

stage also includes the social and environmental studies, such as visual, noise and ecosystem impacts of the proposed project. The technical feasibility allows you to determine the renewable energy resource available and the expected efficiency of the project. Once this is determined, a business case can be developed.
- **Stage 4** – Financing; which requires raising sufficient capital by whatever process you chose, thus enabling the group to proceed to the construction phase.
- **Stage 5** – Construction; where the equipment (wind turbine, solar panels and so on) is ordered, civil works (such as foundations or roads) are built, and the project is installed, and – where appropriate – connected to an electricity grid.
- **Stage 6** – Operation; which is fairly self-explanatory where electricity is being generated; tasks in this phase include technical monitoring and maintenance and financial administration.

It is important to note that while there are reasonably defined stages of the CRE development process, some things will happen throughout. For example, fundraising will need to start as early as the project initiation or pre-feasibility stage in order to be able to pay for the costly feasibility and planning process. Governance is essential the whole way through, as too is community engagement – although community engagement is especially important in the early stages.

The community engagement process

Community engagement is one of the defining features of a CRE project. Community engagement goes beyond standard consultation processes that commercial renewable energy developers typically employ. Good community engagement builds trust, feelings of ownership and a sense of empowerment through providing meaningful opportunities for the wider community to input into the project's development.

Examples of community engagement mechanisms include:

- A survey of your local community, to gauge opinion of different options associated with your project. Questions you could ask include: do you want this project to be highly visible or unobtrusive? Do you want it owned by a majority of local people? Do you want big commercial or government investors? What size is appropriate for us?
- Regular stalls at community events and markets.
- A printed or web-based newsletter.
- Visits to your proposed site and to similar already operational projects; for example a community hydro project or a wind farm.
- A photo montage in a public location of what the project will look like.
- Town meetings or forums; including inviting people to speak who have already developed similar projects.
- Public launches by high profile people at different stages in the project's development.
- A community picnic while the project is being constructed.

- Regular open days and working bees at the site once the project is operational, so people can come and ask questions.
- A participatory and well facilitated community planning process to make key decisions.

It will be important to decide the role of community engagement at different stages in the project and the degree of public participation you want to facilitate. The International Association for Public Participation has developed a useful tool for thinking about this, available from www.iap2.org . (Look for Spectrum of Public Participation under Practitioner Tools.)

CRE projects can take a significant period of time to develop, generally a minimum of 2 years, so one of the challenges you will face is how to keep the community engaged along the way. This will require good planning and thinking about what community engagement mechanisms are appropriate at different stages. See Resources for more help.

The planning process

One of the key tasks in developing a CRE project is getting planning approval. Each country in the UK has its own planning system, so planning requirements will differ from place to place and also by technology type and scale. The trade body RenewableUK outlines the different authorities and legislation that CRE projects will need to comply with at www.bwea.com/planning/uk_planning_legislation.html

Nevertheless, there are some common criteria for gaining planning approval. You will always need to:

- Develop a complaints procedure.
- Undertake an Environmental Impact Assessment. This covers soil, hydrology, wildlife, visual and noise impact, social and economic factors (CES, 2009), as well as technology specific factors, such as the impact on fish life and flight paths for hydro and wind projects respectively. Please note, this process can be expensive and lengthy!
- Have procedures to address any potential impacts.
- Implement a public consultation process.

- Carry out consultation with key statutory and community bodies such as national heritage organisations, water utilities, the relevant Environment Agency and so on.

To get a better understanding of the planning process we recommend:

- Talking to people involved in a similar type of CRE project which has already received planning approval.
- Talking informally to someone in the planning division of your local council – before you make a formal planning application.
- Talking to a CRE support organisation operating in your area.
- Reading up on the planning process described in one of the detailed CRE toolkits, such as Community Energy Scotland's Community Renewable Energy Toolkit, the Plan Local toolkit, or the resources on DECC's Community Energy Online website – http://ceo.decc.gov.uk (see Resources).

Organisation structures and governance
Clear and transparent governance of the project is important. This involves setting up clear decision-making and communications processes and establishing a legal entity.

There are four main legal structures used by CRE projects in the UK, described in detail in the table overleaf.

Different legal structures offer different features and benefits. It will be important to choose a legal structure that fits your desired ownership and member profile, as well as your fundraising strategy. Many groups establish hybrid structures involving a partnership between two different legal entities in order to access the best of two legal structures. For example, in Australia the proposed New England Wind will be a hybrid between a co-operative and a public company.

When you're thinking about how to move forward, keeping the following questions in mind will help you determine which structure will suit your project best. Ask:

- Where will the money for the project come from? How do these legal structures enable or constrain fundraising?
- Where will the money generated by the project go? Who benefits?
- Can only local people be members, or others too?
- Who is included in and excluded from the decision-making?
- Who has power in this process and how equitable is it?
- How do these questions relate to your process and outcome goals or vision for the project?

(For more information about CRE organisational models and hybrids see Hicks and Ison (2011), references on page 216).

Earlier we introduced three organisational models of CRE development: the community organisation, the community investor Co-operative or company, and the community partnership models. In the legal structures table below, we indicate which structures fit best with which organisation models of CRE.

The organisation structures outlined in the table on page 200 can be used to deliver 100% community ownership or to facilitate community ownership in a developer-community partnership. The most common approach to CRE development in the UK has been to set up an industrial and provident society to allow community investors to buy into a large renewable energy development.

The one CRE model that will not necessarily require a new legal entity is an asset-based project. An asset-based CRE project is where a community asset, such as a village hall or school, installs a renewable electricity generation system like a small solar PV array and the electricity generated gets used directly by that community facility (often with any excess being sold to the grid).

Technical considerations
Although we've been largely talking about electricity production, CRE includes projects that produce both electricity and heat. The best technologies currently available for community renewable electricity projects are wind, solar PV and micro-hydro. For

CRE legal structures in the UK

Structure	Description	Example CRE Project	Find out more
Industrial and Provident Society (Co-operative)	Co-operative societies are guided by the seven principles of co-operation (Co-operatives UK). They are founded for the mutual benefit of their members, with the surplus usually being reinvested in the organisation to provide better service (FSA, 2010). One key feature of co-operatives is that their governance is based on one member one vote, no matter how much that member has invested in the organisation. A CRE project using a co-operative structure follows a community investor model of CRE, which tends to be at the larger end of the CRE scale.	Baywind	Co-operatives UK – www.uk.coop Financial Services Association – www.fsa.gov.uk
Trading subsidiary wholly owned by a local development trust or charitable organisation	Development trusts 'create wealth in communities and keep it there' (Locality). They are typically charitable organisations that set up companies limited by shares that can trade and generate wealth. The shares of these subsidiary companies are then wholly owned by the development trust or charitable organisation. This structure works well for the community organisation model of CRE, not the investor model. Given the financing options available (in other words not a share offer) this tends to lead to smaller CRE projects, generally not more than 1-2MW.	Westray Renewables	http://locality.org.uk
Industrial and Provident Society for the benefit of the community (Ben Com)	A Ben Com is an organisation like a co-operative in that it is guided by the seven principles of co-operation. However, they run for the benefit of the community and provide services for people other than their members (FSA, 2010).	Torrs Hydro	Financial Services Association – www.fsa.gov.uk
Community Interest Company (CIC)	Community Interest Companies (CICS) are limited companies, with special additional features, created for the use of people who want to conduct a business for community benefit, and not purely for private advantage' (BIS). CIC based CRE projects tend to lead to community investor models of CRE.	Ham Hydro	www.bis.gov.uk/cicregulator

community renewable heat projects, wind to heat, biomass boilers and other biomass technologies are appropriate. For combined heat and electricity ('cogeneration') projects, anaerobic digestion is the best renewable technology available. In this section we won't go into much detail about the specifics of these technologies, as there have already been chapters dedicated to them. Instead we will pose some questions or technical issues for your consideration when moving forward with a CRE project.

Firstly, there is the question of what renewable energy resources you have available. This one is a deal breaker. For example, if you don't have a river or stream near your community a hydro project is clearly out of the question.

Secondly, you need to ask what electricity infrastructure (grid networks) exists in your community? There are four main answers to this question:

1) There is good network coverage with capacity to integrate distributed electricity projects. This would mean a new CRE project would likely be able to connect into the existing grid infrastructure with few extra upgrades.
2) There is good network coverage with no capacity. This would mean there is a good electricity distribution and transmission network in your community but it doesn't have the ability to accept and export more electricity.
3) There is bad network coverage. This typically occurs at the outer limits of the electricity grid, where supply is unreliable and there is no extra connection capacity.
4) You have no electricity network; your community is off-grid.

Where you are in this list will determine how easy it will be to connect to the grid and to export the electricity you generate, and how much this connection is likely to cost. If you can't connect to the grid you will need to consider energy storage technologies such as batteries or pumped hydro. You may also consider setting up a community owned mini-grid like the one on the Isle of Eigg.

To get accurate information about your local grid network you will need to talk to the local electricity distribution network operator (DNO). Negotiating a good deal with a network company is often one of the most difficult aspects of a CRE project.

The third technical issue to consider is project size: how many kilowatts (kW) or megawatts (MW) will suit your site and need? In part, this question will be determined by the renewable resource you have available but the project size will also be dependent on cost and local energy need. The bigger the project the greater the cost and the more money you will have to raise, but also the cheaper each unit of generated energy is likely to be. There are great economies of scale with bigger projects, as associated costs (such as planning assessments, grid connection, civil works) can be offset against greater generating capacity.

The final technical issue to consider is location: where will you site your project? As with scale, this will partially be answered by the electricity network location and what renewable energy resources you have available and where. For example, if you have a weir in a good sized river and are considering a micro-hydro project using a reverse Archimedes screw, there is no question of location – there's only one place it could be.

However, with wind and solar projects there is often more choice. Motivations that might influence the choice of location include education and level of opposition. If one aim of your project is to raise awareness and public education about renewables, you may want your site to be highly visible and even in an iconic location. On the other hand if there's lots of community opposition to wind in your area, you may want to site the project in a place where it will cause the least controversy (without reducing energy yield).

Many people focus on the technology aspect of CRE because being a renewable energy project is what defines it from other community development projects. Nevertheless, just because it is a 'techy' project does not mean that the technology should dominate and determine the nature of the project.

You have many choices you can make and these technical considerations, while important, should not outweigh considerations about what will best suit your community.

Costs and financing

When developing your CRE project, there are a series of different financing mechanisms available.

As outlined above, the majority of costs for any renewable energy project are capital costs; they come in the pre-feasibility, feasibility and construction phases. As such, finding a suitable financing mechanism to get the project off the ground is one of the biggest challenges a CRE project faces. The main financing mechanisms currently used by operational CRE projects are:

- A community share offer.
- Loans.
- Grants and donations.
- Partnerships with developer or community energy support companies.

Most projects use a combination of financing mechanisms. It should also be noted that some financing options aren't possible with some organisational models. For example, if you want to develop a community trust model of CRE, a community share offer would not be possible as this financing mechanism leads to an investor model of CRE. A community share offer and loan is generally only possible once you have completed technical and economic feasibility studies and proved the viability of the project.

Community share offer

A community share offer raises capital by inviting members of the community to invest in the project. This involves publishing a prospectus and share offer document and distributing it far and wide. Inviting members of the community to invest makes them members of the projects' organisational structure and usually entitles them to participate in formal decision-making (for example, at Annual General Meetings). Different CRE projects have different criteria for who is able to invest, how much they are allowed to invest and what associated benefits (for example, voting rights) investors should receive. Examples include:

- Requiring all, a majority or only partial local investment.
- Defining local in different ways.
- Only allowing individuals, not organisations or businesses, to invest.
- Placing an upper or lower boundary on investment.
- Having only one investment amount, for example £1000, no more, no less.
- Offering lower minimum investment amounts to locals to prioritize local ownership.
- Including or excluding local government.
- Allowing each member only one vote, no matter how much they invest.

Find out more and download a wide range of useful factsheets from www.communityshares.uk.coop

Loans

Most CRE projects are in part financed by loans from banks, co-operative and ethical banks, individuals, organisations or government. Progressive financing institutions in the UK that have a history of providing loans for CRE projects are Triodos Bank, Co-operative and Community Finance, the Ecology Building Society, and the Co-op Bank.

In 2011 the Scottish Government converted its successful Community and Renewable Energy Scheme (CARES) grant programme to a loan scheme (administered through Community Energy Scotland). This scheme allows communities in Scotland to apply for a contingent liability loan to help them get through the early development phases to the point where they're ready to apply for planning permission. If the scheme doesn't successfully receive planning permission the government is liable for the debt. If it does the community must pay off the debt when the project starts to earn income.

There have been calls for this very successful scheme to be extended throughout the UK because it is one of the few ways to raise an unsecured loan without security. This is important because most communities do not have any form of security to offer banks, apart from the earning potential of the project itself, which may not yet be known in the pre-feasibility and feasibility stages of a project.

It may also be possible to secure a loan from a wealthy individual, philanthropic or commercial organisation. Zopa, which matches lenders to borrowers, is one place to look (http://uk.zopa.com/ZopaWeb). Another is the pension funds belonging to local authorities, many of which should have a natural interest in investing funds in local people and projects. Anahat Energy in association with Transition Together is trying to find a way of unlocking this particular pot of money, suggesting that the profile of the investment matches the demands of the pension funds very well. Also try abundancegeneration.com

Grant funding

Grant funding, if available, is very useful, particularly in the early and most risky stages of a project. A grant to help fund the project from the idea phase through feasibility, to the point where you have a firm idea of what the project will look like, is very useful. Grants are increasingly hard to get though, and are often tied in ways that do not fit with your project aims. For example, in the UK it is impossible to apply for feed-in tariff payments if you receive European state aid. This

How much can I borrow?

Conditions of borrowing vary from bank to bank. Triodos will lend a minimum of £25,000 to CRE projects but have the capacity to lend a great deal more. Co-operative and Community Finance will lend less, between £10,000 and £75,000, quite often providing an additional small loan on top of a more substantial loan provided by a larger lender such as Triodos, something to bear in mind if you find yourself with a funding gap. It is quite common for projects to have 60% debt.

might compromise your long term business plan and returns to investors.

Grant makers include all levels of government – council, regional and national as well as philanthropic bodies; a partial list is provided in the resources section, although it should be pointed out that the number and type of grants available changes all the time. For example in 2012 the Scottish Government introduced the Renewable Energy Investment Fund. Checking websites like DECC and the Energy Savings Trust is a good idea.

Donations

Donations are even more untied than grants and are always welcome! To attract donations though, you will need to be able to convince someone your idea is worthwhile and likely to succeed and that you are trustworthy. All easier after you've done the pre-feasibility stage. There are also legal requirements around seeking funds from the public, so make sure if you plan a fund raiser you get some legal advice. Due to the typical size of a donation, even a large one, it is unlikely that you will be able to fund more than a small village hall CRE project from donations alone.

Partner with another organisation

The final possible funding mechanism is to partner with another organisation that takes some or most of the financial risk, and raises some or most of the capital. One example of this is to partner with a conventional renewable energy developer, particularly if they are already planning on doing a project in your area. Another approach is to work with a community renewable energy support organisation, such as Plan Local, Severn Wye Energy Agency (SWEA), Ynni'r Fro (in Wales), Community Renewable Energy (CoRE), Community Energy Plus, Regen SW, or Energy4All. Energy4All and Community Energy Plus both have loan funds, whereby some income from existing CRE projects can be used as seed funding for new developments. It is worth checking all of these organisations to see what they offer. You should also check Carbon Leapfrog (http://carbonleapfrog. org); they provide successful not-for-profit applicants with pro bono advice worth between £10,000 and £100,000.

These partnerships are not stand-alone financing mechanisms; your group will still need to find some way of financing your part in the partnership. Also bear in mind that your group and wider community will have more decision-making power in the project the more financially independent it can be.

Creating the business case for your project

No matter which financing mechanism/s your community chooses, you will need to develop a sound business case for your project, carry out financial due diligence and 'stress test' your business plan. Specifically, banks will need a low risk guarantee that their loan will be paid off. They will want to see that your predicted income streams are robust, that your group has a strong management team and also quite probably that you or someone in your team has a track record in successful business development.

Additionally, most community members will want an assurance that they will get some return on their investment, particularly if it is a large investment. While grants do not require a return, grant makers tend to fund projects that look likely to succeed, and their measure of success will almost definitely include that the project makes money.

The financial basis for almost all CRE projects is the sale of electricity (and sometimes heat energy). This income is only available once the project is operational so the business case for most CRE projects is based on the unit price of electricity sold and the number of units the scheme is likely to generate. Within this framework pricing structures can be organised in one of four main ways:

1) If your project is under 5MW it is likely to be eligible for FITs (though please check this before starting any project as FITs was under review at the time of writing). Under this model, your project will generate electricity which you sell at the FIT rate to an energy retailer. Good Energy and Ecotricity actively seek out small and large suppliers.

2) If your project is over 5MW you can negotiate a Power Purchasing Agreement (PPA) with an electricity retail company. A PPA allows the retailer to buy your project's electricity at a certain price. Also, your project will likely be eligible for Renewable Obligation Certificates (ROCs) which will increase the price you get; however, it is unlikely to be as high as the FIT rate. Note – negotiating a PPA can be challenging.

3) You can sell the electricity generated direct to consumers or your members. This is possible if you own the electricity cable connecting your project to the electricity consumer. For example, the electricity generated by Torrs Hydro is transported by a private wire and directly consumed by their local Co-op shop, with any excess being sold to a retailer. If your community is off-grid, like the Isle of Eigg for example, creating a small electricity grid and selling direct to the consumers may be the most attractive option available to you.

4) You can create your own electricity aggregator or retailer. An electricity aggregator might buy the electricity from a number of community energy projects, such that the electricity is of a sufficient amount for the aggregator to trade in the electricity market or get a better power purchasing agreement. Therefore, creating your own electricity retailer is a way of selling directly to consumers without having to own the electricity network.

In addition to paying back loans and providing a return to investors (if that is the model you go with), most CRE projects that generate revenue also give money back to the community. Typically, the vehicle for this community income is an existing Community Trust (for example, the trust ownership model), or a

dedicated community fund. If you decide to set up a dedicated community fund, this will probably need its own legal entity as well as a separate community engagement process to decide what the income could be used for. Ideas include energy efficiency programmes, funding a new community enterprise, or providing a new social service, such as a school bus. What you use the money for will also depend on how much income is coming in. One hydro project in Wales splits its estimated £20,000 annual profit between a child care project, a coffee bar and a community centre. Another in Scotland invests in energy conservation measures to reduce fuel poverty (see page 98).

Whichever approach to financing, electricity sale and community income you choose, there is one more crucial financial consideration to take into account – cash flow. CRE projects present a cash flow dilemma because most of the costs are upfront and are due before the project starts generating income through the sale of electricity; particularly during the construction phase of a project when expensive items – for example a wind or water turbine – must be bought, as well as civil works paid for. This often comes to hundreds of thousands of pounds.

Preparing a cash flow plan to ensure you have enough money in the bank at the time you need it will help you ensure the success of the project and can form the basis of your financing strategy.

External factors that might affect your project

There are also a number of external factors that are to a greater extent out of the control of your group but that will nonetheless have significant bearing on what is and is not possible for your CRE project. It will also affect specific decisions within the areas discussed above. Key external factors to consider include:

- Energy policy such as Feed-in Tariffs, the Renewable Energy Obligation and CRE support grants, loans and competitions. The government regularly reviews these programmes and changes the terms under which payments are made, as well as the amounts paid. These changes can have serious implications for project financing; a

case in point being the FIT review that occurred in November 2011, which left many projects financially compromised.
- The technical, commercial and regulatory structure of the electricity system.
- Organisation legislation as already discussed in the organisation structures section above.
- The existing organisations in your community – what organisations already in your community could help or hinder the project? What are the internal politics of your community? What are the attitudes to renewables? How will this fit?
- The CRE support organisations that operate in your area; a list is given in the resources section.

Skills and the division of work

During this chapter, a series of skills have been identified as important to the development of a CRE project. One issue you will have to consider is how you will access the skills that are needed. Questions to ask include:

- To what extent do those skills already exist within the core group developing the project?
- Can you recruit new people with specific skills to join the project; do you know anyone who might fit the bill?
- What skills do you need to develop within the group? Who will develop them and what training or mentoring is available to develop said skills?
- When will you need to hire external organisations with specific skills to compliment what you already have and are committed to developing?
- What will be the split between paid and voluntary work?

In addressing these last two questions, no CRE project we know of has been developed by the community without the support of at least one external organisation. The specialist skilled people you may well seek out include lawyers, renewable energy engineers, community development workers, communications specialists, electricians and Environmental Impact Assessors, to name but a few.

DECC are looking at ways to create standardised

legal documents for community energy projects to save different projects repeating the same work over and over again. It cannot be stressed enough how important it is for groups not to reinvent the wheel with each new project but to seek out and gain benefit from other people's experiences. See http://ceo.decc.gov.uk and www.planlocal.org.uk for more advice.

Lastly, while one of the benefits of CRE projects is that many people work on them for the love of it, most (although not all) projects we know of have employed at least one person in a project manager role to ensure that the project gets the attention it needs within the competing time pressures of those involved. Again, funding and recruiting for this position will be an important part of the process.

A final word

Community renewable energy projects are innovative, empowering and achievable. We think that CRE projects are one of the most exciting ways to make a positive change. If and when you choose to embark on a journey to establish your community's own renewable energy project we suggest you remember the following:

Never doubt that a small group of thoughtful, committed citizens can change the world. Indeed, it is the only thing that ever has!

Margaret Mead

Case study

Torrs Hydro, New Mills: groundbreaking community micro-hydro project in Derbyshire

Torrs Hydro New Mills Ltd

'*Archie, Archie, Archie!*'; the spontaneous cry of 100 school kids rang out as they watched the Torrs Hydro reverse Archimedes screw, affectionately known as Archie, start to turn. Looking on, one of the volunteer directors, who had helped install the ten tonne steel screw, was filled with a sense of pride and achievement at how far their community had come.

Three years earlier in the Derbyshire town of New Mills, a group of residents met to talk about the idea of developing a community hydro project. They were inspired by a proposal by social enterprise Water Power Enterprises (H2OPE) to build a low-head hydro power system adjacent to one of the weirs located in the town.

New Mills is a Victorian milling town with a history of harnessing the energy of the two rivers that flow through it, so the idea of generating electricity from the river once more made a lot of sense to people in that early meeting. However, they wanted to see a project developed more locally than that proposed by H2OPE, and to make sure the benefits remained in the community.

By the end of the meeting the residents agreed to contact H2OPE to propose a partnership. So began the process of setting up one of England's first community owned hydro projects – Torrs Hydro, a 63kW reverse Archimedes screw located at the confluence of the River Sett and the River Goyte.

One of the first tasks was to set up an organisational structure that would enable the community to benefit from the project. To that end they incorporated as an Industrial and Provident Society for the benefit of the community, or 'Ben Com' for short. A Ben Com is essentially a form of co-operative underpinned by a similar philosophy and legal requirements, such as one person one vote.

The major difference between a traditional co-operative and a Ben Com is that the benefits of the project are meant to serve the wider community instead of just the membership of the organisation. In this case, it means that the revenue generated by Torrs Hydro funds a community grants programme, rather than being returned as dividends to its membership.

While the project started as a partnership between H2OPE and the community, with H2OPE doing the majority of the technical feasibility and external fundraising – such as negotiating a loan with the Co-op Bank – over time the

Richard Body

The Torrs hydro volunteers

community took on more and more responsibility.

Indeed, while it was initially intended that H2OPE would maintain the technology once operational, it soon became clear that members of Torrs Hydro were better placed to maintain the hydro plant, as they could be available if necessary 24 hours a day, 7 days a week, and also lived in close proximity. Thus, once the screw started turning, the community took on full responsibility for the operation and maintenance of the project. Now, one of the 10+ volunteers is down at the screw every morning at 7am to turn it on and every night at 8pm to turn it off (see below for an explanation of why!).

Within this project there have been three main periods of community engagement. The first phase was focused on getting the community's support for the project, alleviating fears and answering questions. As such, a series of public meetings and an exhibition at the local Heritage Centre were held. The second period involved encouraging interested people to invest in the project through a share offer.

The share offer, which was painstakingly developed by the Torrs Hydro directors and checked by lawyers, ran for approximately three months, during which time prospectuses were distributed to interested people. People found out about these prospectuses by word of mouth, at the local organics store, library and Heritage Centre and through the website. During the share offer period the directors of Torrs Hydro also ran weekly 'Torrs Tours' on a Saturday, whereby they would take interested people down to the proposed site.

The final phase of public engagement has encouraged general support, education of community hydro and

volunteer involvement in the operation and maintenance of the system. Since the project has become operational, the directors have instituted monthly open afternoons during which interested people can be taken round the plant and have a chat with those involved.

One of the concerns expressed early on in the project was the impact on fish and fishing in the Rivers Goyte and Sett. This has been a major challenge for many hydro projects in the UK with both the Environment Agency and the fishing lobby creating obstacles. However, in the case of Torrs Hydro the Environment Agency was very supportive. They provided the funds to install and maintain a fish pass alongside the project. They have also funded the creation of interpretation boards and have also provided information and support for the project.

Between September 2008 and November 2011, Torrs Hydro generated over 400,000 kWh of electricity. All electricity generated is sold and exported by a private wire directly to the local Co-op shop, which uses it onsite and then sells any excess to the electricity grid.

The project has not been without its challenges. Examples include:

- The initial lease for the site of the project not being fit for purpose, such that it required additional negotiation with the Council and thus extra legal costs, particularly as the Council were not very supportive of the project, especially in the early stages.
- Conflicting expectations between H2OPE and the New Mills community group driving the project.
- A starting budget that did not include a series of necessary expenses, such as a sluice gate to stop the water entering the screw at times of low flow and maintenance, which required an extra period of fundraising.
- Discovering a previously unknown noise issue associated with the technology. Specifically, at a power output below 30kW the screw makes a very loud high pitched noise. This has led to a resident complaining to the Council and subsequently to a requirement that the screw shuts down overnight until the noise issue can be fixed.

These challenges, and particularly the technology not performing as expected, have reduced the financial benefit of the project to the community. However, during the course of its development the Torrs Hydro community hydro project has become a site of inspiration, renewable energy education, tourism, community fundraising and, at the simplest level, a site to harness the natural energy of the river.

Index

Resources

This book has been written with help and information from the following organisations, books and websites.

General help and advice

Organisations

Association for Environment Conscious Builders; www.aecb.net

Association of Plumbing & Heating Contractors; www.aphc.co.uk

Biomass Energy Centre; www.biomassenergycentre.org.uk

Boiler Efficiency Database; www.boilers.org.uk

Cavity Insulation Guarantee Agency; www.ciga.co.uk

Centre for Alternative Technology; www.cat.org.uk

Chartered Institute of Plumbing and Heating Engineering; www.ciphe.org.uk

Energy Saving Trust; www.energysavingtrust.org.uk

Forest Stewardship Council; www.fsc.org

Heating and Ventilating Contractors Association; www.hvca.org.uk

HETAS (biomass heating); www.hetas.co.uk

IEA Heat Pump Centre; www.heatpumpcentre.org

Insulated Render and Cladding Association; www.inca-ltd.org.uk

Institute of Domestic Heating and Environmental Engineers; www.idhee.org.uk

Good Energy; www.goodenergy.co.uk

National Energy Foundation; www.nef.org.uk

National Insulation Association; www.nationalinsulationassociation.org.uk

National Self Build Association; www.nasba.org.uk

Passivehaus Trust; www.passivhaustrust.org.uk

Renewable Energy Association; www.r-e-a.net

RenewableUK; www.bwea.com

Retrofit for the future (Low Energy Building Database); www.retrofitforthefuture.org

Westwoods; www.westwoods.org.uk

Woodsure (assured quality woodfuel); www.woodsure.co.uk

Heritage organisations

Cadw; www.cadw.wales.gov.uk

English Heritage; www.english-heritage.org.uk

Historic Scotland; www.historic-scotland.gov.uk

Scottish Natural Heritage; www.snh.gov.uk

Government departments and agencies

Building Research Establishment; www.bre.co.uk

Department for Business, Innovation and Skills; www.bis.gov.uk/cicregulator

Department for Communities and Local Government; www.communities.gov.uk

Department of Energy and Climate Change; www.decc.gov.uk

Environment Agency; www.environment-agency.gov.uk

Highlands and Islands Enterprise; www.hie.co.uk

Northern Ireland Executive; www.northernireland.gov.uk

Northern Ireland Environment Agency; www.doeni.gov.uk/niea/

Scottish Government; www.scotland.gov.uk

Water Regulations Advisory Service; www.wras.co.uk

Welsh Government; www.wales.gov.uk

Websites

http://smokecontrol.defra.gov.uk

www.communities.gov.uk

www.climatechangeandyourhome.org.uk

www.direct.gov.uk

www.fitariffs.co.uk

www.greenelectricity.org

www.londonheatmap.org.uk

www.nef.org.uk/logpile

www.planningportal.gov.uk

www.scoraigwind.co.uk

www.stovesonline.co.uk

Downloads

www.bre.co.uk/sap2009

www.bre.co.uk/media-centre.jsp

www.decc.gov.uk

www.energysavingtrust.org.uk/Generate-your-own-energy

www.english-heritage.org.uk/your-property

www.forestry.gov.uk/publications

www.planningportal.gov.uk/uploads/code_for_sust_homes.pdf

www.ownergy.co.uk/info/

www.spongenet.org/buyersguide

http://info.cat.org.uk/

Community energy

Organisations

Abundance Generation; www.abundancegeneration.com

Big Lottery Fund; www.biglotteryfund.org.uk

Carbon Leapfrog; www.carbonleapfrog.org

Carnegie Foundation; www.carnegiefoundation.org

Centre for Sustainable Energy; www.cse.org.uk

Community Build; www.communitybuild.org.uk

Community Energy Online (DECC); http://ceo.decc.gov.uk/

Community Energy Plus; www.cep.org.uk

Community Energy Scotland; www.communityenergyscotland.org.uk

Community Power Agency; www.cpagency.org.au

Community Renewable Energy; www.corecoop.net

Community Shares; www.communityshares.uk.coop

Community Self Build Agency; www.communityselfbuildagency.org.uk

Co-op Bank; www.co-operativebank.co.uk

Co-operative and Community Finance; www.coopfinance.coop

Co-operatives UK; www.uk.coop

Development Trusts Association Northern Ireland; www.dtni.org.uk

Development Trusts Association Scotland; www.dtascot.org.uk

Development Trusts Association Wales; www.dtawales.org.uk

Ecodyfi; www.ecodyfi.org.uk

Ecology Building Society; www.ecology.co.uk

Ekopia Resources Exchange; www.ekopia-findhorn.org

Energy4All; www.energy4all.co.uk

Fiery Spirits Community of Practice; www.fieryspirits.com

International Association for Public Participation; www.iap2.org

Locality (formerly the Development Trusts Association); www.locality.org.uk

Local United; www.localunited.net

Microgeneration Certification Scheme; www.microgenerationcertification.org

Plan Local; www.planlocal.org.uk

Regen SW; www.regensw.co.uk

Severn Wye Energy Agency; www.swea.co.uk

Triodos Bank; www.triodos.co.uk

Wales Co-operative Centre; www.walescooperative.org

Water Power Enterprises; www.h2ope.org.uk

Zopa; http://uk.zopa.com/ZopaWeb/

On-line community energy toolkits

Canadian Wind Energy Association: Best Practices for Community Engagement and Public Consultation; http://www.canwea.ca/about/communityengagement_e.php

Commission for Environmental Co-operation – Guide to Developing a Community Renewable Energy Project in North America; www.cec.org/Storage/88/8461_Guide_to_a_Developing_a_RE_Project_en.pdf

Community Energy Online; http://ceo.decc.gov.uk/

Community Energy Scotland, Community Renewable Energy Toolkit; www.communityenergyscotland.org.uk/community-renewable-energy-toolkit.asp

Department of Trade and Industry, Community Involvement in Renewable Energy Projects – A Guide for Community Groups; www.bis.gov.uk/files/file48402.pdf

Embark, Community Renewable Energy Resources; www.embark.com.au

Lancaster University, Hydro Resource Evaluation Tool; www.engineering.lancs.ac.uk/lureg/nwhrm/tool/

Wind Works; www.wind-works.org

Windustry, Community Wind Toolbox; www.windustry.org/CommunityWindToolbox

Downloads

www.cse.org.uk/pages/resources

www.communityshares.uk.coop/factsheets

www.localunited.net

www.swea.co.uk/renew.shtml

www.uk.coop/resources

http://ceo.decc.gov.uk/

http://valuesandframes.org/handbook/

Case studies

Ashley Vale Action Group; www.wildgoosespace.org.uk

Bath and West Community Energy; www.bwce.coop

Bristol Green Doors; www.bristolgreendoors.org

Ecomotive; www.ecomotive.org

Fintry Development Trust; www.fintrydt.org.uk

Gamblesby Village Hall; www.gogamblesby.co.uk/village_hall

Ham Hydro; www.hamhydro.org

Hill Holt Wood; www.hillholtwood.com

Hyde Farm Climate Action Network; www.hydefarm.org.uk

North Harris Trust; www.north-harris.org

Superhomes; www.superhomes.org.uk

Torrs Hydro; www.torrshydro.org

Transition Bath; www.transitionbath.org

Transition Brixton; www.transitiontownbrixton.org

Transition Linlithgow; www.transitionlinlithgow.org.uk

Transition Malvern Hills; www.transitionmalvernhills.org.uk

Transition Network; www.transitionnetwork.org

Transition Town Totnes; www.transitiontowntotnes.org

Vauban; www.vauban.de/info/abstract.html

CAT books

Choosing Solar Electricity, Brian Goss

Going with the Flow, Billy Langley and Dan Curtis (New edition 2012 re-titled *Choosing Water Power*)

Choosing Wind Power, Hugh Piggott (out of print)

Home Heating with Wood, Chris Laughton (New edition 2012 re-titled *Choosing Wood Heating*)

Off the Grid, Duncan Kerridge, David Hood, Paul Allen and Bob Todd

Tapping the Sun: A guide to solar water heating, Chris Laughton (out of print)

The Energy Saving House, Thierry Salomon and Stephane Bedel

The Whole House Book, Pat Borer and Cindy Harris

Wind Power Workshop, Hugh Piggott

Zero Carbon Britain 2030: A New Energy Strategy, various authors (Ed. Martin Kemp)

Other books

The Common Cause Handbook, various authors, Public Information Research Centre

Heat Pumps for the Home, John Cantor, Crowood

Renewable Energy: A User's Guide, Andy McCrea, Crowood

Sustainable Energy Without the Hot Air, David Mackay, UIT

The Transition Handbook, Rob Hopkins, Green Books

The Transition Companion, Rob Hopkins, Green Books

Transition in Action: An Energy Descent Action Plan, Green Books

Videos

Wind Of Change, Cornelia Reetz. Produced for Fintry Development Trust

Plan Local; www.planlocal.org.uk

References

For chapters written by Nicky Ison and Jarra Hicks

DWTOA (2009a) 'Past and Present: successful developments followed by stalemate', Danish Wind Turbine Owners Association available at www.dkvind.dk/eng/index.htm, accessed May 2010.

Bolinger, M. (2001) 'Community Wind Power Ownership Schemes in Europe and their Relevance to the United States', download from http://eetd.lbl.gov/EA/EMP.

Gipe, P. (2010) 'Germany to Raise Solar Target for 2010 and Adjust PV Tariffs', www.wind-works.org, accessed 12/4/10.

Gipe, P. (2003) 'Community Wind: the third way', www.wind-works.org, accessed 12/4/10.

Hicks & Ison (2011a) New England Wind Report

Ison, N. (2009), Overcoming Technical Knowledge Barriers to Community Energy Projects in Australia, Honours Thesis, School of Civil and Environmental Engineering, University of New South Wales, Sydney

Network for the 21st Century, www.ren21.net, accessed April 2010.

Sørenesen, H.C, Hansen, L. and Larsen, J (2002) 'Middelgrunden 40MW offshore wind farm Denmark – Lessons Learned', available www.middlegrunden.dk, accessed April 2010.

Walker, G. and Devine-Wright, P. (2008) 'Community Renewable Energy: What should it mean?' Energy Policy, Vol 36, p. 497-500.

BIS (n.d.) Community Interest Company, Community Interest Company Regulator. Accessible at: www.bis.gov.uk/cicregulator

CES (2009) Community Renewable Energy Toolkit, Community Energy Scotland. Accessible at: www.communityenergyscotland.org.uk/community-renewable-energy-toolkit.asp

Co-operatives UK (n.d.) 'What is a co-operative?' Accessible at: www.uk.coop/about/what-is-a-cooperative

DTI (2000) 'Community Involvement in Renewable Energy Projects – A Guide for Community Groups, Department of Trade and Industry.' Accessible at: www.bis.gov.uk/files/file48402.pdf

FSA (n.d) Industrial and Provident Societies. Accessible at: www.fsa.gov.uk/pages/doing/small_firms/msr/societies/index.shtml

Hicks and Ison (2011) 'Community Renewable Energy Research Report, Community Power Agency.' Accessible at: www.scribd.com/doc/65752996/Appendix-2-CommunityRenewableEnergyResearchReport-CommunityPowerAgency

International Association or Public Participation (2004) IAP@ Spectrum of Public Participation. Accessible at: www.iap2.org.au/resources/spectrum

Locality (n.d.) Development Trusts. Accessible at: http://locality.org.uk/members/development-trusts/